Lakeland Walking

The jottings of a fell-walking naturalist in England's Lakeland

by

Alan Gane

Over the hills and far away

First published in Great Britain by Pen Press

All paper used in the printing of this book has been made from wood grown in managed, sustainable forests.

ISBN13: 978-1-78003-011-1

Printed and bound in the UK
Pen Press is an imprint of Indepenpress Publishing Limited
25 Eastern Place
Brighton
BN2 1GJ

A catalogue record of this book is available from
the British Library

Cover design by Jacqueline Abromeit

ALAN GANE, MBE, CBiol MSB FRAgS, having retired from a working life in agricultural research, has since spent much of his time fell-walking, watching and photographing wildlife and giving talks on such subjects, for the benefit of UNICEF, in which he was a Partner. He led a year-round fell-walking group, the 'Mockerkin Mob', on treks over the Cumbrian fells, for 18 years and contributed a series of articles to The Link, *the magazine of the United Benefice of Lorton and Loweswater with Buttermere. It is these articles that are reproduced here.*

Any profit accruing to the author from the publication of this book is to be divided equally between the Cockermouth Mountain Rescue Team and St Bartholomew's Parish Church, Loweswater.

To all who love the Fells,

AJG

JM

'Contents

Prologue

Lakeland walking with wildlife

The cool, fresh air of early morning, the spring of dew-spangled turf, the scent of bracken, the accompaniment of birdsong, the scramble over scree, the security of boot on solid rock and that exhilarating moment of emergence from a rocky chimney onto a broad, expansive top, beset with a panorama of breathtaking views! This is the magic of fell-walking.

In terms of severity, 'scrambling' lies between 'walking' and 'climbing'; it involves the necessity of using both hands and feet, but without the security of a rope. Clearly, therefore, it is not without an element of risk and should only be undertaken by the experienced, who are relatively fit and properly equipped.

While not wishing for a moment to dampen anyone's ardour, or to offer what may appear to be 'nanny-like' advice, it should be stressed that proper equipment is essential in the interest of safety. Fell-walking often extends over rough country, with steep, grassy slopes, rocks, becks and places where there are vertical drops. It is among mountain country, in which the weather is notoriously fickle and may change dramatically in minutes. It is often ten degrees colder on the tops than it is in the valleys. Walking boots are essential, giving both ankle support and good grip. Wellington boots, on the other hand, are totally inadequate, having no ankle support and usually no sideways grip. It is also worth remembering that anyone wearing waterproofs, which are also essential, and who happens to fall on steep grassy fellside, must expect to perform as if on the Cresta Run – a human sledge. One reason why a walking pole should always be carried, and the walker must know how to use it, because it is his only brake.

Anyone who doubts the need to take such elementary precautions should be reminded that the Cockermouth Mountain Rescue Team alone was called out no less than 64 times last year, which was a record, and that this year the number of callouts up to July showed an increase of 80% over the same period last year.

Herein are described both walks and scrambles, but this is a commentary, not a guidebook. Guidance should be sought from Wainwright's *Guides to the Lakeland Fells*. (Wainwright – later referred to as 'AW'.)

Fell-walking and scrambling are made even more enjoyable if an interest is taken in wildlife, whether it be a general interest or something more specialised, such as plants, birds, animals or perhaps lichens or fungi. The broad approach does have the advantage that something of real interest is almost certain to be seen on every walk.

The compatibility of walking and the study of wildlife does depend on the subject chosen. While it is perfectly feasible to seek, find and perhaps photograph plant life while walking, sightings of animals and birds must be expected to be somewhat transitory. Even so, walks as such are useful in providing opportunities for identifying habitats and locations, which may be revisited with the express intention of observation and photography of particular species.

Walks may also be categorised according to the company one keeps. Some consider solitary walking in the fells to be foolhardy, which may well be so for the inexperienced or in really adverse conditions, but at the same time, the lone walker is rewarded with his own uninterrupted thoughts and also has the advantage that his silence greatly increases the chances of coming across bird or animal life that would be long forewarned of human presence by the inevitable chatter generated in a group.

Wildlife apart, there is much to be said for walking in company, whether it is in the form of a dog, another individual or a party. Walking with other people is an experience shared, which increases enjoyment both during and after the event. Each form, therefore, has its merits, and none is to be decried.

Despite, or perhaps because of, all the exertion; the cold – or the heat, the wind, rain or snow, and even the calculated risks at times inevitably involved, it is all so worthwhile. Not only is there the achievement of completing a really good trek and gaining the target top or tops, there is the tremendous feeling of well-being that follows a day on the hill.

Back to base, wherever that may be, a hot bath or shower, a dram, a hearty meal, the day's memories—and the walker is king!

Walk on!

AJG

1. Walkers'wear

Well, really, it was perfectly obvious from the outset that, if I was going to feel anything short of 'odd one out', I would simply have to get kitted out like everyone else. Mind you, I *had* only just arrived in the Lake District for the first time, so how was I to know that fell-walking demanded such ritualistic apparel?

Nothing else for it; a dash to Keswick, chequebook in hand, to seek out the necessary mountain toggery.

Boots appeared to be the fundamental need, so in I went and, having disclosed the required size, I promptly displayed my ignorance by a totally blank stare when asked what *weight* of boot I wanted. I was then confronted by half-a-dozen pairs of varying degrees of ruggedness. Obviously, those light things were no good to me. What did he think I wanted to do, go dancing? Oh, no! He wasn't going to catch me like that! It's the highest tops for me; rock, scree, ice, snow – the lot; they breed 'em tough where I come from. So, into that really big pair went my little trotters; that pair with laces like rope and tread like that usually associated with tractor wheels. They were duly tied up for me—and what an art that proved to be—and up I stood.

"Fine," I said. "Very comfortable."

"Just try walking up and down a bit." Came the reply with a note of disbelief.

Now, it wasn't until later that I realised the significance of a fiendish twinkle in the shop assistant's eye. I moved forward. Well, I don't know if you have ever had the opportunity of watching a deep-sea diver moving about on land with boots encased in lead; nippy, he may be beneath the waves, but out of the water he's about as skittish as a hibernating tortoise.

I moved forward, but it seemed quite some time before I succeeded in getting the boots to follow! Avoiding falling to the prone position, due to the combination of weight and sheer embarrassment, was a close-run thing. Having casually suggested that perhaps something a little less weighty might allow me to climb faster, I moved to the middle range and settled for a more reasonable alternative.

Next it was waterproofs; equally essential if I was to face these sudden mountain storms they keep harping on about, and choosing them was no trouble, except for the colour. I rashly grabbed the green ones, until I was gently, but firmly, reminded that *if* I was climbing to the dizzy heights described, and *if* I was so unfortunate as to get into difficulties ("Not that that is at all likely in the case of so experienced a mountaineer as your good self", the assistant seemed to suggest) then, of course, the bright red, yellow or blue would make it easier for the search parties to find me. OK. Red.

I soon learned that glasses prevent an anorak hood from fitting close to the face at the sides. The rain blows straight in, passes the ears, takes a sharp turn round the back and drips smartly down your neck! But then—the final insult. I had just about got used to getting hotter and hotter in my scarlet plastic summerhouse, peering through my misted glasses while an ice-cold trickle developed down my spine, when the sun came out. There was a clear blue sky above and my storm gear seemed as out-of-place as a rickshaw in Regent Street.

If you paid people to do a job like this, there'd be a strike a week—but this is supposed to be FUN!

All that was many years ago. What do *I* do for fun these days, did you say? Fell-walking, of course. There's nothing like it!

2. Maiden Moor

The crunch of boots on frozen snow

After a long period of grey skies, with dull, low and heavy scudding rain clouds as a daily scene, what a change did February bring: cold, of course; indeed, occasionally bitter in the extreme, especially when accompanied by strong winds, but cloudless skies of cobalt blue and hour upon hour of brilliant sunshine. Compensation!

Of the many walks done at this time, a visit to Maiden Moor and Eel Crags springs to mind. Not that it is a great trek, this, but a good climb and walk on snow and ice from start to finish. The usual ascent from Little Town across Yewthwaite Gill was a veritable sheet of sloping ice, the gill petrified by many successive days and nights of hard frosts, so discretion dictated a safer route through the combe.

And just as well, or we would have missed seeing the biggest icicle of the day. It formed a pillar on Trap Knotts, fully six feet high and 54 inches in circumference!

From Hause Gate to the summit the going was good, although snow was knee-deep in patches; no problem – tho' tiring – except for the danger of being pitched forward when suddenly going deeper than expected – a potential leg-breaker.

Once, when the Maiden Moor route was followed in a clockwise direction after very heavy snow, it was only when glancing upwards while walking back down the valley along Newlands Beck, that the degree of overhang of the snow cornice was appreciated. We had obviously been walking perilously near the edge, and at times would have had nothing below us but snow and a vertical drop! Do remember when walking in thick snow – keep well back from the edge!

The crunch of boots on frozen snow, their ring on iron-hard turf, the rattle of the anorak hood and the whip-crack of toggles; the winter walkers' accompaniment. Between Maiden Moor and Castle Nook lies one piece of track, which runs right along the edge, and, as this stretch was relatively deep in snow with drifts overhanging the side, it served to add a little spice and concentrate the mind! A halt for a bite to eat was brief indeed. Once stationary and with gloves off, the penetrating cold was soon self-evident and there was a return to walking as soon as possible.

But then, as a reward for the effort, a brilliant, sparkling sunlit view from Skiddaw to Scafell and from Grasmoor to Helvellyn, over Newlands; while four jet-black ravens turned and tumbled overhead. So little now is green, but soon brown fells will change their hue, the skylark will be serenading and spring flowers will bloom once more.

February – a month to remember – a jewel in the walker's calendar.

3. The Grasmoor circuit

Along the dashing beck

This longish route, of great variety, begins at Lanthwaite Green, from where the first objective is Eel Crag. Gasgale Gill provides a gentle start, tho' not without the odd scramble. Taking the lower track, the first of these has handholds obligingly provided by the roots of a mountain ash, while this same spot unfailingly produces a fine array of pale green stars of butterwort later in the year. Along the dashing beck, with its scores of miniature waterfalls and cascades, between plump cushions of bright green moss, this fine deep gill has some 20 ribs of Whiteside on the left, and Grasmoor and the great dry hollow of Dove Crags on the right.

Wrens and dippers dart along the beck, ravens soar high above, a resident kestrel hovers over the fellside in search of prey, whilst wheatears dash from rock to rock.

On emerging from the gill at Coledale Hause, the steep scramble straight ahead up to Eel Crag is well worthwhile; a broad and somewhat featureless top after the confines of the gill and with fine views. There can be few spots in Lakeland that give a more extensive panorama. Straight along the ridge, with its rocky ups and downs, to Sail and the long descent to Sail Pass. Once there, it is a pity not to add Causey Pike, which is an ideal target for that well-deserved snack, with Keswick and Derwentwater stretched out far below.

Then back to Sail Pass and left down the Sail Beck track towards Buttermere. A long, mostly easy descent; a good stretch after the earlier scrambles, with a chance of seeing grouse among the heather and, with luck, a ring ouzel or two. Once over the third beck and round Whiteless Breast, an indistinct track forks right and leads upwards between Rannerdale Knotts and Whiteless Pike. Over the saddle and straight on down through Massacre or Bluebell Valley to Lanthwaite Green. A thoroughly recommended route over varied terrain, with excellent views and, especially in summer and autumn, an interesting cross-section of birds and plants.

PS   An attempt of this in mid April 1980, failed at Coledale Hause, where there was a white-out; the only discernible feature was one's own footprints in the snow—and they were fast disappearing. The only sane solution was a rapid return to the gill.

"Oh! To be in England—"

4. The dark side of the mountain

I had made up my mind the night before that I was going to tackle this particular route and, although from the outset the weather looked uncertain at best, I decided to stick to the plan. As I motored up the valley, it was obvious that the cloud was well down; the chance of it clearing seemed remote and I felt that, in truth, it was going to be one of those days not really for 'the tops' – but I was determined anyway.

By the time I reached Honister it had changed little. I grabbed my gear, locked the car and set off, only to find that, as expected, I was well and truly into cloud by the time I reached the Drum House on the old tramway. By the time I reached the start of Moses' Trod I was having to move carefully from cairn to cairn to keep on track and treading warily through the inevitable mix of rocks, peat hags, becks and the like.

Never before had I traversed the Trod without so much as a single glimpse of Great Gable, which I knew perfectly well was towering above me to the left. I know the track like the back of my hand, but even so I had the occasional doubt as, in the eerie light and complete silence, I failed to recognise every step of the way. It seemed so different when I could see only one very short stretch at a time; out of context with the usual surrounding landmarks. The Trod seemed much longer, but I consoled myself with the thought that, really, there was no wrong turning I could possibly take.

Then I suddenly realised I was on rising ground, veering right, and I knew I was coming up to Beck Head. Still no glimpse of Gable or Kirk Fell!

Just over the brow, two ghostly figures appeared from the gloom, coming towards me from the direction of Wasdale; the first people I had seen since leaving Honister. We exchanged greetings and, if truth be known, both parties were tempted to ask,

"What on earth are you doing out here on a day like this?" These two male walkers, in their fifties (so quite old enough to know better!) were aiming to walk over Kirk Fell and return to Wasdale Head. However, on learning that I was bound for the south traverse of Great Gable, they felt that sounded rather more challenging and asked if they could tag along. I welcomed the unexpected company and off we set.

We had a bad start. The beginning of the traverse is never all that easy to locate, even on a good day, except when looking down on it from Kirk Fell, but in these conditions it must have taken me a good five minutes to find it, and then only by criss-crossing the fellside and virtually stumbling onto it. I can't help wondering if my companions were starting to wonder if I had *ever* been up there before!

Having covered only a couple of hundred yards of the traverse, the cloud suddenly parted. We could see Kirk Fell to our right and, ahead and far below, that magical pattern of fields around Wasdale Head and beyond, the shimmering surface of Wastwater. But in a matter of seconds it was gone and we were once more engulfed in the gloom. The View was no more.

In all this heavy damp, the rock was very greasy underfoot and we had to take extra care in selecting footholds. The traverse starts as a fairly level track about a foot wide, across runs of rock fragments interspersed with scree runs and areas of jumbled larger rocks. The scree is not so bad – one expects it to shift beneath the boot, and legs to become accustomed to making continual rapid adjustments to keep the trunk upright, but the mish-mash of large jumbled rocks is a different matter. This is treacherous stuff. After a series of firm steps, one rock will suddenly tilt or slide – many an ankle-breaking trap.

Once round the corner onto the southern face proper, the terrain changes; there are still scree runs extending above and below to a total of 2,000 feet or more, but there are also outcrops of solid rock to negotiate, sometimes up and over, sometimes down and round. Again, the cloud parted momentarily and we could see across the valley to Lingmell, to Mickledore and right down to Wasdale Beck. Thirty seconds and it was lost once more. A little later and it fleetingly cleared above us, just enough for us to catch sight of the famous Cat Rock and there was some apt comment about a very "Foggy Moggy". And then it rained! Not just cloud this time, but serious rain; we were already in waterproofs and were pretty soggy from the cloud, so really, it made little difference.

On we scrambled, eventually beginning to lose a little height, until at last we cut across the Wasdale to Sty Head track. Round a bluff and we could see Sty Head Tarn below and to the north.

Thus we came to the parting of the ways. My companions were off down to Wasdale and thence one to London and the other to somewhere in Wales. There were warm handshakes, albeit with cold, wet hands! We had enjoyed each other's company; we had had a few laughs and had revelled in the scramble.

So, a final wave and I descended the short distance north before turning left for the summit of Great Gable, a summit that was still invisible above me. This is an unremitting slog. Some 1,400 feet of steep, rough and mostly loose going, broken only by one or two stretches where some hardy souls have laid steps. I usually hate these 'improved tracks', but I have to admit that when a track is as hopelessly eroded as this one, steps come as a tremendous relief. On and on, up and up, slither and slide; made worse by the fact that I was in dense cloud and therefore there was no target in view – and 100 false summits!

And then – there it was: the unmistakable summit cairn. Never before have I visited this spot and spent so little time there! I was cold, wet, muddy and hungry, but this was far too inhospitable a place at which to stop. It was like night. Rapidly taking my bearing from the memorial plate in time-honoured fashion, I moved from ghostly cairn to ghostly cairn, swinging right until the ground begins to fall away, gently at first, then over all that slippery, clattery stuff, until those patches of yellow rock confirmed that, yes, I was still on track. Steeper and steeper until hands as well as boots come into play. A large rock appears on my right, with a small one lodged in front – a seat with a shelter! Just right – never was a snack more warmly greeted! I saved the chocolate biscuit for later on – something to look forward to in this dank and gloomy world! Then down over the slabs and round to the left onto that deep red soil and shale – the telltale sign of approaching Windy Gap.

I didn't realise just how tired I had become until I began to climb out of Windy Gap. Only 100 feet or so at most, but it made me puff and pause for breath three times. My thighs were beginning to complain, too, which is rare. The distance, the exertion of scrambling and with little opportunity to relax, was beginning to tell.

Up to the top and away but, although this was, or should have been, very familiar territory, having been covered times without number, being encapsulated in a 'grey-out' of cloud plays odd tricks and precipitates doubts. Rock formations take on unfamiliar shapes and one is not normally conscious of every single up and down, twist and turn; they all fall into a familiar pattern when viewed in the context of the overall route and surroundings, but when viewed in isolation, they fail to trigger that feeling of certainty and security.

However, press on, only twice having to adjust my line and never having to backtrack until I reached unmistakable landmarks. Eventually the old quarry track appeared. Up and over, onto the quarry road, this being the easier descent of the two. As I reached it, I emerged from the cloud and could see the car park down below. For the first time ever, I had walked from Gable to Honister without seeing a living soul!

Back to the car – and steaming hot mug of tea! Bliss! But *what* a day! No views at all to speak of, no wildlife – the camera had not been out of its case once. Cold, wet, hungry, but exhilarated by that wonderful world of silent, sombre crags, the fell's other face – the dark side of the mountain.

5. Ennerdale (1)

The walk

So full of interest is this area that we will deal with it in three parts – the walk itself, its birds and its plants.

It is a superb valley. A massive cleft running east into the fells, open to the west with Herdus and Crag Fells standing guard to north and south respectively of the valley 'jaws'. Eastwards from Herdus run Starling Dodd, Red Pike, High Stile, High Crag and Haystacks. The head of the valley is blocked by Green Gable and Great Gable, and then, returning on the southern side, lie Kirk Fell, the huge bulk of Pillar, Steeple with its tempting, but rather disappointing peak, Haycock and Crag Fell. What a circle of names to conjure with, and every one worth a visit.

The circuit of the lake is straightforward enough, tho' rough on the southern side, involving a scramble at Angler's Crag. For the purpose of this exercise, we'll take the anti-clockwise route, leaving the Bowness Knott car park with the white cottage on our right. However, before leaving this spot, take a long look back at Bowness Knott; surely one of the finest buttresses in Lakeland. At its best in evening light and especially after rain, it positively glows with a host of colours and is a mass of razor-sharp detail.

Round to the end of the lake, past the weir, over a patch of grass and through the gate in the stone wall beyond and the going promptly changes. It is relatively rough from here to the eastern end of the water and the walker's instinct dictates that he should separate the activities of walking and admiring the view! Trying to do both at once invites disaster, because these are no mere stones, but well-embedded rocks, specially designed to stub toes with crushing efficiency and equally adept at twisting ankles.

14

Angler's Crag provides a good little scramble and a choice. Right over the top if you want the best view, across the face if you want the best scramble and, when the water is low, along the shore if you want to make the best time. The track has been much improved in recent years, but one walks continually on sloping ground which drains much water from the fells, a hazard in hard weather when failure to treat the sloping sheets of ice with due respect can turn this mostly very safe walk into something else again.

Once the end of the lake is reached, two fields are crossed keeping close to the stone wall on the right, and then the forestry roads are gained, on which to complete the circle. The latter give a pleasing stretch to tiring limbs and are, in any case, by no means devoid of wildlife interest – but more of that in the next chapter.

6. Ennerdale (2)

Some plants in Ennerdale

Leave Bowness car park, aim left of the white cottage and over the grassy slope there will be found the white flowers of bedstraws and little yellow clumps of tormentil. Down the slope and over the first beck, through the first gate and immediately on the right grow the first plants of earth nut or pig nut, with their delicate white flowers and the 'nuts' below ground.

The next feature on the track is the bridge of concrete sleepers, to the right of which grow marsh marigolds and kingcups. Another 90 paces or so and here are two small gorse bushes on the right by a low bank, and on this there is wild thyme – tiny ground-hugging plants with aromatic leaves and bright purple flowers. Here too is kidney vetch, with its pea-like flowers of bright yellow.

Out in the marshy field on the right are the white tufts of cotton grass waving in the breeze and, in season, there are many orchids here. A little further on and there are plants of sneezewort – a name more reminiscent, perhaps, of a certain Disney cartoon than a botanical monograph. Then comes another beck flowing beneath the track and in the water on the right there is water crowfoot, its small white flowers sitting on the surface of the water, and more marsh marigold. Along the shore is spearwort, its buttercup-like flowers lining the margins of the lake, ladies' smock and, by the low concrete wall that bends to the right, there is horsetail, a non-flowering primitive plant of damp places.

Then comes a wooden footbridge and once over this, the tall and stately stems of bistort grow on the left, with their bright pink blooms in strict contrast to the compact little stonecrop to be found on the stone wall a little further on. Up the stony slope to the next gate, passing deep purple bugle and the cerise of red campion.

Down the slope and on towards the next gate and, just before it, another beck; on the right the lush growth of Indian balsam, or policeman's helmet, growing in profusion with more, as a rule, by the gate itself.

Past the site of the Angler's Inn, the track forks and we keep left. About 80 paces on, to the right, is a patch of common valerian, while also in this area there is foxglove, violet and stitchwort.

Then we go along the side of Crag Fell, with its mosses and lichens then, just past Angler's Crag, parsley fern. Down along the track towards the trees with celandines, wood sorrel and the ever-present tormentil. We reach an area where water flows across the track in more or less degree according to the season and weather, and here there is butterwort and round-leaved sundew; the former with its star of ground-hugging leaves and violet flowers, the latter with its red leaves bejewelled with tiny droplets of sticky fluid and its creamy white flowers; two examples of our small number of insectivorous plants.

Ten yards or so before a shore-side holly there is lousewort, a short plant with pink flowers. Once among the trees it is worth noting the range and size of lichens present here, lichens which, as all the technically-minded will know, are examples of symbiosis between algae and fungi. Around here, too, there are bracket fungi, a devastating fungus infection of silver birch.

Across the fields at the end of the lake and onto the forestry road, and on the right are the large leaves of coltsfoot, whose flowers appear first in spring. There is autumn hawkbit and, where the sloping rock comes down to the roadside, surely some of the finest butterwort one could wish for, along with herb Robert and the brilliant blue of milkwort. On approaching the car park, look out for carline thistles on the bank to the right of the road. These and many more plants enliven the area, as do the birds we outline in the next chapter.

7. Ennerdale (3)

Some birds of Ennerdale

Having observed so many species of bird from the shore of Ennerdale Lake, we are clearly obliged to be selective, or this will be in the nature of little more than a list!

Following our accustomed anti-clockwise route from the Bowness car park, we are reminded of the ravens seen in the vicinity, and of the kestrel so often seen to be hovering above the Knott. No doubt the most uncommon sight, for us at least, was on Saturday 26th April 1985, when, from this spot, we saw high above, a golden eagle, no less, and although we see a great many birds, a seven foot wing-span is rare!

Bowness itself and the trees near the white cottage were frequented in late spring by a pair of green woodpeckers, and the latter spot was the haunt of a tawny owl.

The main island in the lake is a favourite perch for cormorants. We have seen up to nine at one time standing there, some with wings outstretched drying in the breeze. Mallard, tufted duck, pochard, occasionally the odd goldeneye, goosander, red-breasted merganser – both of the last being saw-bills – and sometimes shelduck, which have the distinction of being duck without webbed feet. These and many more, frequent the waters. Great crested grebes are often here and, much less often, little grebes too.

Mireside was the constant hunting ground of a heron until the approach of the breeding season; he (or was it she?) disappeared then and has not yet returned. This is an area well populated with frogs each spring – tadpoles abound – and this ready-made food supply was probably the attraction.

Sandpipers are to be seen around the shore. They often stand on partially-submerged rocks or fence posts and fly ahead repeatedly with a looping course out over the water as we approach. Eventually, tiring of this, they take a longer sweep back to their original starting point.

Wagtails and wrens flit along the shoreline among the rocks, the spearwort and, when the water is low, the water lobelia. Sometimes a dipper is seen here, but more often along the fast-flowing streams. Spotted flycatchers have been busy in the Indian balsam area near the old Angler's Inn site, darting up for their prey and down again in their characteristic way.

The patch of gorse towards the weir is worth watching for the occasional stonechat – that brightly-coloured little sentinel – which typically occupies a vantage point on top of a gorse bush, but which may well retreat within as we draw near. There are one or two reed buntings, too. In summer the male has such a white collar and black bib that I long ago dubbed him 'the vicar'.

A buzzard floats high aloft, soaring with apparent ease, just giving the wings a flap now and then; but when he finds the unwelcome attention of mobbing crows just a little too tiresome, rolling over and presenting them with his talons. Lazy he may seem, but once prey has been selected, his swoop is anything but slow.

However, having turned to birds of prey and to speed, surely the most splendid is the peregrine. This beautiful long-winged bird is the fastest living thing. In its dive, or 'stoop', speeds of up to 180mph have been claimed.

So these are among the birds which may be seen around Ennerdale Water – and there are many more. What an extra interest they provide when walking – not just in this area, but in every corner of Lakeland.

8. Loweswater

Twixt towering fell and shimmering lake

What better picture of a truly English spring than a carpet of bluebells among ancient oaks, dappled sunlight filtering through fresh green leaves, a distant cuckoo echoing its call cross the valley and the gentle lap of quiet waters at the lake's edge? All this and much, much more is there to be savoured at Holme Wood, Loweswater.

Not a place for 'serious' walking, perhaps, but an enchanting spot in which to wander, especially at the quieter times of the day. No specific route is called for; there are paths, tracks and forest roads along the shore and into the wood itself, but its extent is such that unplanned exploration is the ideal, there being no chance of getting 'lost' for long.

One spot worth seeking out is Holme Force, a most attractive waterfall, which descends zigzag and flows beneath a forest road, the beck that feeds it originating high up between Burnbank Fell and Carling Knott. Many folk walk through the wood, especially by the waterside path doing the circuit of the lake, without venturing deeper into the wood and missing this lovely force altogether.

The wood is home to red squirrels, and from time to time we catch a glimpse of them – usually a fleeting one – as they scamper up a tree trunk and away into the branches. Contrary to popular belief, squirrels do not hibernate, but since they spend most of their time in the safety of the treetops, their activities are greatly masked by foliage throughout the summer months. As with birds, the squirrel is most active relatively early and late in the day.

The wood has a good range of birds: spotted flycatchers, pied flycatchers, green woodpeckers, common redstarts, warblers, robins, wrens, chaffinches, titmice, treecreepers and many more. Buzzards drift out from the trees and float aloft over the water and surrounding countryside.

The adjoining lake attracts many birds, too: mallard, greylag, coot, red-breasted merganser, cormorant, dipper, common sandpiper, great crested grebe, heron—the list is a long one.

And talking of the adjoining water, at the north-western end of the lake, water lobelia grows and so, too, does the white water lily, whose beautiful flowers rise and expand as the sun gains strength and close again with the approach of evening.

Viewed from above, on the Coffin Route or still higher on the fells, Holme Wood displays its great variety of trees, especially in the evening light, which serves to emphasise the diversity of shapes, sizes and colours: tall, dark trees; short, pale ones; bulky, rounded ones, ancient oaks and spindly saplings of mountain ash, each with a leaf shape of its own and each with its own particular bark. The silky touch of silver birch, the flaky feel of Scots pine, the ridged roughness of oak—there are those who can identify trees in the dark, by the feel of bark alone!

Mention of the Coffin Route reminds me that we were once up there, above Holme Wood, when a circling flock of teal, that lovely, fast and tiny duck, came swinging and whistling overhead and swooped down to land on the water.

But, of course, the view of Holme Wood we all know best is from the road, from which we dare to glance across from behind the wheel of the car! The reflections of its trees in the lake must be one of the most-photographed views in the area. The water may be still, giving the perfect mirror image of the trees, or dark and foreboding; sometimes covered in a delicate gossamer of mist, sometimes covered in a sheet of ice – but always with the backdrop of Holme Wood in its various seasons.

9. Maggie's Bridge and High Nook Tarn

And look beyond to spring

Starting from the enlarged car park at Maggie's Bridge, Loweswater, and taking the road to Watergate; a number of routes present themselves, which give reasonably short walks of interest. Whatever the overall plan adopted, be sure to look round between Maggie's Bridge and Watergate for a fine panorama, which includes Carling Knott, Hen Comb, Mellbreak, Grasmoor, Whiteside and Low Fell from the unexpected low-lying vantage point from the middle of the valley. Continuing along the main track through Holme Wood is a pleasant enough way to Hudson Place and Waterend, then to complete a circuit of delightful Loweswater by the road or, to extend this a little and take in a fine viewpoint, climb a little by Grange Lane and back by the Mosser road to the lakeside.

If, however, you prefer to leave the tarmac roads behind, leave the forest track in Holme Wood as it veers left towards the gate at its western boundary and instead turn right to the water's edge. This track takes you back along the shore to the stone hut, and shortly after that a track forks right up through the wood and on to join the 'Corpse Road' or 'Coffin Route' above High Nook Farm.

It appears that the so-called Coffin route was probably used to transport the dead from this relatively remote area, for burial at the Abbey of St Bees until 1281, when local ground was first consecrated. That being so, Corpse route is a more accurate term, since at that time shrouds would be the norm, rather than coffins. Whatever the truth of the matter, the route is a remarkably pleasant one.

Follow the road down below Carling Knott and over the bridge at High Nook Beck. Now it is well worthwhile veering right towards Black Crag to visit High Nook Tarn. With the Crag towering high above it, the Tarn may be circled. In summer there is sundew in profusion here, with bog asphodel, bogbean and cotton grass, and the water often hosts mallard and the occasional heron.

From there, return by the track to High Nook Farm and straight on through the yard to Maggie's Bridge, a route which runs alongside a dashing, tree-lined beck.

When in the vicinity of Maggie's Bridge, watch out for the sudden and explosive flight of the resident sparrowhawk as it dashes away with its swinging movement at hedge-top height. Some months ago a barn owl patrolled here every day as dusk approached, but now seems to have moved away.

On approaching the eastern end of the lake, look out for the flock of greylag geese on the water or near the shore. Currently some 50-strong, they have one barnacle goose among them, who sometimes pays dearly for its intrusion by being pecked unmercifully for being 'odd man out'.

The lake is frequented by many birds, including coot and mallard, great crested grebe and pochard, cormorants and herons. The cormorant may be ungainly on land, but its arched dive in which it virtually clears the surface from so low a position in the water presents a picture of sleek mastery of propulsion. Loweswater was also home to red-breasted mergansers, which reared 14 young.

But perhaps it is in autumn when the wood is at its most evocative. Corn-yellow larches, deep green pines with rosy trunks, the treacle-toffee colours of the beech leaves and, high above, bronze bracken cloaks the fellsides. Scarlet rowan berries cling on amongst fast-thinning foliage, and in the treetops a hundred fieldfares rise and fall.

Everywhere that all-pervasive tang of autumn in the air, with becks now gushing full-bore, which merely trickled but a month ago, and lakeside flotsam already lined up high upon the shore. Boyhood memories of gathering conkers on such days, returning home windswept and red-faced to crumpets by the fire! And yet, although the ash is bare once more, its smooth grey limbs exposed, its black buds stand four-square to face old winter's icy blast and look beyond to spring.

10. Burnbank, Blake and Carling Knott

As winter's steely grip once more takes hold

A favourite circuit, providing good variety and fine views, begins at Fangs Brow along the famous Corpse Road or Coffin Route. The first gate leads off the Lamplugh road and the eastward-bound track is too clear to miss. The second lies between two fellside fields and the third has a step-ladder at its right-hand side. At this point the Corpse Road veers left, while we keep straight on and upward with the stone wall on our right. Before long the wall comes to an end and, at right angles to it, an old wire fence is set straight up the fell. Climb over the low fence at the corner and clamber up alongside it, picking a path between loose rocks towards the craggy 'pile of stones' indicated on the Ordnance Survey map. From there, over the grassy slope to the top of Burnbank Fell.

Blake Fell is then clearly seen some 300 feet higher and there is a good and steady inclined walk between the two, easy enough to follow and free from hazards, except, perhaps, for some peat bogs which are best skirted when particularly wet.

From the top of Blake veer left along the southern side of the fence to the first stile; over that, down the fence to the old iron gate at the bottom and from there aim for Gavel Fell, carefully crossing the wet hollow to rejoin the fence, which is then followed to the top. Even then, follow the fence on down in the general direction of Whiteoak. Cross it at a low point where there is outcropping rock and make off along the fellside and gradually down to join the drove road running above and parallel with Whiteoak Beck. This then continues around below Black Crag, with High Nook Tarn nestling in the valley, and Carling Knott, to complete the circuit at the gate-and-ladder and so back to Fangs Brow.

When we did this on 8th January 1987 it was one of the first really frosty mornings of the winter and only a few days before the arrival of appreciable snow; there were serried ranks of hazy fells in the early morning light, like cardboard cut-outs stark against a clear blue sky. They were deep purple in the foreground, and each one paler into the far distance. The low and weak sun cast elongated shadows from tree and rock, picking out each protruding crag along the side of Mellbreak; shady spots where frost survives the fleeting daylight hours; beck sides bedecked with icicles like glistening frozen fingers.

As we climbed towards the top of Burnbank, we were suddenly aware of the furious sound of wing beats overhead, as two swinging flights of mallard swooped and side-slipped to the dark and glassy surface of Loweswater far below. Minutes later the ghostly cry of baying hounds drifted to us from the direction of Low Fell.

Blake Fell, so often vigorously windswept and so often underestimated as a walk and viewpoint, was reasonably still and gave a grand panorama of snow-topped fells and the patchwork of fields and lakes, which never ceases to delight the eye.

Few birds inhabit the tops in winter, but as we began to descend from Gavel, a buzzard rose from beyond a nearby rise, floating lazily skywards with barely a movement of its broad expanded wings. Tempted back in our direction, as they can so often be by an imitative 'meouwing' call, just long enough to survey the scene, it glided rapidly down and away 'til lost to sight towards Red Pike at a speed unbelievable, while apparently so effortless.

A fine invigorating walk, with the ring of iron-hard ground beneath the boot as winter's steely grip once more takes hold.

11. Trouble ahead—?

Despite some very moderate weather, the roadside verges are once again lined with the serried ranks of cow parsley, and the hedges abound with glorious swags of May blossom, a myriad of brilliant creamy-white flowers tinged with pink. The winter dullness of the fells gives way to welcome green and we look forward to warmer times ahead. In fact, with all these encouraging signs, we could be forgiven for thinking that all's well with the world, but, sadly, 'tis not so.

The biodiversity we hear so much about is an incredible feature of planet Earth, with its estimated 14 million different species, little more than one tenth of which have so far been studied, evaluated and classified. It goes without saying that, among the unknowns, there are likely to be species of inestimable value as food, medicines and other uses; we just do not know and, indeed, it may well be a race against time if we are ever to know. There are eminent scientists who are predicting that Man, if not planet Earth, is heading for a catastrophe. Catastrophies have occurred in the past, of course, in the form of geological and astronomical disasters, such as that which saw the demise of the dinosaurs and many other creatures; but the present threat is unique in that it is being precipitated by Man.

One of the basic causes is the explosion in human population, which has grown rapidly and at an increasing rate from little more than 250 million in Roman times to some six billion today. This, coupled with increased life expectancy and increased industrialisation, is causing massive problems. True, the rate of population increase has slowed in recent years and may well level out by the middle of the century; but if not, and if global warming results in some parts of the world becoming virtually untenable, the prospect of the need for mass migration presents another picture of unparalleled disaster.

It is estimated that, of the 14 million species thought to exist, about 90% are to be found in the rain forests, a resource which is being systematically destroyed, year-on-year. Similarly, while we are constantly being exhorted to eat more fish, the majority of commercially-harvested species are already at a dangerously low level, consumption having doubled since the middle of the 20th century.

In the short term the effects of global warming are fascinating to the natural scientist, since it means we stand a chance of seeing species previously associated only with more southern climes. If catastrophe is to come it is unlikely to be in our lifetimes, but it is without doubt up to those who are around today to do everything possible to avoid disaster, or it will be too late for those who follow.

The ever-increasing demand for clean water, for food and for energy presents enormous problems, which call for radical changes in planning and organisation, as does the control of our carbon footprint. Mistakes of the past, including the widespread use of agrochemicals such as DDT and dieldrin, the introduction of alien species to the detriment of native ones, the unbridled release of CO_2 at rates so fast that global warming results, and many other adverse developments engineered by Man, are unsustainable and we continue them at our peril.

12. Lanthwaite Wood, Loweswater

'Neath dappled woodland glades where
sparkling waters flow

Lanthwaite Wood is not so much a 'walk' in the traditional sense of the word, as an 'area' through which to wander. There is no walk of any distance; its length and width can be traversed in a very short space of time, if that is the object; but those who are prepared instead to stroll, look, watch and search may find rewards indeed. The wood cloaks one side of Scale Hill and is bordered partly by the River Cocker and partly by the shore of Crummock Water.

On entering from the car park below Scale Hill one may walk straight down the main track to the lake or turn right and follow the riverside path, and there are a number of variations and circular routes thereafter. Whichever route is taken, it is a profitable place to seek out and observe wildlife the year round.

The river almost invariably sports a pair of dippers between the car park and the weir; those delightful white-breasted, rich-brown hunters of the river bed and shallows, which may be seen bobbing in and out of the fast-flowing water, or in their dashing flight low above the surface.

Goldcrests are to be seen in the conifers near the river, too, their tiny (3½ inch) forms flitting among the branches; their bright crests, orange in the male and yellow in the female, brilliant in the shafts of sunlight filtering from above. Flocks of siskin come here too, among the same conifers and especially in the alders.

In late winter there are snowdrops and in early spring, the banks are decked with primrose, wood anemone and wood sorrel.

Giant woodrush grows profusely, and there is dyer's greenweed and – surely one of the most evocative of common plant names – enchanter's nightshade. Marsh cinquefoil, wild broom, cow wheat and many more are to be found.

The wood itself is home to a variety of birds, from the effortlessly-soaring buzzards to the tiny, but noisy wrens, chattering away in the thickets and on and around stone walls along the northern edge. Startled woodcock hurtle away once their superb camouflage is penetrated; tree-creepers hop their mouse-like vertical ascent of silken tree trunk bark, while the pink, white and black presence of long-tailed tits is announced by their chattering 'tsirrup' call.

And there are roe deer, those most secretive and solitary deer which, as a rule, move singly or at least in very small numbers and which are not the easiest to see. Indeed, one could walk through the wood 100 times and not know they were there at all. But if you move very slowly, very quietly and with frequent stops or, better still, if you stealthily reach a good vantage point and then move not at all, patience may be well rewarded! If, from the corner of your eye, you detect a slight movement and see something, which at first sight appears to be perhaps a sheep in the undergrowth, look again very carefully and you may find that the 'sheep' is in fact a roe deer.

You may, of course, by sheer chance, meet one almost face-to-face. If so, stand stock-still and, for perhaps five seconds or more, the deer will often do the same. If so, you will share an exchange of glances with the dark, limpid eyes of one of nature's most delicate and entrancing creatures before it quickly hops, skips and jumps away, the bright white rump fast disappearing among the trees.

We have seen fox, hedgehog, red squirrel, frog and slow-worm. On and over the end of the lake we have seen cormorant, tufted duck, mallard, kestrel, peregrine falcon, goosander, sandpiper and many more – even a Daubenton's bat skimming over the water in late evening.

Apart from all of which, it is a singularly pleasant wood in which to wander, with a wide range of trees and with wide views of the lake and fells. It is a rich area for those prepared to search out its inhabitants; seek and ye shall find!

13. Grasmoor – the direct route

Lock hand and foot firmly into place

While walkers love walking, the enjoyment of many is greatly enhanced and, indeed, coupled with some degree of feeling of achievement, by reaching the very top of something, even though it is of no great height or difficulty. Few of us have the abilities of a Bonnington or a Tensing, but we can still enjoy our lesser challenges and use them as a means of recharging our batteries by experiencing new routes and revisiting old and favourite haunts.

Whether one is in Lorton, Loweswater or Buttermere Valley, and whichever walk one favours, there can be little doubt that the dominant feature is Grasmoor. Towering above Crummock Water, from which rises its steepest face, Grasmoor stands at 2,791 feet or, for those who have been 'converted', some 852 metres. The highest fell in the immediate district, it is only a little below Great Gable. It is massive, broad-based, imposing and is surmounted by a generous plateau, scoured smooth in the Ice Age with a commodious cairn at its crest.

Geologically, it is of the Skiddaw Slates series, the oldest rocks in the Lake District. It is ringed by extensive screes and has many interesting features, including precipices, rocky terraces, shelves, crags and gullies. In the upper reaches of the northern face, overlooking Gasgale Gill, is a fine combe, a great hollow scooped out of the mountainside and overlooked by Dove Crags. But we digress! There are a number of routes by which to reach the top, some relatively gradual and circuitous, such as those by way of Gasgale Gill or Whiteless Pike. There are others more direct and steep, such as by Dove Crags or Lad How; and then there is the steepest of all, from Lanthwaite Green by Grasmoor End.

If Lakeland perambulations are graded (1) for walks, (2) for scrambles, (3) for climbs and (4) for rock climbs, then this route must surely warrant a (3).

Initially it runs south-east across short grass, threading its way through bracken, getting steadily steeper until the scree is reached. Steeper still now, and the scree rises up some 500 feet and presents the roughest, most tiring section of the entire ascent. There is no escape from the fact that this is a long, hard pull, but every step is one nearer to the enticing rock above and every step increases the breadth of view below. It is large-grade scree of uncertain stability.

But then at last there is that sudden magic change, when boots stand firm on solid rock and reasonable security returns. There is still much variety, in that there are substantial areas of contiguous rock with ample toothy crags, and inviting rakes with strong-growing heather and ancient prostrate juniper. Within this general area there are many 'mini routes' and the choice is sometimes difficult, but if one becomes too hard or awkward, there is always an alternative not far away. It is continually steep, a route to lock hand and boot firmly into place.

Soon after reaching solid rock, the general direction of the route brings one towards the precipitous face overlooking Crummock Water and, needless to say, the view from here is quite superb. However, the steep and rocky climb continues to Grasmoor End at 2,400 feet, where there is a small plateau on which the walker or climber may rest weary limbs; a welcome relief after the exertions of the previous hour or so. The exertions of this climb must be neither exaggerated nor underestimated. At least one may stand upright on this spot without having to hang onto something – and the fact that that comes as a welcome change will serve to indicate the sort of 'walk' to which we refer!

But all is well because from here to the very top is an easy stroll over bare and weather-beaten terrain with little grass, but large mats of heath underfoot which crunches as if one was traversing a carpet of steel wool. On a good day the views are tremendous in all directions, from the coast to Helvellyn and from Binsey to Pillar and Scafell.

Once the viewing is done, the choice of return route must be made. One may drop down to the col between Grasmoor and Crag Hill and then turn left for Gasgale Gill, or right for Whiteless Pike, the former being probably the easier descent, but neither holding anything to daunt the walker who has just scaled Grasmoor End!

This is not a walk we would suggest for a beginner, for the faint-hearted or for those short of 'puff', but for those who are lucky enough to be able to do it, it is a grand climb; well worth every effort. It is undoubtedly among the best – some say it is *the* best – in the Western and North-western Fells. Ideally, it calls for a good day with little wind and dry rock.

Given such conditions and the necessary 'puff', it is, as they say, one for the book!

14. The Buttermere Horseshoe

Dark crags with blue tarns far below

There are many different sorts of walks, and no doubt every walker has his or her preference. Some like ridge walks, some like rock and others grass. Some like to go high, while others prefer the lower levels. It is difficult, to say the least, to find a walk that is everyone's favourite. Still, it is probably true to say that most people like a round trip rather than retracing steps; that most appreciate some good views; and that most like variation in a walk.

Well, those characteristics and more are to be found in the Buttermere Horseshoe. Down the lane to the left of the Bridge and Fish Hotels and bearing left where the lane later forks, over the footbridge across the stream, through the wall and up the track to the left of the lower reaches of Sour Milk Gill—a gill which incidentally is steep and very slippery and which is best avoided. It has been the site of more than one fatality.

Much of the track has received attention, but is quite a pull from Bleaberry Tarn to the summit of Red Pike – steep, red and rough, with the final burst on solid rock. A good climb of some 2,480 feet.

Bearing left from the summit cairn there is a gentle grassy stretch; a welcome change from the previous section, along the ridge and up past Chapel Crags to the top of High Stile (2,644 feet). Provided conditions are reasonable, it is well worth keeping near the edge to glimpse those down-the-gully views of the tarn and Buttermere beyond. A fine place for dramatic photos – dark crags in the foreground and the shimmering blue waters far below, hopefully in bright sunshine. The summit of High Stile is extensive and well worth exploring if time permits diversion from the direct route, but caution is called for in mist, as the northern and eastern faces are sheer.

On along the ridge again to High Crag (2,443 feet), but not without looking back towards Grey Crags, the eastern face of High Stile, a much-frequented haunt of rock climbers. From here too, are excellent views down into Burtness Combe. From High Crag there is a steep scree running two-thirds of the way down to Scarth Gap (1,300 feet); the route then levels for a short stretch where there is a small tarn before continuing down a short scramble over Seat. From Scarth Gap up and over Haystacks (1,900 feet), surely one of the best-loved scrambles with its fascinating collection of features, such as Big Stack, Innominate Tarn, Blackbeck Tarn, Green Crag and, of course, the 'perched boulder' to the south-east of the tarns.

From Haystacks to Dubbs Bottom past the old quarry and the remains of the drum house to Honister Pass (1,190 feet). Doing this walk in an anti-clockwise direction does have the distinct advantage that the biggest climb is done first thing in the morning and the roughest and rockiest walking is concluded in the first half of the day. Nevertheless, it must be admitted that, having completed the southerly part of the valley, the haul up from Honister to Dale Head (2,473 feet) some 1,300 feet of ascent, is a little daunting. The first two-thirds are grassy, but steep. If it is any consolation, the steepness does quite suddenly level off towards the top and there are compensating glorious views of Eel Crags, Maiden Moor and beyond.

Our route turns left at the impressive Dale Head cairn and follows an easy and mostly grassy track along the ridge of Buttermere Fell to Robinson (2,427 feet). Again, it looks to be an easy ridge walk and in normal circumstances it is, but after all that has gone before, the final pull up Robinson is distinctly steeper than usual! Once atop this grand viewpoint, all the early stages of the walk are clearly seen – Red Pike to Honister Pass. In fact, unless my eyes deceive me, Wainwright lists no fewer than 70 'tops', which can be seen from this spot. It may not be a record, but it is certainly an impressive number. From the top, down the stony westerly track, over Buttermere Moss, behind Snockrigg and down the zigzag path to the Newlands road and Buttermere.

Clearly, we walk at different speeds and we all have our own idea of what constitutes 'a good walk', as opposed to a walk that is just too long. Perhaps the best way to describe this one is to say that it would take a fast walker to do it in under six hours. Having said that, those who enjoy a relatively hard walk of that duration are assured that there is much pleasure and satisfaction in completing the Buttermere Horseshoe. Most walkers will have done some, if not all, of the component parts, but to do it all in one is highly recommended. At a rough estimate, it runs to about 12 miles and involves some 5,400 feet of ascent.

It has woodlands, grass, rock, scree, bog, streams, tarns, lakes, ups, downs and fine views to all points of the compass. A walk to remember!

15. Call of the falcon

The bird that stands supreme

Any question as to whether or not it was worth it was soon dispelled. As we parked the car it was still only 5:00 am. We had made good time and, as soon as our feet slipped into our boots and our rucksacks settled on our backs, we were raring to go. Into the wood and along the river bank, with that 'quickly-but-quietly' gait of the hunter who has major prey in mind, but who has no intention of spoiling other sightings by spooking everything else in earshot. The early morning light fell across the woodland carpet of primrose, wood anemone and violet; while at the stream's edges there glowed a warming clump of kingcups. The sombre watery shadows were broken by the bobbing white breast of a dipper, sub-mariner of water-loving birds, as it sought out tit-bits for its young safely tucked away beneath the arch of the stone bridge 100 yards downstream.

A sudden movement among the trees to our left and we froze in our tracks. We were face-to-face with three roe deer, a buck in velvet and two does, a mere ten yards away. For seconds we held each other's gaze and then in unison, as if by some secret signal, they hopped and skipped away into the undergrowth in the exuberant way that makes these delightful creatures so endearing. A few flicks of their white rumps and, with hardly a sound, they were gone.

On approaching the far edge of the wood we noticed tell-tale signs of squirrels – red squirrels in these parts – fir cones half-eaten in the manner so characteristic of our rufous friends. We scanned the trees above in the hope of catching sight of one, and there, sure enough, was the little bundle of red fur, tail over back and ears pricked. And what a tail! Balancing aid, umbrella, parachute, sail – the squirrel's built-in survival kit!

But there was something else, quite large, upright against a pine trunk. Binoculars were brought to bear and revealed a tawny owl, head bowed, eyes tightly closed, clearly fast asleep after a successful night's hunting. But that was not all: there was something strange about the silhouette, and we moved quietly to one side to observe from a fresh angle. We could hardly believe it; it was not one tawny owl, but two, perched back-to-back and both fast asleep!

Out of the wood and to the shore of the lake; a heavy mist was rising from the water and the weak sun was beginning to filter down between the surrounding fells. A pair of sandpipers settled on a half-submerged rock, while two goosanders sailed silently by, like lake-bound Mary Celestes in the eerie light.

Soon we could make out the massive bulk of the fells to right and left, but there was still much ground to cover between us and them. Across a low-lying boggy area, where yellow iris and ragged Robin would later bloom, where scraggy trees survive, despite their sodden roots, with cow wheat, foxglove, reed and rush, and trees that will soon be home to flycatcher and warbler. A wary heron seeking an early breakfast on the plentiful supply of frogs, lifts lazily away on broad grey wings, voicing a ghostly croak of protest on being disturbed.

Gradually the ground begins to rise. An eye-striped wheatear stands proud atop an old stone wall and, as we near, confirms the reason for his name: 'white rear' indeed, as with a flash he drops out of sight. Steadily changes the ground beneath our feet, from leaf mould, sedge and sphagnum moss to sliding, clattering scree; a noisy medium, but one on which both sound and slippage may be minimised by careful, gentle placing of the feet. And then at last that magic moment when boots stand firm on solid rock, making progress economical, giving a good return for energy expended. A thousand feet to go.

Snug among the rocks now, stag's horn lichen, dwarf juniper and mosses cling precariously in what for most of the year is a harsh environment indeed. Many rocks support great plates of lichen, some centuries old, all shades of grey, blue-green, yellow and rust. Tearing wind, lashing rain, ice, hail and snow must all be endured to survive here. Much of the limited bird and animal life of the high fell departs at summer's end and those living things that remain and cannot flee the ravages of winter, must be hardy to survive.

As we climb towards the ragged rim, its tooth-like pinnacles thrust upwards to the skies above, a pair of ravens sail out overhead, their massive beaks parting to emit that deep, deep croak; one rolls and dives, effortlessly climbing again, sheer exuberance and a delight to behold.

But now we near our target, and with weary limbs, approach that vantage point from which, without disturbance, we hope to watch a bird that stands supreme. We are in luck! Almost as we arrive we see the falcon flying in across the valley, steadily descending as she flew and gathering momentum until she was directly over the raven's nest to which our croaking pitch-black twosome had meantime returned. With an instantaneous flick of wings and tail, she flipped into a vertical dive, shot downwards headlong with incredible acceleration and when only 15 or 20 feet above the ledge-borne nest, zoomed upwards with the most dramatic swoop: a simply breathtaking display of aerial mastery.

A further pass or two in which her stoops were accompanied by her frantic 'kecking' call and she went to rest at our own level on the opposite side of a wide and precipitous gulley. The streaked white breast, the blue-grey back, the brilliant yellow cere and talons and those enormous, piercing eyes; a beautiful creature, if ever there was one – strong, efficient, sleek and dashing, a bird of the greatest style and panache.

But minutes passed when the tiercel could be seen nearing the eyrie's airspace, clutching newly acquired prey. The falcon took off to intercept and we were treated to that thrilling spectacle, the food pass. As they closed on what appeared to be a collision course, they finally rose in unison until they almost stalled, and there, right above us, the prey was deftly passed from the talons of tiercel to falcon and carried back to the nest crag. An exhilarating glimpse of avian domesticity.

A magnificent wild bird flying free in the skies of Lakeland, capable of attaining speeds in excess of 180mph in its dive; the fastest bird, master of manoeuvrability, the prince of falcons and the falcon of princes, the Peregrine.

THE PEREGRINE

Well might his chosen colour be
Of slate-blue tinted steel,
As, coursing through the rushing air
His awesome blow to deal.

Majestic head, with gleaming eye
Gold-taloned dashes he,
Defiant, clean-cut, fast and strong
As any bird can be.

Such mastery of flight
Such grace, such poise, such style,
That challenge is there none to him
The monarch of the sky.

AJG
1986

16. Crag Fell, Whoap and Lank Rigg

Where the pleasures of solitude are to be enjoyed

Among the many attractions of the area in which we are privileged to live is the fact that there are many walks of all degrees of difficulty. There are gentle walks calling for a minimum of exertion and of short duration; there are 'walks' which many would claim as climbs, and there are 'horseshoe' and long-distance walks, some of which call for planning and stamina. Then there are intermediate ones, which, although not short, enable the walker to gain height with relative ease and enjoy the benefits thereof – the fine views and the feeling of space and freedom which only height provides.

One such 'intermediate' walk begins at Scarney Brow. Taking the fell road, the first on the left after leaving Ennerdale Bridge on the Egremont road, park the car by the first cattle grid and here the walk begins. Over the stile on the Forestry Commission road, which winds its way gently upward, first flanked by conifers, but eventually to open fell. Soon after, the vistas begin to open up; Grike (1,596 feet) is on one's left, but is barely worth the detour.

Carry on along the forestry road past the radio mast and through the next gate on the left, then aim right for Crag Fell (1,710 feet), which *is* worth the effort. A nice craggy top and, although the ascent has been gentle all the way, on reaching it there are fine views to enjoy. Most of Ennerdale Water may be seen stretched out far below and the panorama includes Murton Fell, Blake, Carling, Gavel and right on to Grasmoor, Hopegill Head, Red Pike, High Stile, High Crag, Haystacks, Pillar, Steeple, Haycock and others. What is more, while walking hereabouts on a Bank Holiday Monday, of all days, only two other walkers were

41

seen all day, while down below could be seen the throngs overflowing from Bowness Knott car park and streaming along the lakeside road! There are still deserted places, if one knows where to find them.

On one occasion when walking in this area, we were descending a steep track across which there was a wire fence. There was a stile, so no problem, at least for us. As was so often the case, we were accompanied by Toby, at that time a large, young, fit golden retriever.

As usual, he was dashing about, always in front, and clearly considering that a mere fence could easily be cleared. He charged downhill and leapt. Now frankly, he had had better ideas! He misjudged the height by an inch or two and succeeded in threading his front legs between the top two wires; his chest struck the top one, his rear flew up into the air, his front legs were caught between the twisted wires and he was hanging there, unable to move a muscle. The only way to release him was to lift him back across the fence, which was no mean task on a steep hillside, but manage it we did – just. Apart from severely bruised and scored legs, he appeared to be no worse for the experience, but just imagine if it had been a lone foxhound, with nobody around.

From Crag Fell, turn south-east to rejoin the forestry road, across the hollow and between the trees to a gate on the far side, and up alongside the stone wall which runs towards Ennerdale Fell. After a few hundred yards the wall turns sharp left, but we veer slightly to the right, striking up the slope and soon bisect a track running east to west, which leads up to Whoap (1,700 feet), from which there is a ridge walk and semi-horseshoe to Lank Rigg (1,775 feet). Between the two we skirt a fine amphitheatre around the head of Whoap Beck, where there are prehistoric cairns and stone enclosures to be seen. There is also a tumulus, or barrow, and a pretty little tarn near the top of Lank Rigg itself. This area of Kinniside Common provides broad and expansive views, including the Solway and the Isle of Man; the walking is mostly very easy and it is 'different' from most of the National Park.

From Lank Rigg roughly follow Long Gill down to the River Calder, which is normally not difficult to cross, and join the track a few yards above Bomary Gill. This takes us back to the fell road, by which the car was parked about a mile and a half to the north.

As for wildlife in this vicinity, well, more than once we have seen foxes along the forest road, ravens around Crag Fell and buzzards quartering the fellsides below Whoap and Lank Rigg, with that deceptively slow glide which can so suddenly turn into a prey-snatching swoop. However, it is not to be claimed so much an outstanding place for wildlife, as for space, for rolling hills and uncluttered expanses; a good place for a day's walking where the pleasures of solitude can be enjoyed. A place where you may indeed wander – 'lonely as a cloud'.

17. Cogra Moss

An area full of interest

Lying as it does between Blake Fell and Murton Fell; Cogra Moss borders Lamplugh Fell and appears on the map to be a somewhat insignificant area of water, while the fact that the lower slopes of the fells are mostly covered with impenetrable conifer forest, might well add to the suspicion that this is an area of little or no interest. Such a conclusion would be wrong. There are a number of different routes and any one of them is likely to yield good sightings of a variety of wildlife. The three main routes are as follows:

A. From the car park at Fell Dyke a track leads up over a grass field and through a gate, where it is at first bordered by conifers. Shortly these give way to a fine line of beeches, where flocks of blue, great and coal tits are often to be seen, sometimes with treecreepers. Down the steep side is a stream where, until three years ago, dippers were invariably seen. Sadly, they appear to have left this site. Follow the track straight past the lake to where it forks; take the *left*-hand fork and follow the forest track all the way round to the northernmost point, from where it continues to the western end of the lake and back along the lake edge to complete the circle.

B. Follow the track straight past the lake to where it forks; take the *right* fork this time, up the hill to the forest road half-way up the fellside. Turn left and follow this road across the back of Middle Fell, Blake Fell and Sharp Knott at the end of which it bears downhill and left to meet the forest track under 'A' above. Repeat the return round the lake end.

C. As (B) up to the forest road, but instead of turning left on reaching it, bear *right* across the road to the southern edge of the conifers opposite and turn left up the side of Middle Fell along the fence to the top. A track follows the side of the fence all the way round to the top of Blake Fell, which is a superb vantage point with fine views in all directions. From the top of Blake Fell bear half-right (northwest), dropping down to the start of the forest road, north-east of Sharp Knott. Follow that road a few hundred yards and it joins the road under Sharp Knott mentioned in (B) above, at the point where it goes downhill to the lake end.

Three very pleasant circular walks; low, medium and high, relatively speaking, are all worth doing. The second and third may also be reached from the road along Harris Side.

A further variation, which adds a little spice, is to follow route (C) along Middle Fell until a minor track is seen branching left around the head of the valley. It is little more than a sheep track, but follow this and it will take you right across the south-western face of Blake Fell. It is less hazardous than it appears and is well worth a try.

The lake attracts a variety of water birds, including mallard, coot, pochard, great crested grebe, cormorant, tufted duck and, occasionally, heron. There are often kestrel and buzzard to be seen; on one memorable day a peregrine falcon stooped on a pigeon down the full length of Middle Fell, directly overhead and so close that we could clearly see its golden talons. There are ample traces of fox and careful scrutiny of the fellsides above the tree line and the area that has recently been cleared will often reveal roe deer.

In the flat and marshy area bordering the north-west side of the lake there is ragged Robin and spearwort and water horsetail, while in the shallows on the south-east side there is water lobelia. There are fine specimens of a wide range of species of lichen on the trunks and branches of trees, on rocks and along the top edges of banks, such as at the forest road side. Demoiselles and dragonflies are there, too, their aquatic larvae living in the lake and climbing the rushes to complete their life cycle.

Not an area for some great trek or rocky climb, but a good one for a two or three-hour ramble, full of interest.

18. 'Dreary December (?)'

Despite the gale-force wind, rain and violent hailstorm of the previous night, the early morning of the 15th December looked promising. The wind had dropped and it was dry – quite a novelty after the weather of recent times. So, in order not to miss such an opportunity, I dashed out at once to carry out the annual 'harvest' of holly and evergreens in preparation for decorating the church, then, as it was still looking good, I set off for a walk.

Certainly, it was fine; but this was December and, as we all know, that does tend to be dark, dank and dismal. I parked the car, but hadn't even had time to close the door, when my eye was caught by a great spotted woodpecker nearby, giving that glorious flash of red, white and black. A hen bird, this, with its scarlet pantaloons, but lacking the red crest of the male. I watched as it landed on the trunk of a tree, hopped up a few feet and then moved off further into the wood, with that undulating flight so typical of the species. My mind went back to 1985 (or was it '86?), when a pair nested in a hollow tree at the foot of Mellbreak and we spent many hours watching the parent birds to-ing and fro-ing with food for their brood. Dark, dank and dismal it may be, but this was a good start to any day!

Off I set and, before I had gone half a mile, what should be sitting in the middle of the track in front of me, but a toad! A young toad, this, bravely enduring its first winter – that great test which claims so many birds and animals. As with frogs, the colour of toads varies greatly and this young chap was almost black, which meant that its golden eyes seemed brighter than ever. Small wonder that fairy stories grew up around the 'jewel' in the toad's head. Having thus passed the time of day with my warty friend, I pressed on, trying hard to ignore the fact that it was getting darker by the minute and that the wind was picking up in ominous fashion, too. Sure enough, the rain was returning and there was no option but to don wet weather gear – just in time. Great hanging curtains of rain, sweeping swags of drenching water were draping themselves along the fellside, and the tops were fast disappearing. Ah, well, so what's new?

Suddenly I noticed a movement above and to my left. I stood stock-still. Yes, there it was again, a long-tailed tit, highly active in a silver birch. And another, and – there were eight or ten in all and among them were blue tits and a coal tit or two; in fact, a typical mixed flock of titmice. How busy they all were, hopping from twig to twig, branch to branch and tree to tree, as if frantically grazing. And no doubt they were; it is unlikely they would expend all that energy without expecting sustenance in return. I climbed a bank and examined some birch minutely, but could find no clue as to their quarry. Over-wintering aphids, perhaps? I gave up and pressed on. Thus far the wind had been at my back, but now I had reached the end of the lake and must turn across it, thus receiving the full blast on my right—and before long I would have to turn once more and face it. But happily it lessened and for a time subsided altogether.

December it may be, but here was gorse in flower, which served to remind me of the old saying, 'kissing's out of fashion when gorse is not in flower'! In other words, kissing is for ever in fashion, as one may always find some gorse in flower. I pass below a crag where in summer there is usually to be found starry saxifrage. Saxifrage, from the Latin meaning 'rock-breaker', so called because at one time it was thought that the roots of this plant, which often grows in the most barren and inaccessible places, could actually break rock in order to gain a foothold. And it is an interesting insight into medieval medicine that, against this background, an extract of the roots of saxifrage was used in the treatment of kidney stones, in the firm belief that it would break them, too.

The fellsides now seem brown and drab at a distance, with the straw-coloured grass and the bronze of the bracken; but if we look closer we can still find some green in the form of moss, fern and lichen. Green, the colour of life – every scrap busy photosynthesising and pumping out that invaluable supply of oxygen upon which our lives depend and which we take so much for granted. The greens of mosses seem to take on an even more brilliant hue at this time of year; is this due just to the enhanced contrast with their dull background, or can they really be brighter through increased photosynthetic activity, using the uninterrupted penetration of daylight due to the much-reduced canopy? I wonder!

The colour of lichens varies enormously; green, grey, yellow, grey-green, grey-blue, orange – and then there is the brilliant scarlet of the *Cladonia* or 'pixie-cup' lichens, which, as we all know, are indeed used as cups by the Little People (Lakeland's equivalent of the Borrowers of TV fame). There are those who doubt their existence, of course, but why else should we have a valley called Borrowdale? Lichens, algae, fungi – all so-called primitive forms of life, but forms that can nevertheless survive the harshest of environments.

And now again it rains – only harder than ever – but who cares? I'm enjoying my walk, just the same. Here in winter grows a patch of wild iris or 'yellow flag', their majestic golden heads held high, a blaze of colour. Three thoughts come to mind as I pass the spot. First, a glance through the microscope at the cross-section of their long, long leaves soon shows how they manage to stay upright, despite wind and weather – their very large palisade cells, rectangular in cross-section – nature's box girders, in fact. Second, the lovely golden flower is the model of the fleur-de-lis – the ancient badge of the French royal house. And third, on a personal note, while I spent 35 years in research on three species of the *Leguminosæ*, a great uncle of mine spent his time on the iris family!

Suddenly there is some activity near some shrubs just ahead; I advance slowly and get quite close before there is an explosion! A charm of goldfinches erupts from a favourite feeding place, some very bedraggled burdock, which clearly still yields some seed. The flash of gold, scarlet, black, white and brown is captivating, even, or perhaps especially, on such a day.

Now it's time for a bite to eat and I settle my back against a convenient birch trunk to hungrily devour those treasured morsels. No, I'll save that chocolate biscuit until I'm round the end and have the wind at my back. What great pleasure comes from such trifles in conditions like these! The weather continues to deteriorate and, by the time I do turn the corner, the tops have disappeared, the wind is howling and the rain is too lazy to form droplets—it seems to be falling solid. And yet, out there in the lake, totally alone, isolated and weather-beaten, stands a cormorant. Despite the weather, he must feed and, with his lack of preen glands, after the allotted number of dives, he must drain his plumage by standing there with wings outstretched. What price the chill factor, I wonder?

But I see that, in fact, he is not quite alone. A valiant dabchick – our tiniest grebe – battles against the increasingly white water of the lake, and a little further on there are half-a-dozen pochard. At least, I think there are half-a-dozen! It is not easy to be sure, because, as soon as one surfaces, another dives. I approach a beck which emerges from a copse and have little doubt that I am a most unpopular intruder, because up from the bed of the stream flaps a heron – displeased, I am sure, at having to emerge from the relative shelter of banks and trees.

And now, three hours after leaving the car, it is in sight once more. Waterproofs (so-called!) are peeled off and thrown in the boot; I jump in and slam the door. Back to a hot drink, shower and hot meal. What a glow! A super walk with lots of wildlife, even in dreary old December. I suppose I could write about it, really—

19. Mellbreak

O'er Crummock's western shore

The fact that a fell is not particularly high or easy to reach does not necessarily mean that it is uninteresting or provides only mundane views. Mellbreak, for example, rises to only 1,676 feet and the walk-in to it is short, but it dominates the western shore of Crummock Water. It provides a fine peak when approached from Loweswater, especially in evening sunlight, and this northern end serves as the best means of ascent.

Starting from Park Bridge, the route passes through Low Park, through the gate at the top of the narrow lane and follows the right-hand wall up through the wood and sharp right around the foot of Mellbreak to where it joins the track leading up from stony Kirkhead Lonning. At this point turn sharp left onto a broad and clear pathway leading to the screes.

Around Park Bridge and immediately beyond Low Park there is a fine annual display of Indian balsam – or, if you prefer, Himalayan balsam or jumping Jack or policeman's helmet! By any name it stands high and flowers pink! The charming wood is home to a variety of birds, including pied flycatcher, great spotted woodpecker, tawny owl and, before now, common redstarts have nested in the convenient holes in the walls. The upper slopes towards the main buttress often echo to the silvery notes of the ring ouzel or mountain blackbird, while the soaring form and mournful cry of the buzzard are seldom absent from the skies above.

The scree is mostly quite stable and, as is so often the case, the climb is not as steep as it first appears, nor is it in any way difficult. There are a number of minor variations, but they all lead onward and upward quite nicely. Keeping towards Crummock side does have a distinct advantage, in that at one point where the track veers right, a grassy ledge may be seen only a few feet away, directly ahead, with a small rock face on its right-hand side. This is a spot not to be missed, as it gives a fine view of the Buttermere Valley. After this small but very worthwhile diversion, we proceed again over the turf, heather, rock and peat and a succession of scrambles to the north top, which is, in fact, a few feet lower than its southern brother.

Move on down from there towards the saddle, keeping on the Crummock side where a narrow track leads to a small cairn. From here there is an excellent view down Pillar Rake – a series of impressive rock pinnacles seldom discernible from below – and beyond to the lakeshore. Ascent via Pillar Rake is a recognised route, but it does involve a lot of scree and in the upper reaches some traverses which are, perhaps, a little narrower than might be appreciated by everybody!

The South Top, too, may be visited, of course, but it is not recommended as a means of descent – not because it is in any way dangerous, but simply because it is a rather featureless, grassy slope, and because there are better alternatives. Nevertheless, South Top gives good views of many fells, Crummock Water and Buttermere and Gale Fell, so named not so much for its exposed position, as for the fact that there grows bog myrtle – another name for which is 'sweet gale'.

We return to the northern edge of the saddle and turn left (ie, west). From here a track leads downwards, but soon forks, and it should be borne in mind that while the left-hand fork is much clearer at this point, the right-hand track provides the more interesting route. It passes just above the very top of the gully and is easily missed. Very soon after the gully, it is quite clear and obvious for the rest of the way. It is narrow, mostly along scree and some rock and presents no hazards. It is a good little traverse, very similar to that across Blake Fell, and it rejoins the broad track where the ascent began below the North Top.

From the traverse there is a fine view of Mosedale and its meandering beck across to Hen Comb. It is an area well populated with wheatears and pipits, while kestrels are often to be seen hovering over the crags and over the valley floor. This is a genuine 'fun walk'; nothing too strenuous, but full of interest, so if you feel like following the famous command of, "Don't just sit there, CLIMB something", why not try Mellbreak?

20. The call of Blencathra

A jagged, rocky ridge

It has often been suggested that, of all the Lakeland mountains, Blencathra stands supreme. It is, without a doubt, a jewel to contemplate and a gem to climb. Its massive southern escarpment consists of a succession of three separate fells, each narrowing from top to bottom as if clawed out by some primeval paw, while in addition Blease Fell and Scales Fell guard the west and east respectively, like a pair of giant bookends. Between these five fells run Blease, Gate and Doddick Gills and Scaley Beck.

On arrival at the Threlkeld car park, follow the signed footpath just below it, even though it starts unpromisingly in a downhill and southerly direction! It soon turns, crosses fields and a wall by means of through-stones, then through a farm and left after leaving Blencathra Kennels on the right. It is a brief and pleasant walk-in, leading to an increasingly good climb all the way to the top. Once through the final gate, swing right across Gate Gill weir and follow the track up Hall's Fell. The way ahead rises more and more steeply until it reaches Narrow Edge, a jagged, rocky ridge with many mini-routes, plenty of solid rock and a little exposure in places; a good scramble to the summit with no particular hazards.

Once on top, aim due north across the saddle from which Blencathra gets its newer, descriptive, but far less evocative name of 'Saddleback', to Foule Crag, where a vital decision must be taken. By now we have had an exhilarating climb, fine views and probably a bite to eat as well! We could, therefore, be forgiven for opting for the gentle way down by way of Scales Fell, and there is absolutely nothing wrong with doing that.

However, for those who prefer to spice their walk with an extra-special scrambler's descent, there is the quite irresistible challenge of Sharp Edge – once known as Razor Edge – a veritable dorsal fin; a spectacular crest running steeply down and away like the back of a prehistoric monster. On a more serious note for once, it must be said that Sharp Edge itself is an acute, jagged rib, well-polished in places, exposed and, although great fun for some, it is really no place for the inexperienced. Nevertheless, for those who do not fancy the crest, there is a track on the eastern side, 15 or 20 feet down from the ridge itself.

For those who do enjoy such places, this really is 'one for the book'; a classic, an absolute fun scramble; but it does border on the treacherous if wet or very windy. The famous 'Step', or 'Awkward Place', is in fact a downward-sloping slab of rock down which runs a hollow; on the right of it is a rock wall and on the left, well—not a lot, really!! The hollow 'chute' has a camber, which tends to run the wrong way (well, it would, wouldn't it?). It is smooth and well-polished, so that, when once committed, gravity is inclined to do the rest. It is quite short, decidedly 'interesting', and concentrates the mind; but not quite the place for Aunty!

Way down below Sharp Edge on the western side is the deep pool of Scales Tarn, a shimmering expanse of water in the basin of an enormous corrie, a clear reminder of the passage overhead of millions of tons of ice in years gone by. Once safely down Sharp Edge, the track descends quite steadily. There is starry saxifrage on the wet sides of the gill, which is precisely the sort of place one would expect to see it. But on a recent visit, it was also growing in a crevice in a totally dry, rocky patch, which seemed quite out of character.

Eventually a stone wall is reached, which runs off to the west. This may be followed along the fellside back to Threlkeld or, if preferred, after a few hundred yards access may be gained to the main road through a gate and a small area of common land. There are a number of routes, but up by Narrow Edge and down by Sharp Edge is a fine combination. The mountain rises to a height of 2,847 feet; the walk is only six miles long, but it is 'steep up' and 'steep down'. Having once visited Blencathra, few will resist the temptation to return.

21. Paws for thought – the badger

A part of our country heritage

It had been one of those warm, still, genuine summer days, of which we seem to have had so few in recent years. The sort of day that brings back memories of school cricket matches long ago; of days by the sea and those car-borne sing-songs as we trundled home, tired, glowing and with the sand lingering between our toes! It had developed into an equally warm, still evening, with a few puffs of cloud in a clear blue sky, the silence broken only by birdsong and the chug-chug of a distant tractor.

As planned, we were in good time, a good hour before the first signs of dusk. We made our way quietly over the fields, round the old tree trunk and then along the hedge. Now *there* was a sight! Many tons of soil and stone had clearly been moved over the years, and now there were positive ramparts punctuated at intervals by gaping holes a hand's span across, sweet-smelling and with signs of discarded bedding around in the form of hay and straw. And who were the inhabitants of these desirable residences? Badgers!

Making sure that such breeze as there was was in our faces, we settled back into the hedge, so as to mask our outline and make full use of natural cover. Comfortably set for a long wait, midge-proofed and camouflaged, the vigil began. After only ten minutes or so our hopes rose for two good reasons. First, a young rabbit hopped out of the hedge only a couple of yards away. He hopped about so unaware of our presence that, although we were only three or four feet apart, he skipped between us quite unconcerned. Second, a pair of wood pigeons flew very low along the hedge, right overhead, with no swerve whatsoever in their flight. Clearly, our cover was not at all bad. A sudden movement to our left – a flash of black and white, and a muzzle emerged from an entrance to the sett only six or seven yards away along the hedge. The boar was emerging, thoroughly sniffing the evening air; a testing time, for if he caught our scent, he would retreat and in all probability we should see no more that night. But no, he seemed satisfied that all was well. He shuffled out, stretched and waddled around to make doubly sure on those stout and somewhat bandy legs and very, very strong paws, so well designed for digging.

The tripod-mounted camera with telephoto lens and ultra-fast film was silently swung onto target and, 'click', the first shot was taken. Despite the tiny sound and the distance involved, the reaction was immediate. The badger's eyesight is very poor, but his senses of scent and hearing are acute. As the camera clicked, he jumped upright on his front legs, head raised and ears cocked and remained motionless for a second or two, straining to detect any further sound. Since none came, he resumed his meanderings. Shortly afterwards, the sow emerged, too, with a pair of cubs, half-grown by now, but still sporting their juvenile powder-puff tails.

Then the evening's sport began! Hide-and-seek, rough-and-tumble, follow-my-leader, and a great deal of boisterous fun was had by the whole family. The habit of standing still and listening at the slightest sound was an observation turned to full advantage. The camera was focused, a faint squeak made – just enough to make the badgers look up and listen – and then the shutter was released while they were standing motionless!

Badgers make very permanent family homes; indeed, some setts in use today were recorded as badger setts in the Domesday Book; hundreds of years of constant occupation. Their diet is one that does little or no harm; their prime food is earthworms, but they are omnivorous and enjoy a very varied diet. One of the very few factors against them is that some badgers do carry bovine tuberculosis – but by no means all – and to condemn a species out of hand on such 'evidence' is unjust, to say the least. Badgers only rarely do damage, but in the same way that the golden eagle was once said to snatch children, badgers have been accused of killing the odd lamb. No proof of such a charge has ever been established, whereas many farmers have sheep and badgers and suffer no such loss at all. Badgers are ancient, native creatures;

part of our country heritage, and to watch them 'at home' is an enchanting experience and a privilege.

22. The Mellbreak Round

A host of crags and gullies

November – and although in recent weeks we have enjoyed some of the best weather of the year, this morning proved to be one on which cloud hung low over the fells and, despite the fact that it was reasonably warm and dry, it seemed not to be the most auspicious start for a day 'on the tops'. So we settled for a short, easy, low-level walk, but one never devoid of interest.

Leaving the Kirkstile on the Kirkhead lonning, we made our way past Kirkhead Farm. Mellbreak's Raven Crag was fleetingly appearing through the cloud, which could be seen well down from Whiteside to Buttermere. Rooks, crows and gulls all called across the fields, and there was just a hint of blue in patches overhead, raising hopes that the day might yet improve with time. There were blackbirds, coal tits, a flock of chaffinches busying themselves and, among bushes set in a 70-yard gap in the stone wall on the left, a group of that pink, white and black favourite, the long-tailed tit, surely one of the most delightful of our acrobatic small birds.

Through the gate and veering right, we are accompanied by the sound of the rushing waters of Mosedale Beck down the slope to our right. The right-hand stone wall is now replaced by iron railings, which together with the old sheepfold a little further on, is frequented by wheatears and whinchats earlier in the year. As we proceed along the bottom of Mellbreak we have Hen Comb on our right, while the end of the Valley ahead appears blocked by the blank wall of Gale Fell. At last, the sun gains ground and sends a brilliant shaft of light down through the gloom, an inverted searchlight piercing the grey beneath.

A glance upwards, over Mellbreak's flank, discloses thinning shrouds which serve to emphasise so well that this, like many sister fells, is not the plain uninterrupted lump it first appears, but has a host of crags and gullies, buttresses and knolls, the low slopes now carpeted with bracken – a panoply of warmest hue; tan, rust, copper, bronze, as if to ward off coming winter's icy chill. The track gradually rises, forking left at the large cairn, and now we once again see Mosedale's famous holly tree, which stands alone and proud as the sentinel of the valley. And proud it well might be, featured as it is upon the Ordnance Survey map of the area. Few individual trees are honoured so!

Now we see a crest ahead, a patch of rushes in which stands a long-disused iron gate. The valley opens out. Red Pike is in view, albeit at an unaccustomed angle; Gale Fell still lies in front, but to the right is a vista which extends past Floutern Tarn to Herdus and beyond to Ennerdale. As a rule, it is possible to go straight ahead from the iron gate towards a post some 100 yards in front, but this is an area best suited to 'long legs and big boots'. It is wet, and among the rushes it is necessary to pick one's way with care; from clump to clump, keep moving! Once through this obstacle, aim for the stiles which can be seen ahead, but beware of yet another 'water jump' just below them. After very wet weather this route may be well-nigh impassable, in which case take a left fork just past the iron gate and detour to the stile via higher ground.

Take the left-hand stile. From here there is a fine view of Buttermere, Robinson and Whiteless Pike: a place where one may sense the silence and solitude of the inner fells. Follow the track down the slope with the gill on the right. A little further and over to the right is the deep cleft of Scale Force, its hurtling water seen to best advantage now the leaves have fallen. Across Crummock Water lies Rannerdale Knotts, this, too, unusually silhouetted by a bank of cloud hanging in the valley beyond.

The lower slopes are home for lousewort, milkwort, sundew, bog asphodel and wild thyme. At the bottom stands an island stile – a stile almost completely surrounded by a sea of mud – but approach with care and the odd rock and log will provide a passage through the mire, and so a grassy track leads on to Crummock shore. To the right lies Scale Island, where cormorants roost, but we turn left (or north) towards Low Ling

Crag, a small peninsula reaching out into the lake, with steep and rocky sides, which allow a view deep down into the crystal-clear water. A spot favoured by Canada geese.

Having visited this, on turning back, aim for two gaunt trees to the right of High Ling Crag and above the lake, and some of the boggiest ground will be avoided. Geese, usually Canada or greylag, may well be heard, if not seen, across the water; a cormorant may be perched or may fly low over the water; buzzards frequently glide along the fellside and stonechats may be seen here, perched on gorse tops awaiting some unwary prey.

Rising finally from lake level lies Green Wood, a haunt of tawny owl, great spotted woodpecker, treecreeper and more besides. Through the gate in the right-hand corner and from there back towards the Kirkstile Inn by the lonning, alongside which there are today a pair of jays in the trees by Park Bridge and a dashing mixed flock of fieldfares and redwings in the fields nearby. Down the lane red campion flowers still bloom, whilst the afternoon sun lights up the scarlet rose hips in the hedge. A pair of buzzards sail across the greying sky, their plaintive cry drifting gently down as evening stillness falls.

23. Hen Comb

A shroud o'er Haystacks' craggy tops

The last of these short articles having concentrated on Mellbreak, it seems logical to turn attention to what might be described as Mellbreak's sister fell, Hen Comb, a little-visited mountain of closely-similar height.

It proved to be one of those very mild January days, far more like October or April than 'winter' and, indeed, unlike many of late, it was reasonably light, with a dappled sky in which patches of pale blue were to be seen. The cloud was quite low; felltops appearing and disappearing as rolling billows of cloud slowly came and went, like some great tide seen in slow motion. It drifted gently down Gasgale Gill, thickening as it rounded Grasmoor and trailed its way the length of the valley to lay a shroud over Haystacks' craggy tops. Utter stillness, except for the bleat of distant sheep and the gurgle of well-filled becks; clear reflections in the lakes, a day to savour Lakeland's calm serenity.

The walk began along the Kirkhead lonning to the very end of the stone wall on the right-hand side, where there is a small gate. Through the gate and down the slope to Mosedale Beck. A delightful spot, this, especially after heavy rain when the dashing waters froth, tumble and foam over the rock-strewn bed, giving a gentle roar in the confines of the valley bottom. For those not looking for a long walk, this place alone is worth a visit; it provides a gentle stroll from the village, with just enough height being gained to provide views to Lorton and Loweswater, and with the dominant form of Mellbreak close by.

But we digress. Having reached the beck, if the walk is to be pursued, it must be crossed and the ease with which this is done depends on the flow of water, but is no problem for the agile. Once over this single obstacle, bear left along a track which slopes obliquely to the summit of Hen Comb, a vantage point reached without further difficulty, it being a mostly steady incline rising to a little over 1,600 feet.

It is another of these delightful, underestimated fells, which provide solitude and splendid views. Bordered on the west by Whiteoak Beck, on the east by Mosedale Beck and with Floutern Tarn to the south and a considerable area of bog linking the three, the head of Hen Comb rises high above a watery and desolate expanse, from which the very name 'Mosedale' is derived. Perhaps surprisingly, the view takes in a broad sweep of Grasmoor to Robinson, Fleetwith Pike, Red Pike and on to Pillar, with many more tops in between, as well as at least parts of Loweswater, Crummock and Buttermere lakes.

The best return route is straight down the ridge to Little Dodd, thus having the full view of the Lorton Valley, Low Fell and Loweswater laid out below. From Little Dodd it is a simple, if somewhat steeper drop to the crossing point over Mosedale Beck to rejoin the Kirkhead lonning.

An alternative, if rather wetter, route is to start as before, but follow the Kirkhead lonning straight on instead of turning right through the gate, until the first rock cairn is reached. Then keep right and follow the track down to, and then along, the beck, crossing it below Thrang Crags. It is then possible to walk right round the end of Hen Comb, gaining height all the time until the summit is reached on a virtually spiral route. This has the advantage of giving a fine 'surprise view' looking north as you finally come over the top.

If time permits, a diversion towards Herdus will allow a visit to Floutern Tarn, and between Hen Comb and the tarn is a clearly-defined ancient stone pit circle.

Buzzard, kestrel, dipper, heron, wheatear and stonechat are all to be seen here, while grass of Parnassus is to be found in the region of the famous solitary holly tree mentioned previously. A solitary place, yet one which has a charm of its own and which is not without its points of interest—but then, if there *is* a fell devoid of interest, I have yet to find it!

24. Walk and LOOK

And snowdrops danced their snow-white heads

Few would dispute the fact that the great joy of walking is not just the physical exercise, the exhilaration of attaining heights and exploring new territory, great though that is, but the veritable wealth of interest that abounds in the observation of nature. There are few country walks – one is tempted to say there are *no* country walks – on which nothing of interest is to be found. Such pleasures may be increased greatly by the old habit of taking notes and transferring these to a diary in due course. As the years go by it is fascinating to turn back the pages and recall past observations: where we found that particular flower or saw that falcon, fox or deer; how early some events occurred, or how late, compared with the current season. A further aid is photography, which can provide a permanent pictorial record in colour. Without such records, even those of us with the best of memories – and there are those of us who would not lay claim to membership of that elite band – cannot expect to have total recall. Diaries provide a series of benchmarks; but more than that, they serve to alert us to events that are about to happen once again as the seasons turn, thus giving us a second chance to witness the many special events with which the natural year is so richly sprinkled.

After a very mild winter, March seems to have been a mixture of very stormy days and bright and sunny ones in the strongest contrast, as if we were having to pay for one with the other. Snowdrops long since danced their snow-white heads; there are celandines, coltsfoot, primroses, daisies, dandelions and many more, but he who looks only at the flowers of plants misses much.

It is only a little more difficult to identify plants at the seedling stage – and think how that extends the season of interest! Similarly, if we wish to extend our season still further, at the other end it is equally possible to identify flowering plants from their seeds. (There are those of us who have been expected to do just that, in order to establish the presence of impurities in agricultural seeds.) For those with the necessary equipment, it is also possible to identify plant species from their pollen grains. Just now there are catkins to be seen and if we touch a ripe one, a cloud of yellow 'dust' drifts away. Dust it may appear to be, but under the microscope it is soon quite obvious that this is pollen – tens of thousands of minute pollen grains – and those from each species are unique.

When someone mentions tadpoles, it conjures up a picture of small boys with jam jars, intrigued by the black wriggly mass fished from the depths of some much-favoured pond in sunny spring. We first saw spawn this year on the 19th of February, but we know from others that, in fact, there was some about in the previous month. Much less often do we see the frogs themselves. They hibernate in holes in the moss, in the mud and even under water at the bottom of the pond. Oxygen from the water is their sole income at that time, taken in through the skin; just enough to keep their hearts and little else ticking over until they emerge in search of a mate at the start of the year. Not that the life of a frog is all fun and games. Fox, badger, buzzard, peregrine and heron all take their toll, and around the spawning grounds there is ample evidence of the unlucky ones' swift demise.

While recently scanning a fell buttress, a raven sailed into view, its great black form gently floating round a crag, legs dangling, a long twig in its beak, slowly and gently descending, manoeuvring its way onto a rocky ledge selected for its now part-completed nest. It landed, pushed and pulled the twig until it occupied just the right place in the enormous tangle, and then effortlessly drifted off into the wind with two deep croaks of satisfaction.

Lakeland is a bountiful hunting ground for the naturalist at all levels and in all degrees, from pond to fell top and from mountain to microbe. To say 'let's hope' that current environmental threats will recede is no longer enough. There is something every single one of us can *do* to achieve that end. Can any of us afford to fail?

25. Haystacks

A magic place—a place apart

Of all the fells in Lakeland, large and small, smooth and craggy, can it be that there is one fell dearer to more hearts than Haystacks? It really does seem most unlikely, because Haystacks is within the scope of such a high proportion of walkers, and yet provides not only the greatest possible variety of terrain, but manages also to have a certain indefinable aura all its own. To analyse it too deeply might serve to break the spell and so suffice it to say it is a magic place whose call is more than just its crags and gullies, tarns and streams; it has an extra element which makes it somehow quite a place apart.

The best route of ascent is the direct one from Gatesgarth via Scarth Gap, returning by one or other of the two tracks from Little Round How or Dubbs Quarry to Warnscale Bottom. But it can also be reached from Ennerdale, the longest way, or from Honister, which involves the least climbing once the initial steep section is conquered. The first-named is the route followed here.

The climb to Scarth Gap is mostly rough and rocky; it is steep in the early stages, but has a relatively level stretch part way up, which offers a degree of respite for tired limbs and overworked lungs! There are compensations, in that there are good views all the way and there is, therefore, every excuse to stop and admire them, never admitting for one moment that to continue without a break is well-nigh impossible!

High Crag towers above and to the right; while behind rises the ridge of Fleetwith Pike, with Robinson beyond and back towards Buttermere. There is a natural amphitheatre formed by Fleetwith, Green Crag and Haystacks, and the white plumes of

65

the tumbling waters of Black Beck. During the ascent, the appearance of the face of Haystacks and Green Crag depends on the weather, the time of day and the quality of the light. It may appear quite simply as a solid wall of drab brown and purple hue, devoid of interest; but if, on the other hand, the elements are favourable, the 'wall' is seen to be punctuated by dozens of lesser crags, gullies, pinnacles and clefts in sharp relief. Big Stack, the main pillar of Haystacks top, is especially impressive.

Scarth Gap is a pass linking the Buttermere and Ennerdale valleys, with Haystacks on the left and with Seat, a subsidiary of High Crag, on the right. On reaching the pass itself, cut across towards Haystacks and a track appears which leads on round the side. Look out for worn rocks on the left, which indicate the way up through rock-strewn heather, scree and eventually solid rock. A rock wall is reached on the left-hand side and from here there are a number of variations. They are all good scrambles; none difficult or dangerous. Simply follow whichever well-worn way appeals, but remembering that, as usual, the top you can see is not really the top at all, but just another step along the way aloft! Nevertheless, with a little perseverance, the summit is eventually reached – and what a top it is! Something of a moonscape among tops and surely quite unique.

From the many vantage points along the length and breadth, there are fine views, including Scafell Pike, Great Gable, Green Gable, Helvellyn, Dale Head, Fleetwith Pike, Robinson, Skiddaw, Whiteless Pike, Grasmoor, Mellbreak and many more, as well as Buttermere, Crummock Water and Ennerdale Water. Whilst here, even if only for a short time, it is well worth visiting the top of Big Stack, or at least one of the edges overlooking Warnscale, from which there is a dramatically precipitous drop to the valley below, a sight denied those who stick to the well-worn track.

The return route takes us along the top of Haystacks past Green Crag on the left and Great Round How on the right. Shortly before Little Round How, bear left and downwards by a cairn from whence a narrow, rocky track leads all the way down on a zigzag course. Throughout the descent the view is enchanting – but be sure not to miss the towering crags of Haystacks on the left. They are most impressive from below, but on bright days, and only if the eyes are shaded against the bright light from above, as the glare robs one of all the detail. Also not to be missed are the glorious pools and cascades of Black Beck, which is close by on the right as the bottom is neared. Again, leave the obvious track and wander over to the water – worth every extra step, even at this stage of the walk.

Perhaps on first acquaintance, this walk is best done 'straight', without too many diversions or breaks, apart, that is, from the obligatory break for refreshments on top! But, really, the top has so much to offer that on at least one occasion, time should be allowed to explore it, rather than just cross it. It has a number of tarns, some named and even one named 'Innominate Tarn'. On good days, the views of Pillar Rock and Great Gable are especially fine, while another feature of interest is the balancing rock, seen to best advantage when looking back on the approach to Great Round How. From there it is quite unmistakable – a large boulder which appears to be perched precariously on the skyline.

With all its many attractions, Haystacks is very popular and the only chance of enjoying it in solitude is in early morning, late evening or winter. It is a special place, understandably dubbed by Wainwright, 'Dear Haystacks'! If you once visit it, you may be sure you will return.

26. September thoughts along the lonning

The gossamer of autumn enshrouds the ghostly trees, as fainter and fainter into the distance they all but merge in greyness beneath the diffuse ball of fire that gently bids adieu to yet another glorious day. Silence settles over all, only to be broken fleetingly by the rasping, bark-like call of a heron as it lazily flaps its giant wings to skim the glassy surface of the tarn.

Hedgerows are but sparsely brightened now by the occasional surviving blooms of red campion, buttercup, herb Robert and a few more; the splendour of the summer flowers has all but gone, the greens are tinged with yellow and move towards the gold and copper soon to follow.

Yet hope is ever-present in the natural world. Next year's seeds have already set and many have dropped, ready for germination. Some, like cleavers and burdock, will have attached themselves to passing animals, only to be knocked or scratched off at a fresh location. Others, like Indian balsam, will have been dehisced, propelled through the air by the 'explosive' mechanisms of their pods. The winged seeds of sweet Cicely will have fluttered down sideways, rather than simply dropping to the ground beneath, while the tiny black seeds of campion will have been shaken out of their capsules by the wind, as if from a pepper pot. All this and more to ensure distribution and the survival of the species.

Such 'preparation' for the winter and the coming spring is by no means confined to the plant world.

The local peregrines have been busy 'training' their eyasses in the art of aerial assault, then stooping and feinting, soaring and somersaulting, to strengthen the wing and quicken the eye, to gain maximum manoeuvrability against the fast-approaching time when they must fend for themselves. We recently watched as a pair of buzzards 'schooled' their young in like, but more leisurely, fashion.

Similarly, the fast-growing badger cubs have had to learn how to hunt for earthworms in the dewy grass, how to recognise the sound of a tasty beetle rustling nearby and how to supplement their autumn diet with blackberries.

This education of the year's young is in fact a most urgent activity, for time is short between spring birth and the onset of the potentially lethal cold, wet and windy months, during which a host of wildlife perishes annually. A good schooling in survival will often make the difference between life and death.

And then again, we have the magic of migration. The incredible flight of the swallow across the Sahara and beyond, and the southward flight of those wonderful skeins of geese. Can there be a sound and sight more evocative of autumn than the distant honk of geese and the thin arrowhead formation, purposefully drawing its line down the coast to warmer climes?

A hundred such survival stories surround us every day and, '—thus doth Mother Nature guard her own 'gainst fatal loss thro' Winter's cruel and perilous assault'.

27. Red Pike

A prince among fells

The northernmost peak of the High Stile range, Red Pike is a well-known landmark, clearly visible for miles and from most directions, except from Buttermere itself, where it is obscured by Dodd.

The popular route of ascent is from Buttermere village, passing to the left of the Fish Hotel and later taking the left fork, rather than the right-hand one, which leads to Scale Hill Bridge. Once over the new wooden footbridge across the stream, Buttermere Dubbs, the start of the climb is signposted, and a considerable climb it is. Just to the right of the sign is the foot of Sour Milk Gill, a relatively new jumble of rocks resulting from a substantial fall only a few years ago – a fall which I heard one evening in the Bridge Hotel, where I was staying at the time.

The ascent may be divided into four sections. First there is the part from the valley floor to a welcome grassy shelf at about 1,600 feet. Time was, to reach this point necessitated a constant scramble over very rough, boulder-strewn and, in parts, unstable terrain, caused partly by the natural construction of the fellside and partly through the erosion resulting from tree-felling and the tramp of many thousands of pairs of boots. Sadly, the erosion became so bad that it was deemed necessary to 'repair' the track, so that the way is now far easier, much of it 'laid' with stone and even protected by small sections of walling. Essential, no doubt, but what a pity it is that the very wildness of a place attracts so much attention that repairs are necessary which reduce a mountain track to something approaching a 'Roman road'. The climb to the grassy shelf is still steep, of course, and gaining the shelf is still something of a relief.

Stage two starts here. The track levels off, relatively speaking; it runs close to Sour Milk Gill, a pretty spot with its rushing waters and cascades, but beware; the rock therein is wet, greasy and slippery in the extreme and has proved fatal in the past. From the shelf then, the track crosses the stream, which feeds into the gill and leads on into the combe with its splendid backdrop of Chapel Crags, beneath which nestles Bleaberry Tarn. Skeletal fish, probably arising from eggs inadvertently deposited from the legs of duck and heron, eke out a meagre existence in its dark and rock-bound depths.

But then, after the rest afforded by the combe floor, begins stage three; a loose, rock-strewn section rising steeply from tarn level to the saddle lying between Red Pike and Dodd. In short, a section that is 'rough and tough', with no great feature save the view of combe, tarn and crag; a long and trying haul.

Stage four, the final assault in which soil and scree at last, if only for a few blissful yards, give way to solid rock, where boots may firmly grip and propel the weary limbs aloft to the summit cairn at 2,479 feet and, of course, to the superb views over Buttermere, Crummock and Ennerdale and some 50 tops. And, by the way, the soil and rock *are* red – hence the name, Red Pike.

There was a time when it seemed a good idea to tackle this climb early in the day in order to get photos from the top while the sun was still towards the east. After the effort of an early rise and a climb at a determined and purposeful rate, arrival at the summit coincided exactly with the arrival of the rain! Ah, well, if you can't take a joke—!

From this fine vantage point, once duly savoured and with breath restored, a number of excellent routes are available. There is the glorious ridge route described over High Stile and High Crag to Scarth Gap from whence to Gatesgarth and Buttermere, or, if you've the puff, on over Haystacks, Dale Head and Robinson – now, there's a walk!! Or there is the track down to High Gillerthwaite in Ennerdale, from where a return route may be made along Ennerdale Water and on towards Whin, just short of which is a signposted route to Floutern Tarn and Buttermere via Scale Force. This latter route is usually very wet and always very rough. This is a grand round trip, but assess the mileage first

– it is not short. Alternatively, there is a track along Lingcomb Edge, which is quite spectacular, and which eventually veers left and finally gives a descent along the side of Scale Force, the highest waterfall in Lakeland. (A good route in reasonable weather, but a dangerous traverse in icy conditions, because of the sheer drop into the gill. This is mentioned only because a certain scribbling walker who shall be nameless once lost his footing on ice here and spent some unforgettable seconds suspended above the gill by one hand, and does not propose repeating the experience.)

Then there is yet another way from the saddle between Red Pike and Dodd down through Lingcomb. This used to be very indistinct and one could get in a muddle in deep heather, but through increased usage it is now much clearer and can easily be seen from above. Any of these routes is likely to prove interesting from the point of view of wildlife. There are a number of birds of prey in the area; wheatears, ring ouzels, duck and geese on the lakes; and in the Scale area, many cuckoos in spring. There are a number of lichens and wild flowers, including sundew and butterwort.

Red Pike, a grand mountain, perhaps seen to best advantage from around Lanthwaite Green on the approach to Buttermere. An absolute must for any walker in the Buttermere district and one that may be incorporated in a number of good circular walks. A prince among fells!

28. Scafell Pike

The highest in the land

Well, we did make a reasonably early start, but by the time we were at Seathwaite there was little doubt in our minds that we were in for another hot day. However, the plan had been laid and, come what may, we were determined on returning to the highest place in England, Scafell Pike.

We set off along the broad and well-worn track along the River Derwent, now reduced to little more than a trickle, and over Stockley Bridge, where that deliciously blue pool already looked most inviting. In fact, we jokingly said, "Oh, let's spend the day here instead!"; but with great resolution on we went, turning sharp left along the old wall, leaving the Sty Head route on our right, and gradually the steepness increased. Surely, these tracks have never been dryer. Fine dust puffed up around our boots and every stone and rock was loose instead of stuck in the customary plastic bed of wet soil. With Glaramara on our left, Seathwaite Fell on our right and the massive bulk of Great End in front, this is a striking, if not spectacular, route. Once past the old sheepfold there are normally some fine cascades, but now they are much reduced by drought.

The next section is one of the steepest parts of the walk and borders on a fine, but apparently unnamed, gill, home for one or two interesting plants and accessible only to sheep or some adventurous and well-roped soul. However, a telephoto lens makes a useful monocular, and with its aid it seemed that one such plant was orpine or livelong, a sedum (*S. Telephium L.*) – and, by the way, in case there are any readers who are of a scientific turn of mind, that capital letter for *Telephium* is intentional! – although the flowers did seem rather more bronze than purple. A fascinating ravine, this, worth returning to specifically to explore, but one cannot combine that activity with a visit to the Pike!

And then over the hump, soon gaining a view of Sprinkling Tarn below and to the right, and joining the track coming up from Sty Head and Wasdale Head. Dead ahead stands the enormous solid wall of Great End, rent asunder down the centre of its face by the south-east and the central gullies. We turn left up to Esk Hause and then bear right for Calf Cove, then on to Broad Crag. A short stop here where a most welcome little beck obligingly crosses our path and offers an irresistible cooling splash or two; the last drop of water to be had on the ascent.

By now it was blisteringly hot as we approached the roughest section of all – indeed, one of the roughest areas in the whole of Lakeland. Between Broad Crag and the Pike lies a wilderness of large, tumbled, jumbled, jagged, ragged rocks. Despite their size, it would appear that they have been most carefully arranged to make quite sure that a very high proportion look perfectly safe and stable, but they are not! They will tip, they will almost balance, but not quite, and there are as many ankle-twisting sections as in the rest of the fells put together. Woe betide he who hurries here! A scene of the utmost geological chaos.

There is, as so often happens, some small descent before the final assault – arranged by the planners of such terrain to make certain that the ultimate pull up is as protracted as possible! A glance back gives a fine view of Green Crag – and then on up to the Pike itself – another good jumble of rocks, which, on the day in question, reflected the heat and the glare to the full. The great, round, flat-topped cairn is a masterpiece and gives a firm foundation on which to stand and declare that, if only for a moment, one really is the Highest in the Land!!

This day can hardly be called typical. So much more often is Scafell Pike wreathed in mist, drenched in rain, deep in snow, windswept and inhospitable. At 3,210 feet, little survives here. A pair of ravens glided by and the only other living things (apart from a few intrepid walkers) were the occasional misguided lichen, a solitary tuft of grass and, of all things, flies. Why something as mobile as a fly should opt to make its home up here is a mystery. What *do* they live on, and why ever don't they find somewhere more comfortable?

It was very hazy now and the view was not all that extensive, but Great Gable, Hell's Gate and Napes Needles showed up dramatically well across the valley. We've said it many times before—"The best way to see any mountain is from the top of another!"

Scafell Pike is not alone in having a confusing 'top', and care must be taken before starting on the descent to make doubly sure that the correct route is selected, otherwise the sheer drudgery of back-tracking, or worse, may befall the unwary. (We once met a chap coming down Gasgale Gill late in the afternoon who pointed down at Crummock Water and said, "That *is* Derwentwater down there, isn't it?" The sight of him trudging all the way back to Coledale Hause and beyond haunts us still!) From the summit we dropped down to Broad Crag col and turned left down a sea of unstable rock and scree, all of which seemed bent on the descent too, in the direction of Piers Gill, then right past Round How and so on down to Sty Head. From the region of Round How there is a most impressive view of Great End's Long Pike above and to the right, a really grand, bold and jagged pinnacle.

Scafell Pike's prime claim to fame is, of course, its superior height. It is rough and barren; it is bare, rugged and hardly beautiful. However, it does provide a certain grandeur of its own and a stimulating 11-mile walk. A good place to visit, especially in relative solitude, to gain a new perspective and '—to lose all thought of this world's Pygmy pomp'.

29. Pillar

Atop some turret crag

The long approach to Wasdale Head, skirting as it does the often
black and forbidding depths of Wastwater with its backdrop of
enormous screes, serves only to encourage the walker by giving
promise of even more dramatic scenes to come. The dale
improves as it is penetrated, opening out, 'tis true, but with what
an encirclement of mountains. From its head there is a clear view
of Scafell Pike, Great Gable, Yewbarrow, Red Pike, Pillar and
more besides.

But today Pillar has been selected as the prime target; that
massive bulk of fell that stands four-square between Wasdale and
Ennerdale. Still, on leaving the tiny hamlet by the track parallel to
Mosedale Beck and then veering right along Gatherstone Beck, it
is Yewbarrow which attracts attention away to the left, for enough
of its impressive Stirrup Crag may be seen to ensure that it is
promptly marked down with the immortal words – "I shall
return!"

However, to proceed. The ascent to the first feature is quite
long, but it is relatively gentle. Just below Black Sail Pass we
cross Gatherstone Beck, which is just about the last drop of water
on the way up. Here we bear left and upward towards the summit,
but shortly after reaching Looking Stead on our right, watch out
for a fork in the track marked by a small cairn. Fork right across
the north face of Pillar on what is known as the High Level
Traverse. Up to this point the route is almost entirely broad, but,
as one might expect, the traverse is hardly that; it is narrower
throughout. It has numerous ups and downs, some gentle and
some far from gentle; it has scrambles, jumbled rock and solid

rock. In fact, it is very variable indeed, which is part of its charm. It is a fine scrambling-walker's route and is great fun.

Nevertheless, it must be said that, while there is nothing really difficult, it *is* a scramble in places and there are spots where a trip or a slip could prove rather nasty. There are some sections where there is a sheer drop to the right and others where solid slabs of rock sport an 'adverse camber' – no problem in dry conditions, but care is needed when the rock is greasy or icy. So it's grand, it's superb – but do be careful!

Quite suddenly on approaching Robinson's Cairn, an unmistakable structure perched right on the edge, there it is – Pillar Rock! So clearly seen from way down the far end of Ennerdale Water, but hidden from view until now on this route. And what a Pillar it is! The sheer grandeur of this massive column rising up from the side of the mountain, its very size, its rugged declivities and towering buttresses conjure up a picture of some Lakeland castle guarding the approach to Great Gable. Half close the eyes and there is the standard fluttering bravely in the wind, and is not that the clink of armour drifting up from the floor of the valley far below?

On the southern side is Pisgah, and then a great cleft, Jordan Gap, followed by High Man, the true summit of Pillar Rock, with Low Man beneath and forming the northernmost point before the precipitous drop to Green Ledge. On the approach we pass over Shamrock and then left, steeply up to the top of Pillar Mountain some 400 feet above the top of the Rock, but pausing frequently, not so much to catch breath as for the sheer delight of looking *down* on the Rock and beyond it, right down to the miniature trees, the forest road and the Liza, all far, far below. This section, the High Level Traverse, is, without doubt, one of the most outstanding stretches of terrain in Lakeland, a four-star route, if ever there was one.

And so to the top, with its inevitable cairn affording welcome shelter, for although we had climbed most of the way in the lightest gear on quite a hot day, the bare and windswept top was cold and bleak and found us immediately donning sweaters and windcheaters. Here we had our usual top-of-the-hill snack and just as quickly made our way southeast to rejoin our original route just above Looking Stead, from there to retrace our steps to Wasdale Head. What more can be said? A nine-mile walk, climbing 2,700 feet to the top of the highest mountain west of Great Gable, standing 2,927 feet above sea level. But statistics are soulless things compared with the great satisfaction of visiting such a place—and to be able to do it all from home in a day! Aren't we lucky?

30. Extinction is forever

It is now a good many years since I gave up trying to think of a new title for every talk and lecture I give up and down the country against the background of fell-walking; long ago I adopted the universal one of 'Walking with Wildlife' and, although that remains constant, no such talk or lecture has yet been repeated in its entirety. The subject is so vast that there are always changes that can be rung and different combinations of aspects and species to employ.

The vastness of the natural world is one of its great fascinations; tens of thousands of species of plants and animals, from celandine to the sequoia and from the hydra to the hump-backed whale. Even the common celandine is worth a second look – we can find it with seven, eight, nine, ten, eleven and twelve petals! But that is nothing compared to the dandelion, which can be found in over 100 different forms!

At the same time, there are still many species to be identified, named and classified and whose part in the overall scheme of things is yet to be evaluated. From a purely selfish point of view, therefore, it would clearly be unwise for Man wittingly to allow the destruction of species that might be of great value for some as yet unsuspected purpose.

Some degree of biodiversity has already been lost, but at least we are now alive to the problem and, indeed, some species have been pulled back from the brink. In this very area we very nearly lost the peregrine falcon, that fabulous raptor, the fastest bird in Britain; but, thanks to the introduction of less persistent pesticides, the voluntary guarding of nest sites and the introduction of severe penalties for egg thieves, the position was reversed. It was a close-run thing. We got down to ten pairs.

Tales of the peregrine becoming too numerous are, of course, nonsense. Population will be limited naturally, as it always has been, by the limited number of suitable nest sites, by the availability of suitable food and by severe winters. We may well sympathise with the pigeon fanciers, but the fells are a natural habitat for these birds and the maintenance of biodiversity for universal benefit must surely have priority over the hobby of a small minority. But all is not yet well, as a mere sample of facts and figures will illustrate:

1. Ponds are important habitats for a wide range of species, but it is estimated that in the UK we have lost a million in the last 100 years.
2. We have lost 20% of bird species in the last 2,000 years and 11% of those species remaining are currently under threat.
3. Song thrushes are in decline; so are lapwings, skylarks and yellowhammers. The corncrake is endangered. The number of frogs and toads is falling worldwide.
4. Planting conifers close to watercourses increases the acidity of the water; this reduces or even eliminates crustaceans and invertebrates – the food of dippers – and fish.
5. Oak woods are one of our most important habitats. We have felled much of our ancient woodlands (it took 2,000 mature oak trees to make one man-of-war); each mature oak can hold some 200 gallons of water in its root system. Absence of such hillside woodland accelerates erosion and reduces habitat.
6. The effects of acid rain are well-known, but in 1986 we in Britain released four million tons of sulphur dioxide into the atmosphere, a degree of pollution now much reduced.

A lot has been done and is being done to halt the slide, but much more must be done as a matter of urgency. True, world governments must accept a high degree of responsibility, but none of us can pass this particular buck entirely. Conservation is an attitude of mind we should all adopt, from saving newspapers, cans and bottles for recycling to supporting the major conservation bodies by subscribing to the enormous sums of money on which their work depends. We may not agree with all that they do, but their overall effort is undeniable. The National Trust, the RSPB – which alone spends some £20 million on conservation projects – the Wildlife Trusts and others create and maintain nature reserves, which serve as havens and reservoirs for wildlife, which are essential, but they also serve as vital teachers, watchdogs and pressure groups. The bigger the membership, the more notice government will take of the expert and professional views which such bodies can express.

The combination of personal, regional, national and international activity can make all the difference. It is needed now. Tomorrow may be too late, for there is no escape from the old conservation adage that, *'extinction is forever'*.

31. The Liza Path

A place of solitude

Having sung the praises of Ennerdale on at least three occasions, we trust we shall not bore you by returning yet again, especially as this time it is to describe a different route.

Bowness Knott car park is again the starting point, and we set off along the forestry road in the direction of Black Sail. We simply follow the road, but that does not mean to say that this part of the walk is devoid of interest. Keep an eye open on the left among the conifers and there is every chance of seeing blue tits, great tits, coal tits and the tiny goldcrest, too. You may well see a kestrel or a buzzard soar out and away from the treetops. There are always wildfowl at the end of the lake and you will hear the unmistakable cackling 'laugh' of the mallard. The area is not so devoid of wildlife as one might expect. One day in late November, while doing the circuit of the lake, we recorded 18 species of bird! In the main we tend to find bird calls far from easy to identify—with the obvious exceptions. One that we do know well and which always stops us in our tracks is that of the peregrine falcon. We heard it on this latest trip and there, sure enough, stood the female on her lofty perch high above the crags; just discernible to the naked eye, but seen to best advantage through binoculars.

But I digress. Along the lakeside road past the concrete Irish Bridge on the right, straight on past Gillerthwaite and past the signs on the left for Red Pike. Soon now we have a fine view of Steeple, its pointed top reaching up into the mist and its upper flanks powdered with snow. Next we draw towards the base of Pillar and have superb views of this glorious mountain with Pillar Rock silhouetted against the overcast sky.

As we near Pillar there is a fork in the road – we go right and down a slope to cross a bridge over the river and turn immediately right along the bank. This is the Liza Path, opened by Chris Bonnington in 1985, and there is a large plaque to remind us of the fact. Now, this is a place at which to linger. At this point the Liza is confined to a relatively narrow rocky gorge and, especially after heavy rain, there are rushing, foaming torrents, which at one point divide to encircle a massive central rock. There are deep pools and the water appears an eerie aquamarine greeny-blue: a place of solitude with the steep-sided high fells all around and not a sound, save that of running water. The track ahead runs roughly parallel to the river, finally turning right again to the Irish Bridge, where we rejoin the forestry road.

But the track is quite enchanting alongside the rushing water; water, which fans out to wandering shallows through conifer forest, open heathy glades, over emerald moss and a narrow rustic bridge and with continual glimpses of the crags above. Sometimes there is a dipper, sometimes a flash of watery take-off as red-breasted mergansers splash into the air, and sometimes a solitary heron, standing motionless, awaiting the approach of prey.

The Irish Bridge will always bring back memories of a particular incident a year or two ago. Simba, my golden retriever, is naturally forever in and out of the water and regularly dashes into the river at this juncture. Well, at the time in question we had had a lot of rain and, of course, the river was in spate. He was gaily swimming around, but the current was strong and I suddenly realised to my horror that he was in some difficulty. He was upstream of the bridge, but he was being drawn to it by the force of the water and towards one of the pipes that take the water beneath the bridge. There was absolutely nothing I could do but stand and watch and, swim as he might, he was clearly losing the battle. With gathering speed he was sucked into the pipe and disappeared from view! After what seemed like an eternity he suddenly came gushing out of the other side, like a cork from a bottle, looking very surprised and not a little relieved. He swam to the bank and gave a very strong shake, looking round at me as if to say, "Well, I made it – but I don't think I'll try that one again!"

However, such adventures apart, this little circuit, which takes three to four hours, is well worth a try. It is easy going all the way and delightfully varied.

ICE

Wan sunlight filters through
The morning mist,
But barely warms the chillsome air;
Deep blue the cloudless sky
And all is still, as Jack Frost stands
O'er his night's work
To survey and admire,
As row on row the spiny crystals gleam.
But walkers do beware
This crisp and sugary scene,
Which so beguiles the senses
And the boot, that in a trice,
From 'neath the unwary
Deftly pulls the rug and
Sends one earthwards with a thump;
All's chaos in a second,
Struggle, thrash and grab
As well we may,
The trick's so quick
We're horizontal in a flash
And wondering how
The ground came up so fast!

AJG

32. Lakeland lanes

As the seasons turn

To many of us the high fell is the ultimate walking country, especially when wandering way off the beaten track rather than on the all-too-well-known and 'popular' routes, exploring those distant gullies usually frequented by fox and buzzard rather than humankind. But none of us can be right up there all the time; we have to have 'routine' walks closer to home, if only to achieve the regular excursions demanded by our four-legged friends. Such perambulations are also invaluable in periods such as the recent ones when storm has been followed by severe gale, gale and just plain strong wind! At such times the local lonnings are useful, to say the least, and although they may be traversed regularly, there is always something of interest to note. Roadsides, banks, hedges, trees – and the fields just over the hedges, too; the sky above and the watery ditch, each provides a habitat suitable for something; there is always something to remember, to see or to anticipate as the seasons turn.

Roadside snowdrops have been in flower for weeks now and, having reached early March, the celandines, too, are in flower. That is, the lesser celandine; the greater celandine is unrelated and does not appear until May.

The rich gold of the gorse is always with us, flowering as it does in every month of the year; a wonderfully showy member of the *Papilionaceae* – the butterfly-like flowers. The systematic botanists are always finding excuses for changing the classical names of species of both plants and animals, if only to confuse us and make things difficult by altering the terminology of a lifetime! Gorse, whin and furze always used to be *Planta spinosa*, an easy name to associate with gorse, because 'spinosa' immediately reminds one of the spines of the plant. But no, that was too simple, and now it answers to the name of *Ulex europea* – not quite so memorable.

Not that we need to wait for the appearance of flowers to appreciate that plant life is well and truly on the move again. Just look along the banks and you will find the developing leaves of dog's mercury, violet, herb Robert, red campion, primrose and many more, not only emerging, but increasing in leaf area at a tremendous rate. Much of this early plant growth, as with the onset of germination of seeds, is triggered by accumulated day degrees or heat units – accumulated warmth, if you like. Once we have a certain amount of 'warmth' above a certain base level, away they go. The reactions of some seeds and plants to day degrees, is very critical and can be used to forecast with great accuracy the development of seeds in the seedbed, or even the emergence of that great pest of summer days, the midge. Current development is not confined to plants; we have frogspawn again in ditches, ponds and puddles and some birds have been busily building their nests.

The hedges are frequented by lots of birds: robin, wren, chaffinch, blackbird and blue tit, all searching among the twigs and litter for scraps of food. The hedges are hunting grounds for others, too. The sudden swish and swoop of something larger skimming the top of the hedge in the hope of flushing out the small birds, heralds the attack of the sparrowhawk, often so fast and fleeting that it is identified more by its method of attack than by any single physical feature one has time to see.

A sudden jerky rustle and darting movement in the hedge itself or among the litter beneath may suggest something of fur rather than feather. Stand absolutely still and watch and you may well find that you are face-to-face with a stoat. If you move a muscle he is likely to be gone in a flash, but stare him out and you may be able to enjoy fascinating moments of mutual inspection. A hunter to be often seen atop a roadside tree, is the kestrel, our most common bird of prey, but so beautifully marked. Often seen when motoring, it is likely to stay put on its perch as long as your car keeps moving, but if you dare to slow to a stop and reach for the camera, it will usually drop from the tree and swoop away.

We have the bleat of lambs around us once more, and soon that evocative sound will be accompanied by the warbling call of the curlew, that large wader with the long, downward-curving bill, which returns to the higher ground each year to breed. And soon the trees will begin to burst their buds and once again we shall see that welcome mantle of green begin to deck our woods and hedges. What incredible things trees are – and let's hope Man begins to respect them a little more before it's too late. A single 100-year-old beech draws up and transpires 20 tons of water a year through its 500,000 leaves! The oak tree harbours around 280 different species of insect – a small wonder oak woods are happy feeding grounds for so much birdlife! Conifers, needless to say, harbour a fraction of that number.

So, next time your walking is confined to the local lonnings, remember that they are edged with many wonders of nature; plant and animal, large and small, common and not-so-common, and aplenty if you really *look*! Whatever else they may be, they can never be accused of being boring!!

33. Watendlath

—once contorted, now serene

A walk in the vicinity of Watendlath calls first for a drive to Keswick and out on the B5289 alongside Derwentwater, forking left just past Falcon Crag. This narrow twisting road, with its many ups and downs, takes us all the way to Watendlath through enchanting scenery. A grand array of ancient woodland, crag, beck and force; deep defiles, rocky outcrops and dashing rivulets falling to Watendlath Beck. An area ruggedly moulded through a combination of volcanic action and the Ice Age, it is so clearly 'once contorted, now serene'.

Watendlath – which means 'the end of the lake' – is a very tiny hamlet made famous in literature as the focal point of Hugh Walpole's *Herries Chronicle*. It is remote indeed, but is so great a favourite with walkers and others that there is a mini-café here in 17th century surroundings, which provides a very excellent cup of coffee and other delights for consumption before or after the main event.

Once here, there are a number of possibilities. There is a walk past Watendlath Tarn to Dock Tarn, for example, or the circuit of Brand Fell, from which there is a direct view down onto Castle Crag, the site of an ancient earthwork. Not for nothing is the area called 'Borrowdale' – the valley of the fortress.

But we have elected to go higher, starting due east from the car park up the steep and much-repaired fellside track, turning right along the wall towards Blea Tarn.

Depending on the length of walk required; there is then a further choice between going to, and indeed beyond, Blea Tarn; before turning back along the ridge, over Shivering Knott and

Middle Crag and on to High Tove, where a sharp left turn brings one down the western slope again to the aforementioned stone wall.

Or, if this is longer than required, the distance may be much reduced by turning east part-way along the southerly leg and aiming across the fell, straight for Shivering Knott. This is rough, tussocky stuff, with humps and hollows, wet spots and outcrops, but the distance is not great.

On the descent from High Tove in late May and early June, we pass through an area rich in sundew, butterwort and milkwort. The latter is often classified simply as *Polygala vulgaris*, but it is very variable in form and in colour; blue, pink and white flowers being easily found. Some authorities differentiate between the forms and describe no less than five different species—but whatever the truth, the depth of colour of the blue is fabulous.

The view from the ridge is superb, taking in the Helvellyn range to the east; Glaramara, Great Gable and the Scafells to the south-west; Eel Crags, Maiden Moor and Grasmoor to the west; and to the north a view right along Bassenthwaite Lake. There are over 40 tops to be seen, but to identify them all is a stiff test indeed.

One word of warning – this area is inclined to be very wet underfoot, so it's best to enjoy it in a dry spell – or be prepared.

On the return from Watendlath by car, look out for the 'Surprise View' – a magnificent viewpoint above Derwentwater, which suddenly appears through a gap in the trees on the left. This is a wonderful vantage point and should not be missed.

Another highlight of our particular day was to see and hear, albeit at some distance, an occupied nest site of our favourite companion, the peregrine falcon. Through binoculars we watched the frantic flapping of young wings as this year's brood flexed their muscles in preparation for launching themselves from the rocky ledge. Yet another element that went to make up a great day in a fascinating part of Lakeland.

34. Sheer magic

The combination of high temperatures and very short periods of darkness combined to make us all, I am sure, wake early and perhaps realise that, by adhering to the normal hours of activity, we were missing something special and very probably the very best part of the day. Well, at least that seemed to be a theory worth testing, so, nothing daunted, I decided to get up really early for once and venture out into the big wide world before most folk were about their daily round.

Three o'clock in the morning seemed about right, and so it was that at that delightful hour I tumbled out of my bed on Wednesday 25th July and sped from Mockerkin. My planning did go a little awry, in that I sadly omitted to warn my neighbours of my intentions and learned afterwards that at the first click of the car door, protective souls to left and right were leaping from between the sheets, convinced that cars were being broken into yet again! I do apologise!

However, oblivious of the alarms in our wake, I sped to Lanthwaite Green and duly left the parked car there at 4:15. There was very little light at this point, but just enough for me to be able to distinguish between grass and rock as I crossed the Green and made my way to the footbridge. The familiar climb to the top of Whiteside was undertaken in the eerie stillness of approaching dawn, and never has it been dryer underfoot. As I neared the top there was a strange roseate hue to Dove Crags – it seemed almost as if it came from within, instead of from the as-yet unseen rising sun. It showed up, in far greater detail than is seen later in the day, the gullies and buttresses of that rocky precipice. Similarly, the steep northern face of Eel Crags was illumed with a warm blush, which emphasised its detail in turn.

Down to the right this strange light flowed horizontally towards Gasgale Gill, and the shadows it cast there clearly showed a moraine, which in full sun would easily pass unnoticed. Just as I approached the summit of Whiteside at 5:50, I first caught sight of the sun itself; a dazzling golden ball immediately above the stark point of Grisedale Pike, while to the north-west there lay below a series of lesser fells, paler and paler into the distance, each one a mere silhouette with a golden rim. Ahead and to the right of Grisedale was the protruding stump of Causey Pike.

Prostrate juniper, Lakeland's answer to the Bonsai tree, seems to be gaining ground up here, and a very good thing, too; it appeared an unnaturally blue-green at this time of day.

So I made my way upward to Hopegill Head, a superb vantage point from which to survey the scene of glowing landscape: and the point must be made that in fact this was no exceptional dawn. What must it be like up here on those rare early mornings when we have genuine red sky? But no matter, this was the one I was witnessing and it was breathtaking. Down the long descent to Coledale Hause, where I breakfasted at 7:30 by the rushing beck. The bell heather was brilliant purple over much of the clearly-defined 24 ribs of Whiteside, and its delightful perfume hung heavily in the air. Along the well-worn downward track through Gasgale Gill I was surprised to find a recent heavy fall of rock – or more accurately – the recent fall of a heavy rock; a massive boulder, which had lain undisturbed for many a long year, had finally succumbed to the nagging efforts of wind and weather.

There was little to note in the way of wildlife, except that a small flock of grey wagtails had joined the inevitable dippers along the beck, while beyond the gill there were yellowhammers on the bracken tops. Again, in the still relatively early light, the *Polytrichum* moss seemed an even more brilliant emerald green than ever.

Stillness, incredible clarity, the strange shades of light, beauty, peace and tranquillity. Sheer magic.

Please Don't Mock the Turtle

A group of local birdwatchers recently went to sea to observe the seabirds along the cliffs in the St Bees area. While good birdwatching was no doubt had by all, the greatest excitement was caused, not by a bird, but by the persistent presence of a turtle of considerable proportions!

Whilst I was not there, the description given leaves little doubt that it was in fact a leathery turtle, or lupe (*Dermochelys coriacea L.*), a beast whose carapace, or shell, measures anything around six feet, with an overall length of some eight–ten feet and a weight of about 800–1,000 lbs.

(Had the vessel been a small one, clearly a collision could have caused it to turn turtle—!)

The lupe is something of a rarity. The British Museum (Natural History) keeps records of all turtles reported in British waters, and it has been reported only 40 times throughout the period 1767–1966. With an average frequency of sightings of only once every five years, the chances of seeing one in all that vast area of water are remote indeed.

PS   Had I failed to report it, I would have been in the soup!

35. Dawn's early light

No matter with what determination and enthusiasm the prospect is considered the night before, when the moment arrives to actually get up, really early in the small hours, things are different! I am convinced that at that time we weigh more than later in the day – levering oneself away from the sheets can be so difficult. Once the break is made, movement rapidly accelerates and the initial lethargy is overcome in a trice. Hard it may be – but *so* rewarding.

Timing is vital. Too early is simply a waste, while too late leads to terrible frustration. I rose one day this summer when it was still inky-black, but by the time I reached Fangs there was just a glimmer in the eastern sky, enough to give a scarce delineated edge where felltops met the blue beyond. The night was still distinct, but little by little it surrendered to the advancing day. There was a velvet blackness through which the eerie dawn crept silently into view. Then, as at dusk, there is an awesome twilight zone, when objects float 'twixt sharp reality and the all-embracing darkness of the night, and when accompanying sounds are likewise muffled between the clarity of wakefulness and the oblivion of slumber. A transitional point in time – a pause in life itself.

There is a slow and gentle lightening of the sky, a gradual change, barely discernible; a subtle paling of shade, an orange streaking in the blue, a creeping glow, until that sudden moment of transformation. Until then the night is dominant, the coming hours of daylight the barest hint on the horizon. But in the next instant a shaft of light beams forth, as the very first vestige of the sun's circumference rises above the crest of the distant fell.

The suddenness is amazing. One second there is no sun to be seen – but in the next there is a blinding flash. A 'shaft' of light indeed – as sudden and as piercing as any clothyard shaft at

Agincourt or Crécy. What a contrast between 'dawn' and 'sunrise'.

On another day such scenes were witnessed from the slightly greater height of the Coffin Route, above Holme Wood, but on that occasion all below was pure white. The rumpled blankets of mist lay carelessly along the bed of the valley, as if tossed aside by the awakening day, then slipping slowly and silently towards the sea, an echo of the glaciers of 10,000 years ago. The route was the same, but what a contrast in style! The one as soft as gossamer and as silent as the grave; the other as hard as iron, crushing and grinding its thunderous progress. And yet each in its own way enveloping all in its path; the one leaving no trace within the hour, the other creating lakes and mountains to survive the centuries.

Fascinating early hours, when most that can be seen has altered little since prehistoric times – Man's impact being merely to scratch the surface and occasionally to burrow a little.

So stand the fells; sombre and grand in their simplicity, still half in shadow with wisps of mist ascending, so that at times it is difficult to distinguish between the material and the transient. A scene of pure tranquillity reflected in the mirrors of the lakes. It is a beautiful world.

36. —onto the rim like a cork from a bottle!

Among the many interests that abound in so varied an area as Lakeland, is botany – partly because the wide range of habitats allows a great number of species to find acceptable homes and partly because, as a result, it has its rarities.

One such rarity is the red alpine catchfly (*Viscaria alpina*), which is unknown in any location other than our own Hobcarton Crag. The very fact that there is the possibility of seeing such a plant is excuse enough for some to 'have a go', and since Wainwright says, 'Don't', the challenge becomes even more irresistible!

A little over a mile east of Scawgill Bridge in the lower reaches of Whinlatter Pass lies Swinside House, and a fifth of a mile east of that, on the southern side of the road, is the start of a forestry road where there is ample room to park the car. Reference to the Ordnance Survey map will show that from this point there are tracks in a number of directions, including one which goes due west, virtually parallel to the B5292, and then suddenly doubles back along the west side of Hobcarton Gill towards Hobcarton Crag. This latter points one precisely in the right direction, and when it runs out it is simply a matter of continuing in a straight line along the side of the fell.

The valley gradually narrows, with Ladyside Pike on one side and Hobcarton on the other. Ahead, the end is entirely blocked by Hobcarton Crag, a broken, shattered cliff with numerous gullies, ledges of grass and scree, bilberry and heather.

As the end of the valley is approached, a gill of considerable size appears on the right, having previously been screened from view by a rocky buttress. This provides a route all the way to the top. It is full of loose soil, scree and rock, and much of it and the surrounding wall is unstable, moving beneath the feet and coming away in the hand. Quite safe, provided one is aware of its condition, and provided that in consequence complete reliance is never placed on the foot or hand alone!

It is quite a stiff climb; the gully narrowing dramatically in places, but decidedly interesting, and then suddenly, at last, emerging onto the rim of Hobcarton Crag just below the summit of Hopegill Head. Having reached this superb vantage point, however, the walk is by no means over—more delights are to follow. Round the rim of Hobcarton Crag and on to Grisedale Pike, over the top, down the ridge towards Hobcarton End, Black Crag and, eventually, the forestry road and the car. But this is all good walking and not without interest.

Whatever you do, keep looking back across the valley towards Hopegill Head to savour yet again the gill climb so recently achieved! From this angle it doesn't just look steep, it looks almost impossible – giving one a (quite false!) sense of pride—even more so than popping up over the rim like the proverbial cork from a bottle!

The descent from Grisedale Pike is not devoid of interest. On the upper slopes plant growth is sparse indeed. Cladonia lichens, bilberry, bearberry, crowberry—and alpine clubmoss grow here; a suitable diet for reindeer, which just serves to remind us once again that the upper fells are classed as sub-alpine and have the flora to support such a claim.

Nearing the end of the descent it is possible, though probably not advisable, to take a shortcut straight down the steep fellside. Not advisable because of two hazards in the intervening stretch which are not immediately obvious until one is committed.

First, there is an area of quite the deepest moss imaginable. It is springy in the extreme and the first step or two are great fun, rather like walking over feather beds, but the novelty soon palls as high-stepping through this entangling green mass becomes increasingly hard work.

Second, there is a stretch of forest brash, which is a veritable entanglement of twigs, branches and stumps, each one so trained as to trip and snare the boot of the weary ones who dare to penetrate the patch. Much easier to go a little further round and avoid them both!

37. —just around the corner!

The vast majority of walkers would agree that winter walking generally provides the best and the most exhilarating of the year. Given the appropriate clothing and the initial energy and enthusiasm to lever oneself out of the armchair and away from the comfort of the fireside, the rewards for braving the elements far outweigh the hazards and discomforts. It is all a matter of degree and contrast.

Look out at night from a brightly-lit room and there is nothing but inky blackness; but venture out and in half-an-hour much of the darkness has melted away and there is much more to see than one might think. In the same way, get up and go, on what appears to be 'a dreadful day', and return with a great internal glow that no fireside can reproduce.

We must admit that this winter, so far, we've had but few of those truly glorious brilliant frosty days which light up the lakes and fells in a sparkling panorama and in the starkest detail. No, it has been a bit drab, but then it is no bad thing at times not to be distracted by a lot of detail and to view the broader outline scene alone.

What about those hedgerows – laden with berries – scarlet ribbons along the roadsides and alive with the clatter of flocks of fieldfares and redwings? A really great crop of berries, which folk used to say heralded a hard winter ahead. A nice thought, that a bountiful Mother Nature stocked up the larder for our feathered friends when the going was going to be tough – but in reality it reflects the fact that there was rain at just the right time, when the blossom was setting. Many more flowers set successfully if water is around at the right moment. (The yield of some vegetable crops can be doubled by irrigation during early flowering and the early stages of maturation.)

We've also had a bumper crop of beechmast, and the woods have been busy with highly-active blue tits, great tits and coal tits, as well as flocks of chaffinch.

One of the great advantages of late autumn and winter is that, as the trees become denuded of foliage, we stand so much better chance of seeing what wildlife is among them.

The treecreepers are seen more often, hopping their mouse-like way up the trunks, searching for insects in the crevices of the bark. And of course it is the most likely time at which to catch sight of that great favourite, the red squirrel, partly because the wood offers them much less cover than throughout the spring and summer months and partly because they spend much more time than usual on the ground, busily collecting and storing nuts and acorns in preparation for the onset of severe weather. Not that they remember where they create their caches, but the scent of buried stores, the very concentration of the nuts, allows them to locate them when the need arises.

We don't catch sight of very many red squirrels, which is hardly surprising. As is the case with so much wildlife, the density of population depends very largely on the food supply, and it takes some five acres of mixed woodland to support a red squirrel. Looking for a pair in ten acres is no mean task. They are not very big; they spend by far the greatest part of their time in the treetops, where lies their most constant food supply and where they are safely away from most predators, and in addition, they have a habit of staying very still when we are about.

So, late autumn is the best time of all to see squirrels, because cover is minimal and the fall of nuts brings them down to earth more often and for longer than at any other time.

The ratio of population density and food supply has been studied in relation to a number of species. Four or five acres is said to be sufficient to support an urban fox, while it may well take some 2,000 acres to support a mountain fox.

Midwinter it may be, and we may be reduced to about six hours of what passes for daylight, but already there are ample signs of spring. Buds swell; bulbs emerge; ravens will soon nest and once more the peregrine's call will echo from the topmost crags. Keep walking, keep smiling and remember the words of the old song – 'Spring is just around the corner!'

38. Along a stone wall crest

Parking the car at Bowness Knott seems to be the starting point for so many walks that there is hesitation in repeating so well-worn a phrase, but bear with me and a substantial and relatively uncommon 'perambulation' will be revealed!

So, having thus parked, we pursue the well-worn route along the forestry road towards Black Sail, turning right or due south at the end of the lake. But then, instead of turning right again and over the stile, as if to do the circuit of the lake, keep on through the gate, through the plantation, and the sound of rushing water will announce the meeting point of Deep Gill from the left and Silver Cove Beck straight ahead. Keeping the water on the left, continue up the bank of Silver Cove Beck.

It would be a pity to rush this section unduly, because here are rushing torrents, steep gullies, falls and pools amid overhanging trees, bracken and heather. Something of a scrambling start, but full of change and interest and totally different from the rest of the route.

And so, having savoured this little area of character, it is onward and upward, emerging from among the trees and levelling off a little; a wettish area this, with deep moss along the beck side and some flat and water-worn rocks of no mean size.

A broken stone wall appears and there's debate as to whether we should be on its right or left, but, no matter, keep gaining ground and pass through Silver Cove, with Caw Fell, Haycock and Steeple off to the left. Gradually swing right and we emerge on the top of Iron Crag.

Now here's a vast expanse, and along its ridge runs what must surely be one of the best stone walls in Lakeland. Newly-restored, this massive wall extends for miles. Keeping on its northern side until the gate is reached, then swapping for the southern, we continue the full length of Iron Crag, dropping finally to Black Pots and then up to the summit of Crag Fell.

From here we have the superb view of the whole of Ennerdale and beyond. The whole of the ridge from Banna Fell to Haystacks, Pillar and Steeple is before us.

Part-way down the western slope of Crag Fell we double back across the face, down through the famous Pinnacles to Angler's Crag, the lakeshore and round the western end back to Bowness Knott.

Now, this is a good walk! It is varied, with wood, water, rock, grass, scramble and a fine stretch along the top. A climb to 2,000 feet and some grand views.

When walking in a group we do not seriously expect to see much in the way of wildlife; that is a treat more likely to be enjoyed when alone or perhaps when there are only two of us. Suffice it to say that our own sightings along this route have included roe deer, raven, peregrine, buzzard, kestrel, goshawk, curlew and, of course, on and near the water, common sandpiper, dipper, cormorant, great crested grebe, pochard and many more. We were once long-entertained by an inquisitive stoat!

Apart from the walk outlined above, the northern face of Crag Fell is well worth exploring, having once been the sight of much mining activity. Tracks and spoil heaps remain and there are even odd bits of machinery to bear silent witness to the industry of many years ago.

A largely unfrequented area, where the pleasures of walking may be savoured well away from the madding crowd.

39. When morning is breaking

After the gloriously hot summer of 1995, it seemed as if the summer of 1996 would never arrive! The weeks slipped by, signs of spring were few and far between, what little sunshine we had was tempered by cold winds and we were well into June before any summer dawned.

Then, quite suddenly, there were the familiar and long-awaited blue skies. We had passed literally from winter to summer in a few days, spring being largely omitted!

However, when such precious days do arrive so late, they must at once be savoured to the full, and so the 'early and late' routine is quickly adopted. Already there are few hours of darkness, and when one needs to be out at dusk and at dawn, the period for sleep in between does get a little squeezed! Getting back from badger-watching at 10:30 pm means that getting up time at 4:45 am comes round rather quickly!

Is it worth it? Well, as I approached the wood, young rabbits dived for cover through the dewy grass – and there are a great many rabbits around just now, much to the delight of the local buzzards.

I wandered into the wood in the dappled sunlight, the bright green leaves of beech dancing in the gentle breeze; a massive buzzard drifted overhead, its broad wings outstretched as it glided silently above the treetops; a cuckoo called softly from some hidden perch way up the hill, while tits and warblers chattered among the lower branches. Primroses had all but disappeared now, and were replaced by a carpet of bluebells.

Only a few minutes after my arrival, a sudden movement caught my eye. Fox! The unmistakable silhouette against the top edge of the wood. It was no more than a momentary sighting; so much so that, although the camera was 'at the ready' on its tripod, there was just no chance of getting in a shot. However, that fleeting impression was of a furtive and protective stance, which suggested that this could well be a vixen with cubs, so a mental note was made to return another day, with very great care, in the hope of perhaps getting pictures of the whole family.

Five minutes later there was another movement, one that made the early start to the day even more worthwhile.

A pair of roe deer ambled into view, one attended by a tiny fawn, clearly only a day or two old. There can be few more beautiful sights in nature than deer and fawn meandering unconcernedly through an English wood in the early hours of a spring morning. The doe looked directly at me. Sleek of coat, black of muzzle, with those limpid, doleful, pleading eyes; surely the most elegant of our wild animals. The fawn, its ruddy coat gleaming in the sunshine, tottered on its spindly legs and nuzzled close to its mother as they picked their way daintily through the still-short bracken, with the characteristic flick of the tail. Slowly they wandered off, unhurried, to disappear among the undergrowth.

Soon afterwards there was much rustling as an excited red squirrel dashed along the hedgerow straight towards the spot where I had taken up position against a tree trunk to minimise my 'visual impact' on the scene. Only a few feet away he shot up a hawthorn, scrambled through its branches, leapt to the lower limb of an oak and away into the tops. Such agility and confidence in his aerial roadway!

A kestrel silently side-slipped from a tree and hovered over a group of rushes in the adjoining field, its pale plumage clearly showing its flecked and spotted underwings against the brightening sky. Incredible how they can hover and maintain their bodies so very still, no matter how great the buffeting of the wind.

But it was the deer and fawn that captured the imagination and plucked at the heart strings that day. He who could view that scene and remain unmoved would be a cold fish indeed. That peaceful, tranquil sight of mother and young; a pair of nature's gentlest and most appealing creatures epitomising the arrival of another summer, rebirth, renewal and the eternal rotation of the seasons.

At such sights as these – 'Then sings my soul'.

40. Old Man of the Fells

A massive bulk of a mountain, standing to the north of Keswick, Skiddaw is the oldest of fells and presents a well-rounded outline; lacking in crags and gullies, but soaring to over 3,000 feet, the fourth-highest summit in the District.

There are a number of recognised routes, but one of the most solitary is that from Peter House, a farm adjoining the road from Bassenthwaite Village to Orthwaite. Just before the farm there is a pair of gates, one on each side of the road. That on the left is a way-marked route to Bassenthwaite Village, while that on the right opens onto a tarmac road towards Dash Falls, Skiddaw and Threlkeld.

Parking near here we set off towards Dash Falls, along the road that passes through four fields before really starting to climb. A delightful area, this; a succession of sheep pastures with a few well-spaced farmsteads dotted through the valley. The valley itself gradually narrows and the surrounding fells gain height and steadily encroach, and for quite some time along the route, Dash Falls is in sight straight ahead. We pass Dead Crags on our right towering above us, a great slice out of the side of Bakestall, while the falls lie ahead and to our left. The cascade and the falls are quite spectacular, but the greatest drop is obscured from view at the nearest point. Lively falls, these, the main drop being preceded by a good cascade, with its fan-shaped sprays of spume.

Up past the falls, by which time the tarmac has given way to a rough and rocky track, we reach a gate, the point of decision! Ahead lie some miles of good walking, past Skiddaw House (the most isolated building in Lakeland?), set among its shelter of conifers, and on, all the way to Threlkeld. Devotees of Sherlock Holmes will recall the phrase, 'a two-pipe problem' – well, Peter House to Threlkeld could well be classed 'a two-car walk' – one to get you to Peter House and one to meet you at Threlkeld!

However, today Skiddaw is the target, so we turn right at the gate and up along the wall-and-fence, all the way to the north col, from where the summit is in sight. It would be very difficult to get lost here, except in thick mist, the way being abundantly clear; it is not all in view at once, but opens up steadily.

It is a long, steady climb virtually all the way and, although Skiddaw may not be the most exciting of mountains, it does offer good height and superb views. It is bare and rather inhospitable and when the wind blows (and it usually does!) there is no shelter but the odd cairn or two along the ridge. However, the ridge is quite sharp, so it is always possible to get out of the worst of the wind by ducking down one side or the other for a few yards.

From the top one may see many a fell, including Helvellyn right through to Crinkle Crags in the Langdales some 15 miles off; across the Solway to the Galloway Hills – indeed, if time and weather permit, there's a host of fells to identify from here. Close to hand lies Mungrisdale Common – that vast expanse of heather and peat moorland – and a fine look at Blencathra, the outline leaving one in no doubt as to why it is also known as 'Saddleback'. Below lie Derwentwater and Bassenthwaite Lake.

Unfortunately, there is no easy round trip, so it is a matter of retracing steps, but this is not without its rewards. The views northwards are grand, not least that of Overwater nestling below Bakestall. The latter has its own little cairn, by the way, lying only 100 yards off the route down and it *is* worth a visit.

Not so much an area in which to wander and explore hidden nooks and crannies, more a spot to visit when you really feel like stretching those limbs and exercising muscles. At a brisk and steady pace, allow two hours to the top from Peter House and 80 minutes for the return. Recommended!

41. —above the magic Munro mark

Helvellyn! What a lovely ring the old name has; so Celtic, it could as well be in the heart of Wales. But, name apart, this fell is well-known as one of the very few which rise above the magic 'Munro' mark of 3,000 feet; in fact, it exceeds that figure by some 118 feet and its height is such that it commands breathtaking views in all directions.

Of the various recognised routes of ascent, that from the east has the reputation of being the most imposing, at least in part because it includes the famous challenge of Striding Edge, a graceful rocky ridge which sags between two points like the trapeze artist's high wire. A scrambler's delight in good weather, but not without its hazards when wet and windy.

However, it's a long way round by car to the start of that approach, so on this occasion we opt for the nearer way. Leaving Keswick southwards on the A591, we park by the Swan Inn at Thirlspot, about a quarter of the way along Thirlmere. From here there is virtually no walk-in at all, the climb being signposted from the start. The track swings left and then right to Lower Man and provides a reasonably clearly-marked route all the way.

Apart from the necessity of the occasional pause for breath, it is worth glancing back, down and across. The A591 soon retreats to form a narrow ribbon and the traffic takes on dinky-toy proportions, the sparkle of Thirlmere glints in the sun and gradually a vast panorama opens up. The summit is broad and largely bare, but there is much to see. Catstycam stands off to the north-east, and between this and Striding Edge lies Red Tarn, from which Red Tarn Beck runs all the way down to enter Ullswater at Glenridding.

It would be far too boring to list all the tops that are to be seen from the top of Helvellyn. Suffice it to say that 'AW' lists over 50!

Just east of the summit cairn overlooking Striding Edge is a touching memorial tablet which records an event early in the 19th century. One was when a Kendal man, one Charles Gough, was unfortunate enough to fall to his death from Striding Edge in 1803. He was by no means the first, nor the last, to do so, but what makes this so poignant a story is that, although his body was not found for some three months, his faithful dog remained by his side, watching over his dead master and no doubt surviving on scraps of grass and snow.

We retraced our steps along Swirrel Edge, which in May sported a substantial snow cornice, and it was here that two favourite and familiar sounds assailed our ears from opposite ends of the scale – sounds as typical of the high fells as those of wind and rain. First, the high-pitched silvery notes of the mountain blackbird, or ring ouzel, the blackbird with the white collar, a plaintive sound, but one which carries so far across the expanse of the open fell; and second, that other evocative call, the deep-throated guttural croak of the raven. We didn't manage to spot the ring ouzel, but the raven glided right overhead and then indulged in one of those wonderful tumbling rolls which seem to be the raven's way of saying, 'What a glorious day!'

From Lower Man we veered north to enjoy a good limb-relaxing stretch along the smooth and springy turf to Raise (2,889 feet) before descending the gill, which runs down from Sticks Pass. A long descent, using first one side of the gill and then the other, but with the reward of spectacular falls towards the bottom before a left incline for Thirlspot.

A fine walk, this, with a host of fells to see as well as Ullswater, Bassenthwaite, Coniston, Windermere and, of course, Thirlmere.

42. Wastwater at dawn

Although plans had been laid for an early start, waking at 3:00 am did not inspire immediate action! However, by 3:45 there was a glimmer of light, so in no time at all it was a case of out of bed, downstairs, in the car and heading south.

Mockerkin to Wastwater was achieved without sighting a single other vehicle travelling in either direction!

The car was parked, the camera was set up near the water's edge and a few shots were taken without delay. Not the most dramatic of dawns, perhaps, but not at all bad. The water was like a millpond, the rocks in the foreground were black against the shimmering lake and Great Gable and Kirk Fell were darkly outlined against a fiery red sky streaked with white cloud—altogether a scene of contrasts. July it might be, but it was cold, very cold.

That done, a move was made further up the valley to Wasdale Head, the car parked again and the walk began at about five o'clock. Over a somewhat depleted Gatherstone Beck, on up to Sail Pass and left towards Pillar, calling in at the little tarn near Looking Stead which provided another good picture of bog bean in the water and a pair of sheep drinking from the opposite bank, all illuminated by the still almost horizontal light of early morning.

On a little higher, forking right onto the High Level Route across the northern face of Pillar. Looking back, another shot presented itself across the northern flank of Kirk Fell to Gable, and yet another towards Brandreth, with Black Sail Hut glistening on the floor of Ennerdale far below. On along the tortuous traverse, with all its ups and downs, its rock and its scrambles, passing starry saxifrage, mountain yellow saxifrage, goldenrod and many more botanical niceties, clinging in their crevices and thankfully mopping up the welcome sunshine.

Under the end of Hind Cove was a tent where a young couple were having breakfast – a little surprised at seeing anyone approaching at that hour. I jokingly ordered eggs and bacon, without success, but I was at least offered a cup of coffee! Onwards and upwards behind Pillar Rock and that exhausting scramble to the summit (2,927 feet).

It *was* a glorious morning, with a clear blue sky, a wonderful freshness and brilliant sunshine slowly but surely warming by the minute. Straight over the top of Pillar and down to Wind Gap (2,600 feet), a very rough and steep descent made a little easier by keeping towards the right of the ridge where there is some solid rock, as opposed to the loose jumble on the other side. Into Wind Gap, with Wind Gap Cove falling away to the west and Mosedale to the east; then on up to Scoat Fell (2,760 feet), veering left for Red Pike (2,707 feet) with that super view down to Scoat Tarn, over to Wastwater, the enormous bulk of Kirk Fell and Great Gable beyond, the Scafells and others too numerous to list.

From the rocky top of Red Pike down to Dore Head and right along the full length of the flank of Yewbarrow to the Gosforth-Wasdale road, then just 1½ miles back to the car; some 11 miles in all. Now, that is a good walk and, at that time of day on a fine morning, a good walk becomes superb!

Crummock Water

Ennerdale from Crag Fell

Grasmoor from Whiteside

Storm over Blencathra, from Skiddaw

Red Squirrel

Fox cub at dawn

Badger

Roe deer

43. Strange habits!

The vast majority of green plants obtain the necessary nutrients from the soil and combine oxygen, hydrogen and carbon to form carbohydrates. This 'manufacturing' process continues ceaselessly throughout the hours of daylight in the presence of chlorophyll and with the energy provided by the sun; photosynthesis – a fundamental process, vital for life on earth. But there are some plants that feed partly or wholly in other ways, some species of which occur in our own district. Perhaps the best known are the sundews and butterworts. The round-leaved sundew (*Drosera rotundifolia*) and the less common English sundew (*Drosera anglica*) ensnare small insects in the sticky globules on the ends of their leaf hairs, then dissolve the soft parts of their captives in enzymes and absorb the resulting 'soup' to supplement their diet of the poor and acid soils in which they live. The common butterwort (*Pinguicular vulgaris*) has sticky leaves that enfold tiny insects, to deal with them in a similar way.

Other plants, such as lousewort (*Pediculata sylvatica*) and marsh lousewort (*P. palustris*), common cow-wheat (*Melampyrum pratense*) and yellow rattle (*Rhinanthus minor*) and others are hemi-parasites, drawing some nutrients in the usual way, but also adding to their 'diet' by fixing some of their roots onto the roots of other plants and 'robbing' them of some of their foods.

Then there are some plants that are wholly parasitic, depending entirely on other 'normal' plants for their food supply. One such is dodder (*Cuscata epithymum*), which is rare in the north, but less so in the south of England and in Wales. The bulk of the dodder plant consists of a mass of pink or maroon leafless stems, which entangle and entwine themselves through the host plant like a mass of fishing line. It is parasitic on gorse and heather and has tiny stalkless flowers, which appear in ball-like heads. The amount of growth it produces and its colour is such that a gorse bush infested with dodder may be identified at 20 paces!

One aquatic plant that depends on insects and small crustaceans for its existence is the greater bladderwort (*Ultricularia vulgaris*). Its bright yellow flowers appear above the water of pond or stream, while below the water there are air-filled bladders or sacs on the stems, with fine hairs or bristles nearby. When a small creature such as a cyclops or a water flea touches the hair, the bladder springs open, the 'prey' is sucked in with the rush of water and the lid closes. As the prey decomposes, the 'juices' are absorbed.

These and other species with 'unusual' feeding habits occur quite commonly in the Lake District, except for dodder, which is rarely seen here, and form one of the innumerable groups of plants to be seen, as the fell walker 'homeward plods his weary way'.

44. A place in which to stretch and breathe

No doubt we all prefer some form of circular route, however irregular that 'circle' may be, to those on which one is obliged to retrace steps, which is one factor immediately in favour of the Fairfield Horseshoe. Having said that, whether the route is best done clockwise or anticlockwise is a matter of some debate. Our own preference is always to climb *up* anything really steep rather than down and, wherever possible, to gain height as early in the day as we can. That being so, we tackle the Fairfield Horseshoe clockwise. 'AW' recommends the reverse approach, preferring a gentle start to the day. Well, "You pays your money—!"

First by car down the A591 to Rydal; turn left at the sign for Rydal Mount and park almost immediately on the left. Then, setting off on foot past Rydal Mount itself, up the very steep hill and left again through the signposted gate. Here begins the ascent of Nab Scar (1,459 feet), by no means the highest point of the day, but almost certainly the hardest pull. A rough and narrow zigzag track among old oaks and bracken, with lovely views soon opening up over Rydal Water and the woods around High Fell nestling in the valley bottom.

Having reached the top of Nab Scar there is little respite, because clearly standing straight ahead is Heron Pike (2,003 feet), the two separated by an area of humps and hollows, twists and turns, which all help to maintain interest. On approaching Heron Pike, the silvery ribbon of Rydal Beck shimmers in the early morning light as it meanders southwards along the floor of the deep dale far below.

Once again the old trick is played – as we gaspingly reach the top of one fell we are at once confronted by another! Beyond Heron Pike stands Greatrigg Man (2,513 feet) – and then Fairfield itself, rising to 2,863 feet, with some inevitable loss of height in between.

So far we have been travelling north, but from the top of Fairfield we turn due east to close the 'horseshoe'. On the way up we have had grand views of Helvellyn, Striding Edge, Dollywaggon Pike and Grisedale Tarn over to the west.

The next top is Hart Crag (2,698 feet), but before reaching that we skirt the northern end of Rydale and the southern end of Deepdale. Immediately after Hart Crag we have Dovedale also running off north-east, and between the two stands Erne Nest Crag. Fine little dales, these; with moraines in the bottoms, some fascinating crags surrounding them and when we were there, they were being systematically scanned by both kestrels and ravens.

Next comes Dove Crag, and from there lies a good springy stretch on which one may happily step it out and move on apace before starting on the main descent to High Pike (2,155 feet) and Low Pike (1,657 feet).

Near Low Pike a stone wall runs obliquely down the western slope and if this is followed it takes us down to Rydal Beck. Following the beck is a further delight, a gentle and peaceful way to make the closing stages of the walk as memorable as the high tops.

The beck travels energetically through impressive deep ravines strewn with massive boulders, its previously-placid waters turning into roaring and churning torrents and cascades punctuated by deep, deep pools of dark green-blue. It passes through an area of wooded glades of the old Rydal Hall estate and, incidentally, the path is an officially-designated National Park access route. Eventually there is a footbridge and crossing this brings us to the point at which we started up Nab Scar, some six hours earlier.

A good, sound, circular route of some 11 miles and a total of eight tops; occasionally rough, but never hazardous, and without difficulties other than those occasioned by tiring limbs and shortage of 'puff'. Thoroughly recommended without reservation, it provides a good day's walking among very varied and always delightful scenery, with grand views near and far of silvery becks and tarns, the lush hummocky tops of oak woods o'erlooked by sometimes rounded and sometimes craggy, wild, expansive fells.

A place in which to stretch and breathe, to wander and savour yet another of Lakeland's scenic jewels.

45. Sounds natural!

A couple of days ago I was out with Toby, giving him his morning airing, when two sounds caught my attention in quick succession – hence the theme of these few words.

One sound in nature which never ceases to thrill me is the distant call of wild geese as they wing southwards; it is surely one of the most haunting calls, and one which I seem to pick up on my 'radar' when the birds themselves are the merest specks in the far distance. This was one of those occasions. A fine, crisp morning, when Jack Frost had delicately painted every vein on the fallen leaves of oak and sycamore, and when the skein of geese was no more than a thin black line moving slowly down the coast. No sooner was silence re-established, than a raven flew high overhead, emitting that deepest of croaks from that enormous bill.

The combination of the two set me thinking of other sounds to be heard 'in the wild', and just how much is missed by those unfortunate folk who spend all their lives in the towns. The whickering of badgers from way down within the sett; the chuntering of a red squirrel at being disturbed when tackling a particularly promising nut; the agitated 'thump' of the hind leg of a suspicious rabbit and the busy rustle in the autumn leaves as a hedgehog urgently seeks a suitable winter shelter; the eerie bark of a fox at dusk and the answering hoot of a tawny owl as it scans the ground in the gathering gloom for some unsuspecting rodent for its evening meal.

The cacophony of sound produced by a brood of great spotted woodpeckers, deep in the hollow tree, and the 'clatter' as a flock of fieldfares takes flight from a berry-strewn hedge in autumn; the abrasive 'yarrrrk' of the heron as it drifts aimlessly across a lake surface at dawn, its massive wings reflected in the shining water.

Two other sounds that never cease to excite me are the 'meouw' of the buzzard as it soars effortlessly among the thermals, and the unmistakable call of the peregrine falcon, that master of flight and undoubted king of the Lakeland skies.

And, of course, there are many 'lesser' sounds, too; the rasp of the grasshopper, the constant hum of hoverflies in the canopy of the oak wood in high summer – and even some plants join in the chorus—the rattle of the seeds as Indian balsam pods explode, or of the well-named 'yellow rattle' – increasingly rare, but still to be seen and heard at Sossgill.

There was once a nature programme on the box called *Look*— what about one called 'Listen'? In fact, perhaps we could adopt and adapt an old code, 'Stop, Look—and *listen*'!

46. Gently does it

The prospect of traversing no less than seven felltops would perhaps cause instant hesitation in many a walker, and yet that is in fact what is done in a distance of only some 2½ miles on this particular walk, which runs from the Whinfell road, ie the old road between Lorton and Mosser, and which is signed at both ends as being 'Unfit for Motors'. In fact, it is sufficiently fit to be used by car, with care and at a steady pace. Park near the end of the stony track, which runs south-east up Whinfell, and pursue this track on foot. It does not last long, finishing at a gate and stile and already the walker is at a height of about 900 feet.

More or less straight on along an obvious grassy track and a second gate and stile are reached. Immediately over this on the right is the tumbledown ruin of Hatteringill, little more than a heap of stone now, but once a high-perched little farmstead, isolated, but with a remarkable view over the Lorton Vale to Lord's Seat, Grisedale Pike, Whiteside, Grasmoor and the rest. Whinfell falls away steeply here and the panorama is superb.

Turn right, or west, immediately round the ruin and along the wall as it wends its way up the hill. On the right at the top there appears a striking rocky outcrop, Hatteringill Head, from which the aforementioned farm got its name. Over a stile to the right and immediately over a ladder to the left and there then follows a further climb along the fence to the top of Fellbarrow (1,363 feet). It must be stressed that this little series of felltops presents no problem throughout – the ups and the downs are not great and it really is simply a matter of straightforward walking all the way.

And yet the rewards are considerable, as indeed they so often are on many of the not-very-high, often ignored and undervalued fells. So close, so well-known at a distance, so local, that many a local has never set foot thereon!

Along the approach to Low Fell there are fine views to the north, east and west, but this walk keeps the best 'til last, because the view from the little summit crags of Low Fell itself is a view apart. It is without doubt one of the very best viewpoints in the district, and some go so far as to say that it is *the* best. It encompasses Loweswater, with the backdrop of Burnbank, Carling Knott, Gavel and Mellbreak, but more than this, it offers a sighting of the full length of the Crummock-Buttermere valley, from Grasmoor and Mellbreak to Haystacks and Great Gable, with the sylvan waters of the lakes shining below. A view right through from Pillar to Lord's Seat and a quite remarkable series of tops to identify.

Even that is but the tip of the aesthetic iceberg, because of the sheer grandeur; dramatic and imposing, impressive beyond mere words. Needless to say, much depends on the day, the time of day, the light, the cloud formation, the season and so on, but it is a place from which to see at its very best that area which has so special a place in all our hearts, the spot we all love so dearly, The Valley.

47. Survival

Midwinter may indeed be bleak at times, but it does seem to me that it is always bleaker when looking out from indoors! Once out and about, it's not so bad; there is always something of interest to see and always some sign that spring is on the way.

The recent circuit of a lake, for example, gave sightings of a variety of birds. Scores of mallard, the rich, green heads of the drakes glistening in the weak sunshine; every now and then the flock would dissolve into that peal of cackling laugher, as if one of their number had just cracked the funniest of jokes!

And there was a flotilla of pochard, with their red-brown heads and that lovely dove-grey plumage. Maddening birds to try and count, because they are divers and the number on the surface is constantly changing.

There was a pair of great crested grebes, too, gliding along, their bodies low in the water and their crested heads perched high on those long, thin, vertical necks, like ornithological periscopes!

The unmistakable tufted ducks were in evidence, also, blue-black, with that striking brilliant white flank and that funny little trailing crest on the head.

On the same circuit there were red-breasted mergansers, a heron, a buzzard, a peregrine flying high above from crag to crag, and from a nearby copse the intermittent hammering of a woodpecker.

It never ceases to amaze me how small birds manage to survive the cold, the wet and the wind of our worst winter nights. I know some, such as wrens, join forces for mutual warmth and protection, while others find tree holes and barns; but there are many who do not. Imagine one of us, however well-clothed, clinging onto a branch from dusk to dawn, night after night, maybe for weeks on end of bad weather.

Nevertheless, the ravens nest in January, peregrines are courting now and before long these and many more will undertake the great annual gamble, the race against time to lay, hatch, rear, fledge and train young before the onset of the next winter.

In the animal world, too, the race is similar; to bring on the young sufficiently well for them to be able to look after themselves and survive the lean times which follow all too quickly. In the natural world, survival is the name of the game, and the first winter in a young life is a great challenge, a challenge that many are unable to meet.

The gamble is not confined to birds and animals, but is as great for every individual seed – but then, that's another story!

48. Where once the eagle soared

The name 'Eel Crag' occurs many times in Lakeland, not unnaturally, since it is derived from 'eagle crag' and clearly in days gone by the population of golden eagles was far greater than today's, which until recently boasted a mere single pair near Haweswater.

However, the Eel Crag to which we refer here is that which lies due east of Grasmoor and which, for some curious reason, is labelled Crag Hill on the Ordnance Survey map. Starting in Newlands, it represents the penultimate in a series of steps of increasing altitude. Rowling End is 1,500 feet high, Causey Pike, 2,035 feet, Scar Crags, 2,205 feet, Sail 2,503 feet, Eel Crag, 2,749 feet and Grasmoor, a grand 2,791 feet. While it is probably seldom climbed for its own sake, it is a top which is traversed while engaged on a number of well-worn routes, but which really deserves a little attention in its own right.

When walking from Lanthwaite through Gasgale Gill, Eel Crag appears ahead, beyond the fine cascades towards the top of the gill and, indeed, the upper section of one way of ascent is seen most clearly from this point. Once up out of the gill it becomes obvious that the initial climb is over scree, half-left towards the ridge, and that the ridge itself is scaled through a rocky gully. There is nothing difficult in this, but the usual warning should perhaps be sounded, that what one may see from the start is *not* the top! (How many times have we noticed *that* little trick before?) Once above the gully, there is still quite a long cairn-studded walk to the summit.

A second approach is over Sail, which in turn can be approached from Buttermere along Sail Beck, or over Whiteside from Causey Pike or from Braithwaite via Outerside, which serves to illustrate the pivotal nature of the fell. These are all well-worn routes known to thousands of regular fell walkers and holiday walkers alike, but there is another way which appears to be little-used, despite the fact that it is certainly one of the best—and probably *the* best.

If we approach from Gasgale Gill, on reaching Coledale Hause we go straight on; this gives us the northern face of Eel Crag on our right, while going down on our left is the uppermost stretch of the miners' track which leads all the way down the valley to Braithwaite. From this point there is a rather indistinct track – little more than a sheep-trod – which traverses the fell horizontally. It tends to run out in places, but when it does, a few steps higher, will reveal further stretches above patches of scree and rock.

Following this track leads us to a minor ridge, from which a much more imposing one may be seen a few yards ahead. This second is Tower Ridge and on reaching it, we turn right up the ridge itself. This presents a first-class scramble over solid rock, between narrow gaps and out into exposed places, from which excellent views open up. We need to use hands as well as feet at times, but it is a grand and exhilarating little climb; it is not difficult, but adds just that little bit of extra excitement to the scaling of so well-known an old friend. There are good views of Whiteside, Force Crags, Grisedale Pike and Skiddaw – and, of course, the superb panorama once we reach the summit itself.

So, next time Eel Crag comes into sight and your inner self is heard quietly to murmur, "What—*again?*", try this for a route. A highly recommended variation you will not regret.

49. More plants in Ennerdale

The 'Mockerkin Mob', that small group of intrepid explorers who traverse the mountainous nooks and crannies of the district once a month throughout the year, have just completed their 88th walk and, just for a change, it took the form of a stroll around Ennerdale with an eye on the plant life (not to be confused with a floral dance, you understand!).

We made no earth-shattering discoveries, of course, but we did casually identify some 40-odd flowering plants, plus the inevitable mosses, lichens, liverworts and a few birds for good measure.

One of the most fascinating aspects of plant life in an area, is just why a particular species thrives where it does, rather than in some apparently identical site close by. There are a host of factors which may be involved, such as aspect, water table, soil type, soil acidity and so on and, of course, combinations of such factors, too.

Similarly, why is it that some species are so much more prolific in some years than others? This may be influenced by weather conditions in the previous year, when fertilisation was taking place, or it may be due to weather conditions in the current year, perhaps, when seeds were germinating. Germination is a highly complex process, starting with imbibition – the uptake of moisture; once the process starts, it must continue without a break if the seed is to produce a seedling. If it stops, because the soil dries out, say, it cannot restart.

We saw all those plants we would expect to see, such as tormentil, earth nut, water dropwort, spearwort, heath bedstraw and so on, and some which are perhaps a little less well-known. The northern shore sported a couple of plants of sweet Cicely, which, although common enough, seldom appears here. There were two twayblade orchids, which again are not uncommon, but which are very few and far between in this valley. Carline thistles usually appear on the northern shore of the lake, but now there are some on the southern side.

Among the grasses there were no surprises, cocksfoot and sweet vernal among them, and I suppose a little less usual there, soft brome. Aromatic species included some fine patches of wild thyme and one good area of sweet gale, for so long used in brewing. One or two members of our party were brave enough to try chewing wood sorrel, to experience the sudden outflow of flavour, which occurs after a few seconds. But there were no volunteers to make the famous Cumbrian Pudding from the leaves of bistort!

Cotton grass and bogbean were in full flower, as was butterwort, proudly displaying its tall bloom and making it quite clear why its second name is 'bog violet'.

The bird life was not very extensive, but we did see some greylags at close quarters, shepherding their goslings out among the waves of a very rough lake on a very windy day and, I am sure, hoping we would pass quickly by so that they could return to the shore. There were a few mallard and one or two common sandpipers, but the star turn was a group of red-breasted mergansers.

An enjoyable walk, renewing acquaintance with old friends!

50. 'All that glisters—'

An excellent round trip – or more of a horseshoe, really – is afforded by the combination of Robinson, Littledale Edge and Hindscarth and, while it can be done in either direction, the one hazard on the entire route may be minimised by doing it in this order, rather than the reverse.

Having parked at Little Town, the walk begins with a stretch of road straight past Newlands Church and on up the lane past Low High Snab and eventually through the gate at the road end. There follows a stretch of 100 yards or less which is heavily trampled by sheep and is in any case soft, wet and very muddy – but if consolation is sought, it may be found in the fact that it is both the first and the last of such areas on this walk!

Once through the mire, turn right up the broad and clear track, straight up the fellside; a very steep grassy section this, and therefore one which gives every excuse to stop at intervals (short ones!) to admire the view. On reaching the ridge, turn left along High Snab Bank, throughout whose length there are fine views. Down to the left lies Scope Beck and the little reservoir built by the miners of many years ago, while among the steep slopes of Hindscarth one may pick out the old workings of Goldscope Mine. It did indeed produce gold at one time, but such amounts as there were have long since been removed. Definitely *not* worth packing your pick, shovel and pan!! Beyond the reservoir are some good waterfalls before the valley opens out into Little Dale.

On leaving High Snab Bank the hazard referred to earlier is soon found to the west of Blea Crags. It is in the form of three rock 'steps', each about 20–30 feet in height and, while two of them are not at all difficult to negotiate, the third is inclined to be smooth, polished, slippery and affording few firm holds. It is certainly better to go up than down, hence the aforementioned choice of direction, but either way, care is needed – be warned!

However, having safely scaled the three 'steps', the way is clear to scale the remainder of Robinson—a mere 800 feet of ascent to the summit, which stands at 2,417 feet and is a superb view point. The panorama stretches from Helvellyn to Blake and from Binsey to Scafell; Robinson has a great broad and bare top, but the view is outstanding.

We then proceed in an easterly direction down a steep fence-side descent along Littledale Edge at around 2,000 feet and up again to the southern end of Hindscarth, at whose cairn we reach 2,385 feet. The descent from here to Little Town provides an excellent and varied walk. It begins near the massive cairn just below the summit and for a while is on loose rock, but soon on grass and among heather. All the way the views are grand to left and right, and ahead to Skiddaw and Blencathra. The Scope Beck valley is now on the left, while to the right or east stand High Spy and Maiden Moor – with a wonderful view of those fells' western flanks, the dark ramparts of Eel Crags and the Newlands valley and beck far below.

Finally, the route takes us round the lower end of Hindscarth, past the eastern spoil heaps of Goldscope Mine, through Low Snab and down the road past the church to the car park once again. An excellent walk with lots of points of interest along the way.

51. Miterdale

Living where we do, with so many fine walks of every description in the immediate vicinity, it is perhaps only to be expected that we seldom venture far afield. Probably not often enough because, although the home area offers great variety, still greater variety is available if the catchment area is extended a little further, especially bearing in mind that it is not far to any point in the Lake District! One excellent walk in the south-western corner, for example, entails a few miles in the car, but is well worth the effort.

First, drive to Gosforth and pass straight through the village, past the Wastwater turn, to Eskdale. Note the Bower House Inn on the right. Soon after that a large stone house appears on the left and hard by that, between two trees, there is an unmarked left turn. Follow this narrow lonning for a mile or so, when it leads onto a broad flat green area where the car should be parked. We are now in Miterdale, along the floor of which runs the river Miter. (Incidentally, there was once – following the Ice Age – a Lake Miterdale, in which Muncaster Fell was an island – but that is another story!)

From here the lonning becomes a farm road and then a footpath. We follow this past the remains of Miterdale Head Farm, gradually leaving the trees behind and skirting Tongue Moor. The scene becomes more and more open and desolate. Then we come across Burnmoor Tarn off to our right, which is overlooked by Burnmoor Lodge, a sizeable building which is surely one of the most isolated houses in England. All this time we have been gently climbing along the south-east flank below Illgill Head and at around 900 feet we turn up left or south-west for Illgill Head itself, which stands at 1,998 feet. As we approach the turning point, however, the view that opens up ahead encompasses Wasdale Head, Kirk Fell, Great Gable and Scafell – a grand panorama from an unaccustomed vantage point.

Once the ascent is accomplished there lies ahead a superb ridge walk with no further serious ups or downs; there are some very wet spots, peat bogs and hags to negotiate, but nothing worse. This is, of course, the topmost ridge of the Wastwater screes and, given a good day, there is a marvellous view down over the screes and Wastwater itself, especially from the best viewpoints, such as that just before the two small tarns which appear as we near Whin Rigg. There are also good views to the south, particularly of the great isolated dome of Harter Fell.

After Whin Rigg the track leads gradually down, over a stone wall and out onto a broad, grassy stretch, to the left of which is a plantation. Part-way across, the track forks and we take the left one through a gate into the plantation. A very muddy patch, this, but short-lived and then we can complete the descent either on the forestry road or more directly by adhering to the track itself. Either way, we regain the narrow lonning up which we travelled by car. Turn left and the car is soon reached.

Having once been caught on the ridge in thick cloud, it should perhaps be said that in such conditions the track can be very difficult to follow in places, and that one must bear in mind the precipitous drop over the screes.

Nevertheless, this is an excellent walk of probably some seven miles, with varied terrain and gaining sufficient height to give fine views in all directions, some of them quite dramatic, with relative ease.

52. A beneficial climb

After weeks of wet weather it was an incredulous group of members of the 'Mockerkin Mob' who assembled at Lanthwaite Green on a fine morning on 14th October; not very bright, but it was *dry* and the clouds appeared to be lifting from the tops. Across the grassy slope to Gasgale Beck, over the footbridge and up to the start of the higher of the two tracks into Gasgale Gill, along the length of which the beck was in full spate, the water rushing and tumbling in a foaming cascade as it dashed downwards from the sodden fells above.

On reaching Coledale Hause (1,900 feet) we veered left and made use of a little-used and therefore ill-defined traverse across the north-east face of Eel Crag, leading to the foot of Tower Crags. Although not very extensive, Tower Crags provides a spectacular and most enjoyable scramble. Viewed from the approaching traverse and, indeed, from directly below, especially when, as on this occasion, the summit is but fleetingly seen through swirling cloud, it appears somewhat menacing. It is undeniably steep; a ridge of grassland and rugged outcrops of rock sloping off to the east, but with a near-vertical drop on the western side. As is so often the case, however, there are a number of 'routes' upwards, none of which is too arduous, and each of which opens up as it is followed. Probably the best is up the sharpest part of the ridge, because this is free from really tricky spots and affords good views to the west over interesting rock formations, similar in form to the Pinnacles of Mellbreak. Not surprisingly, after all the recent rain, the rock was treacherously slippery and called for some care.

On gaining the rim of the crag, a little below the summit (2,749 feet), the cloud had mostly lifted to the north, revealing Coledale, Braithwaite, Keswick and on to Ullock Pike and

Skiddaw, although to the south cloud lingered and Helvellyn was still masked.

Incidentally, until recently I was of the opinion that 'Eel Crag' and 'Crag Hill' were adjoining tops, but it seems the two are one and the same.

From Eel Crag we dropped some 300 feet to cross the arête and climbed 100 feet again to the top of Sail, then down the long and rough 700 feet to Sail Pass. From there we set off on the two-mile gradual descent above and parallel to Sail Beck, eventually forking right up and over into Rannerdale and on to Lanthwaite. Keeping up no more than a reasonable pace, we regained the cars in five hours, having covered some 12 miles with 2,500 feet of ascent. Not too bad for eight fit young folk, only seven of whom have long since retired!

This particular walk was all the more satisfying as it was the subject of sponsorship and donation for the benefit of UNICEF and raised over £450, enough to immunise 50 children for life against an important group of potentially fatal diseases.

On behalf of UNICEF and, above all, on behalf of the children, warmest thanks are due to all who supported this little effort, whether in terms of money or sweat – or both!

53. Some of England's grandest country

Once or twice a year a very good friend comes up to the Lake District from Croydon and stays somewhere in the area. During each stay he and I go off for a fairly strenuous day in the fells. This year was a little different, in that the walking party was joined by his rock-climbing son and we decided to visit the Scafells. I did explore this area before, but this time had in mind a different route.

Having made a reasonably early start, we abandoned the car at Seathwaite, that narrow gateway to the enchanting and challenging region of the Scafell massif. The valley is narrow and edged by towering fellsides from the start. We soon progressed to Stockley Bridge, which spans the infant River Derwent as it passes over and between a mass of solid rock, worn smooth by the rush of countless millions of gallons of water. Then on past Styhead Gill and Styhead Tarn which, like the lakes, has many moods; brilliant blue and placid when shimmering in summer sun, or black as ink when reflecting stormy winter skies.

The route so far is usually well-peopled – it is so popular a way to so many walks and climbs – and indeed the track has become so very worn that much of it has been re-laid with stone to conform more to a Roman road than a fell track. In view of the wear and tear being inflicted, no doubt this has to be; but there are a good few miles of it here and it is very tiring and trying stuff to walk on for any distance. There is in fact an alternative and much less-worn parallel track on the other side of the beck, which involves just a little scrambling.

By now we have passed Glaramara on our left and Green Gable and Great Gable on our right, a distance of about 1½ miles. Ahead and to our left stands the unmistakable hulk of Great End, beneath which lies another Lakeland jewel, Sprinkling Tarn. But we ignore that for the moment and press on south-south-west, approaching Scafell as directly as possible. On arrival below Mickledore, the start of our prime target begins to come into view. An enormous fan of scree runs down from Mickledore towards Wasdale Head. Keeping to the right-hand side of this, we round the lower buttress of Scafell Crag and as we do so a great chasm opens up on our right. This is Lord's Rake, a long and very steep fissure, narrowly confined between walls of solid rock.

But it is neither the steepness nor the narrowness that present the problems here; rather, the state of the 'ground' underfoot and one particular rock step. Underfoot we have scree of a kind, but it is more than just scree; it is a jumble of soil and stone and rocks of every size and virtually anything and everything, other than the walls, is likely to move under the boot, creating a cacophony of geological flotsam. Approach with care and assume from the start that nothing is secure! It is very important to be aware of anyone climbing above, because the steepness is such that anything which they unavoidably disturb must be expected to come down in your direction. Similarly, if responsible for serious dislodgement – be not shy or slow to give an instant warning shout – "Below!"

Then there is 'the step'. This is an almost vertical rock face which bars the way up the Rake and which is – and here I am guessing – probably ten feet high. Holds are small and few and far between; it's a job for fingers and toes. It is a hazard that certainly wouldn't suit everybody, and I never cease to wonder at the fact that it doesn't seem to be mentioned by Wainwright. Mind you, it could well be that, as the Rake has become increasingly worn, more and more 'scree' has moved downwards and that, as a result, the step is gradually getting higher. In any event, while it is nothing to a rock climber, we lesser mortals who merely content ourselves with walking and scrambling find this just about as hazardous as we want! However, the main point on today's route is that, not only are we going *up* Lord's Rake—but back down it as well!

So, after all that we duly reach the top of Scafell (3,162 feet), where we have a short rest and the compulsory bite to eat. And now—down Lord's Rake. All's well, more or less, until we reach the wretched step, and here we must approach the edge with great care, especially as it is covered in the loose scree on which one may so easily slide. Once there, it's a case of going in reverse, facing the rock and seeking out those elusive foot and handholds as best we can. Even those who, like me, love a scramble may well find this operation just a little daunting. It surely concentrates the mind for a few minutes!

But there, we managed it without mishap and moved along the very top of the scree, traversing from Lord's Rake to Mickledore and thence up to Scafell Pike, and savoured for a time the thought of being the very highest in the land! (3,210 feet). The summit of Scafell Pike is virtually bare. There are a few discernible stony tracks, but for the most part it is strewn with layer upon layer of boulders, spewed heavenwards by volcanic eruption in the very distant past, only to fall back to earth to form this precarious jumble. Pock-marked by bubbles of gas, the boulders must be crossed with care; many will rock and turn, on being stepped on.

Now we leave Scafell Pike, topped by its massive circular cairn, swinging round east, north-east and then north-west right round Great End and then on to Stockley Bridge and the starting point at Seathwaite.

A walk of some 11 miles among some of England's grandest mountain scenery – and with the double challenge of Lord's Rake thrown in! Another great day to remember!

54. A vast and tranquil scene

While there can be little doubt that the conical summit of Red Pike is one of the most popular targets for walkers in the Buttermere valley, it is perhaps less often viewed as the first port of call on the more extensive route described here.

Setting off in the usual way from Buttermere and up the most-used approach, we first scale the steep and rocky ascent to Bleaberry Combe, a track recently much restored with carefully-placed rocks and therefore hard and unyielding to the boot. However, in August this ascent was made the more pleasurable by the exceptionally brilliant carpet of heather. In fact, it has been the year, rather than the route, which has been exceptional for its heather − all the heather has been unusually heavy with blossom, an intense purple, and giving off the sweetest of heady perfumes. The deep combe is surrounded on three sides by a graceful rim involving Dodd, Red Pike, Chapel Crags and the ridge to High Stile, while in the bottom lies the placid jewel of Bleaberry Tarn, where once volcanic eruption rent the air.

On approaching the lower rim of the combe there is a choice of routes. The track levels off at about 1,300 feet and meets the upper section of Sour Milk Gill at right angles. Unless in exceptional spate, the beck may easily be crossed at this point if desired or, if there is a preference to visit the tarn itself, turn left along the southern side of the wall. The two routes meet again at the start of the next steep section, leading directly to the Pike.

As we climb and look back, the combe becomes even more impressive; a fine corrie scalloped out of the mountainside by the receding glacier long ago.

The climb from the floor of the combe is not easy; here, too, an attempt has been made to arrest the scouring of loose soil and scree by laying stone 'pavement'. On approaching the base of the conical Pike itself, the going gets even steeper and it is a relief to turn right into the little gully which runs up to the top, since here one is on reasonably steep and solid rock where both hands and feet may be brought to bear and easy progress made. At 2,479 feet, Red Pike is a superb viewpoint, falling away sharply in all directions and giving sight of five lakes and a host of fells.

From here we travel a few yards due south down a gentle slope and then turn south-west along a clear and often rough descent, crossing Gillerthwaite Beck and joining the main Ennerdale forestry road just above High Gillerthwaite. All the way down, Ennerdale Water lies before us, with the towering expanse of Haycock, the Side and Crag Fell above, all equally displaying their glorious mantle of purple heather.

There now follows a road walk of some four miles, past Gillerthwaite Farm, Bowness Knott and Routen Farm to take the public footpath on the right to Floutern Tarn. Here begins a steady climb to some 1,400 feet; first through a very narrow, wet, stony and overgrown stretch reminiscent of the smugglers' ways of the Devon coastline, but which soon opens up and leads onto a well-defined track between Banna Fell on the left and Herdus or Great Borne on the right. By now the long and narrow water of Floutern Tarn has appeared on our right, with Floutern Crags, the northern face of Great Borne, high above. This area is inclined to be wet underfoot, but is not too bad up to this point. For those with an archaeological bent (as opposed to that caused by too much weight in the haversack!) it should be noted that there is a splendid example of a pit circle directly between the tarn and Hen Comb – worth a short detour if time permits.

We now draw level with Hen Comb, which stands at 1,661 feet on our left and reach the southern edge of Mosedale. Here the terrain opens up ahead and below to reveal a vast saucer bounded by Hen Comb, Mellbreak and Gale Fell and it is at once clear that this area is likely to be *really* wet! Extensive areas of rush abound and there are the tell-tale bright green patches, which spell bog. A vast and tranquil scene, without sight of human habitation in any direction, numbering snipe, kestrels, buzzards and peregrine among its visitors, the occasional heron and even a cormorant on passage from Crummock to Ennerdale, or vice versa.

Down the slope we go, over the stile and on again to the right, where wetness underfoot begins to become very marked. This is the time to look out for a way off at right angles, due south, to gain the safety and comfort of the higher ground along the foot of Gale Fell. Failure to do so lands us in a dangerously soggy situation with nothing solid underfoot, where much of the vegetation is virtually floating and will move for yards around, at the touch of the boot.

Once opposite the full length of Mosedale, there appears an unexpected and sometimes dramatic view of Low Fell framed between Hen Comb and Mellbreak; on this last visit it was bathed in sunlight.

There is a good track along the side of Gale Fell, well above the main water table, and which leads on to pass over the footbridge at Scale Force – Lakeland's highest waterfall. From here the well-known and well-worn, but decidedly rough track leads all the way to Scale Bridge, which crosses over Buttermere Dubbs – that delightfully deep, sparkling and fast-running stretch of crystal-clear water – and on up the lonning all the way to Buttermere itself.

A distance of some 14 miles, this is not a walk to be undertaken lightly, but it is certainly highly recommended. A *real* walk, full of interest and quite unforgettable.

55. Glaramara and beyond

Although I was parked at the foot of Glaramara by nine o'clock, it was already both warm and clear, thus announcing that before long it would be positively hot. There were still long shadows, creating strong contrasts and throwing every view into sharp relief as I set off through the dewy grass, beset with diamonds, which slowly melted before the rising sun. Dappled sunlight among the trees on the lower slopes gave cool shade at first, but soon I was up onto the open fell and into the unremitting glare from a cloudless sky. Glaramara rises steeply from the start and a great combe gradually appears on the left. From a buttress came the call of young peregrines and before long I was to be accompanied for some time by a silently-gliding falcon, its boomerang wings scything through the air with consummate ease and grace.

The summit is reached by means of a lovely little scramble and ahead lies that deceptive route to Allen Crags. Deceptive, because it looks short and quite flat, whereas in fact it is not so short and is punctuated by hidden and considerable undulations which include quite steep and rough descents. On this higher ground there was still hardly any movement of air at all. However, on to Allen Crags, down to Esk Hause and left along one of these 'improved', 'conserved' or otherwise 'mended' tracks; good for conservation, maybe, but bad for feet! The bang, bang, bang of boots on these solid slabs soon drains the springiest of muscles. Then a somewhat indistinct left turn down towards the Langstrath—easily missed. At this upper end the track is narrow and gives the impression that it is little-used. On the right at this point is a small beck and before long there appears a mountain ash on its rocky bank. An ideal place to pause for lunch, providing, as it does, one of the very few bits of shade. Once this descent is started, it is immediate and substantial. Height is very soon lost; the floor of the valley is soon reached and the beck steadily widens. In places lower down there are the most beautiful limpid pools, which beckon the weary walker to their depths! But make no mistake, this is a very long, long valley, with a number of surprise twists and turns; do not think for a moment that, on reaching the valley floor, the walk is nearly over! It does go on – and on!

Eventually a little cluster of houses appears which is Stonethwaite – a welcome sight of habitation at last, where there is ice cream to be had, among other things to delight the tired traveller! A short road walk now, and the car is regained at Thornthwaite. On my own, this walk took me just seven hours, car to car and it does have much to recommend it. Fine views of great End, Esk Pike, Bowfell, the Langdales and right round to Gable, Grasmoor, Skiddaw and many more. A fine walk, but not one to be undertaken when short of time or energy!

56. Lingmell

The long and tortuous approach to Wasdale Head does have its compensations! It is certainly a very lengthy, narrow, twisting and undulating ride from Gosforth, but bordered by rocky scenes which promise more delights ahead and, of course, there is the ominous sight of Wastwater. So often dark and foreboding, with such extensive and gaunt screes plunging all the way to the water's edge, this is not only the deepest of English lakes, but its bottom is over 250 feet from the surface and is thus below sea level.

On arrival at Wasdale Head we take the track signed Lingmell and on this occasion follow the Shoulder Route up this deceptive mountain. Deceptive because on this side Lingmell presents merely a long and steep grassy slope, albeit with outcrops of rock here and there as we progress. But the northern and eastern slopes are quite different, being of substantial crag and scree and, comparatively speaking, a far more rough and rugged scene.

Apart from the fact that this fell may be used as a staging point on more extensive routes to Great Gable, Scafell, Scafell Pike, Esk Hause and beyond; it is in itself a fine viewpoint from which to see some of the grandest scenery in England, including our highest mountain.

The view back down to and over Wasdale Head is superb, while the overall vista takes in, amongst many others, the western Red Pike, Scoat Fell, Pillar, High Stile and even Grasmoor and Grisedale Pike. The view of the southern face of Great Gable, featuring Napes Needles, is one of the finest. Similarly, to the south and south-east lie Scafell, Mickledore and Scafell Pike, their massive crags, buttresses, gills and screes showing up to great advantage; near enough to see all the detail and yet far enough away for the broader scene to be appreciated, which is impossible when on the Scafells themselves. A place from which to gain a greater insight into the placing of and the relationship between the components of this glorious area.

This was one of the many Lakeland areas occupied in Neolithic times, and it is not unknown for stone axe heads to come to light.

From the summit of Lingmell, which stands at 2,649 feet, it is possible to complete a circular route via Sty Head and the track which leads from there due west along the northern edge of Lingmell Beck back to Wasdale Head. Sty Head should be reached either by joining the Corridor Route, or the track along the eastern and south-eastern edges of Piers Gill, the latter being the shorter, but less distinct of the two.

One further attraction in this area is that an energetic day's walking may be rounded off at the Wastwater Hotel, a renowned haven for walkers and climbers, where thirsts may be slaked and starvation averted by good beer, good bread and fine cheese, in a unique and fascinating bar which has echoed to walkers' tales for many a long year.

A fitting way to complete another great day!

57. Fleetwith

Petrified the tumbling waters

The morning of Thursday 5th March looked highly promising. It was one of those bright, clear days when it seemed that it really was set fair; visibility was going to be good and it was a day on which to gain height and make the most of ideal conditions. Rising heavenwards at the head of the valley stands Fleetwith Pike, a broad-based mountain towering above Buttermere, presenting a clearly-defined ridge from Gatesgarth all the way to the summit at 2,126 feet. There is virtually no walk-in at all, the climb being immediate and steep, and the track, such as it is, is concealed from below. In fact, it is one of the most tortuous zigzag routes to be found anywhere in Lakeland.

It begins by skirting Low Raven Crag, on the western face of which stands the white cross erected in memory of one Fanny Mercer, who fell to her death here in 1887.

From here the route progresses steadily up Fleetwith Edge with little respite; just the odd little shelf where one may stand on level ground and admire the ever-extending view to the west – and what a view it is! It stretches over Buttermere, Crummock and Loweswater and before the top is reached it encompasses the Solway, too. Thrush Bank shines forth as a white patch below Low Fell.

The climb itself varies from steep walking to scrambling, and in some sections it is certainly necessary to take care – especially on this particular day, as we were climbing into increasing snow. At times the track is clearly defined, but in places it is much less obvious, especially through snow-covered scree! In parts we are reduced to scrambling on hands and feet, but it is broadly a case of 'onward and upward' along the ridge, with a few obvious diversions to avoid vertical rock. Some parts appear quite daunting as they rise ahead, but as progress is made the route gradually becomes apparent. To the west we have the ranges to left and right of Haystacks to Red Pike and from Dale Head to Grasmoor, with Low Fell in the distance, whilst to this, on reaching the summit, must be added all those fells to the north, east and south, including Causey Pike, Skiddaw, Helvellyn, Fairfield, Great Gable, the Scafells and Pillar – in fact Wainwright lists some 50 tops which may be seen from this superb vantage point. On this particular day the vast majority were well and truly snow-capped, sparkling brilliant white under a cobalt sky.

Having reached the summit cairn, the track goes on along the top of the Pike, which rapidly broadens out after the sharpness of the ridge, but it must be borne in mind, especially in mist, that to the left or north is the precipitous face of Honister Crag. There is ample evidence of the old quarry workings, where the famous green slate is extracted; further quarry workings may be seen from here on the southern face of Dale Head across Honister Pass, a mountain which has also yielded copper along its northern flank in days gone by. Before long, as the track gradually descends, it will be found to swing round to the right and travel south-west and then south to Dubbs Quarry, joining the well-known and abundantly clear sledge-way down to Warnscale Bottom and on to Gatesgarth.

Again, on this particular day we were treated not only to sunshine, blue skies and brilliant snow, but also to the most impressive array of icicles, especially on the northern face of the higher reaches of Warnscale Beck. Row upon row, and in places great clusters of icy columns, where Jack Frost had petrified the tumbling rivulets; nature's organ pipes, many of which must have been six or eight feet in length. The descent is rough and rocky, but has the distinct advantage of giving the grand view of Green Crag and Haystacks towering above to the left, and further ahead, High Crag, High Stile and Red Pike, with the still waters of the lakes below.

But at last the boot sinks into soft and level turf and a glance round reveals most of the route, both up and down.

Another great walk, right on our doorstep. A must!

140

58. The Pond – haven for wildlife

It was some 60 years ago that I changed forms and form masters, too. The new man had a horrendous reputation for discipline, but I soon found that he kept an aquarium on his windowsill. A guy who keeps an aquarium can't be all bad! Little did I know on that first, timid meeting that he, Teddie Archer by name, who, incidentally, came from Cumberland or Westmorland, I forget which, would become a firm friend and that he and his aquarium would so fire my imagination that it would lead me into biology and 35 years in agronomic research!

A well-stocked and well-balanced aquarium is a pond in miniature, providing a habitat in which microbes, plants and animals can thrive. My first book on such matters is still on the bookshelf today; *Life in Ponds and Streams*, by W.S. Furneaux, still bearing its pencilled price of six shillings and the legend, 'New Impression, 1935'!

Like all other forms of habitat, ponds vary enormously; in fact, it is tempting to say that each one is unique. Variations in surrounding soil, aspect and, in particular, the acidity of the water, influence just what will grow there. The depth of the water affects its temperature and the rapidity with which it fluctuates. The type and density of plant growth influences which animals will adopt a particular pond, since, while some depend on open water and their own speed to escape predators, others rely on secluded hiding places.

The 'ideal' pond has areas of different depths and at least one area where amphibians may easily emerge from the water onto dry land. Ponds fulfil a vital role in the countryside, attracting not only aquatic species, but many birds and animals to drink, bathe, preen and, of course, to hunt. They are an important element in the maintenance of biodiversity. Sadly, however, the number of ponds is falling rapidly; indeed, it is estimated that, while in 1880 there were 1.3 million ponds in Britain, there are now only 300,000. The reasons are many and include pollution from industry, roadways and farming, and the fact that it is the nature of things for some ponds simply to dry up. Garden ponds have thus become a valuable resource, providing relatively safe oases in which aquatic life and those dependent on it may be conserved.

They provide a constant source of interest, too, with the annual reappearance of frogs and their spawn, the brilliant colours of dragonflies as they emerge and hover on a summer's evening and maybe even a hedgehog, fox or badger venturing in to drink. Such water is also much appreciated by birds; and so it goes on, an addition of great interest to adorn any garden and another little aid towards conservation.

The Pond – long may it survive, this jewel of the countryside, this oasis for wildlife.

59. Steeple

—where ravens soar, in Mirklin Cove!

Rising to a tempting peak west of Pillar stands the well-named summit Steeple, an unmistakable landmark on the skyline when viewed from the western reaches of Ennerdale.

Probably the most popular approach is from Bowness car park along the forestry road towards Gillerthwaite. We turn right over the first bridge, crossing the Liza, and over the stile at the top of the road. Left here, along the forestry road that runs along the southern side of the valley. Quite soon we find a broad drove road on the right, a clearway flanked by trees on both sides, and this is the start of our climb.

(There is an alternative – proceed further along the road to the bridge over Low Beck, where there is a sign on the right, which simply says, 'Path'! This does lead more directly to the foot of Steeple and is less steep, but the going gets rougher and, on balance, is no easier and less attractive.)

The drove road gets steeper and steeper. It starts on grass, but higher up it consists of slumped peat, roots and rocks. Keep left along the fence for the easiest ascent. This is, in fact, a shoulder of Lingmell (about 1,400 feet), and once the top is reached there is a good clear way in the general direction of Steeple, although a little height is lost in dropping to cross Low Beck. There is a zigzag here, right along the beck side, over and back a bit. Once this far, the general form of Steeple can be seen and, although the summit is not always in view, the way ahead is reasonably obvious.

Steeple is really a ridge running northwards from the slightly higher and much broader Scoat Fell; the former rises to 2,687 feet, while Scoat is 2,760 feet; the two being connected by a short arête. There is the usual series of false tops, but nothing particularly hazardous, except in mist, when there are precipitous drops to look out for. It is very much steeper to the east than the west and, apart from its distinctive sharp peak, its greatest features are perhaps the great drops into Wind Gap and Mirk Coves, which lie between it and Pillar, and into Mirklin Cove on the opposite side. This is dramatic stuff, with fine crags, deep fissures and a balancing rock; twin buttresses erupt from the floor of Wind Gap Cove and, indeed, a visit to the coves themselves is recommended – but that is another walk!

From Steeple itself we cross the arête to Scoat Fell, quite an easy scramble, and turn right or west along the rim of Mirklin Cove. Here we have a fine view over the cove itself, the length of Ennerdale Water and on to the Solway and beyond. We travel round the rim of the cove and swing down northwards towards Tewit How and aim for the top of the drove road on which we started. This is quite a long section in which the track, such as it is, frequently disappears and progress depends upon making something of a beeline through heather.

Total distance is probably about nine miles of varied walking, and in good conditions there are excellent views to Causey Pike, Miterdale, Ravenglass and the Galloway hills. There are ravens, grouse and a number of items of botanical interest. A good walk, but it must be said that it is best done in good conditions, because of the steep drops and because of the difficulty of finding the downward route in mist—a point we proved for ourselves on one occasion!

60. Haweswater

A visit to the far eastern fells in the region of Haweswater calls for quite a long trip by car; a circuitous route round many fells and then a southerly and finally a south-westerly drive. This latter leg is along the tortuous lakeside road, among scenery of increasing grandeur, and always in the back of one's mind is the fact that we are now in eagle country.

A car park at the farthest end of the lake road is our starting point on foot and we set off round the lake end and back along the opposite shore for a while. Once a natural lake, Haweswater has been dammed to form a reservoir, submerging the village of Mardale in the process, a project undertaken by Manchester Corporation. It is difficult now to imagine that in the mid-19th century, a ton and a half of butter was being sent off every week from Mardale Green to be spread upon the Manchester bread!

We cross the foot of Riggindale and follow the track towards Low Raise, a steep, but mostly grassy climb and on from there to High Raise, which stands at 2,634 feet. Throughout most of this climb we can look back to our left over Riggindale to Riggindale Crag, the site of the most productive golden eagle eyrie in Britain. During the breeding season we can also pick out on the valley floor the group of wardens and enthusiastic birdwatchers guarding and watching the adults and their young. It is, of course, a matter of taste, but to some at least the eagle is not the most exciting of birds. Eagles are inclined to have a really good feed and then simply to stand about, rather like vultures. They do remind us of the old saying, "Sometimes I sits and thinks, and sometimes I just sits"!

If, however, you are fortunate enough to see an eagle in flight and at reasonably close quarters, and especially when hunting, that is a very different matter. By our normal bird standards, the eagle is huge; it has a wingspan of some seven feet and recorded speed of up to 90mph, which is a breathtakingly exciting combination. However, in an area like ours, where there is usually only one pair – the only admitted breeding pair in England – you may wait a very long time before seeing any action at all. Needless to say, excitement mounts, too, when they have successfully reared young and the chick is about to fly. It can be seen staggering around the massive nest, flapping its wings and obviously very frustrated until eventually the great moment comes when it half-falls and half-jumps into space. If you are lucky enough to be able to spend a lot of time there, then clearly it is rewarding in the extreme, as recorded by Mike Tomkies in his captivating book, *Golden Eagle Years* (Heinemann).

Once High Raise is mastered we veer left along a clear track, keeping to the left of the wall, along High Street, over Mardale Fell to Nan Bield Pass, round the summit of Harter Fell and then almost doubling back down to the end of Haweswater where we began. This is a fine walk with an excellent high-level stretch between good climbs up and down and with extensive views. It feels rather, as a mere walker, that one is very much a visitor, if not an intruder in this glorious expanse of fells rolling under a cloudless sky and echoing to the call of the skylark and ring ouzel – and with always the chance of seeing our largest bird of prey, the Lake District's equivalent to Mike Tomkies' 'Atalanta', the golden eagle.

61. Simba – A 'Fine Feller'

Little did I know, on that memorable day, what lay ahead for the new arrival. I was still working at the time, in a city, and there was little or no open or wild country readily available. The new arrival was a small bundle of creamy fur with two large and deeply-appealing eyes and a wet nose, which I was assured would one day grow up to be a golden retriever, and whose name was 'Simba'.

From the very beginning he was a great character; highly intelligent, full of fun and yet an excellent house dog. Friendly to a fault and yet very protective. I was once walking through a wood when, unknown to me, another walker, quite innocently, was coming up behind. Simba stood full square and barred his way until I had turned round to pass the time of day with the newcomer. I was delighted!

He was nothing if not an enthusiast, whose warm companionship brightened any day and who could always be relied upon for a great welcome.

I used to take him on holiday to Buttermere, in the very heart of the Lake District, where walkers really are spoilt for choice! He walked the fells and loved every minute of it. Happy days!

But then, quite unexpectedly, early retirement became a possibility and, in no time at all I had moved house, lock, stock and barrel, to a small village tucked in among the western fells of Cumbria, only a few miles from the favourite holiday haunt of Buttermere.

What a life for a dog! I walked and climbed, roamed and wandered, much to his obvious delight! At low level he was constantly in and out of the water, romping through the shallows and gamely swimming to fetch sticks which were thrown as far out as I could manage. At medium level he would be coursing the fellsides; enjoying springy turf, exploring every trail through bracken and gorse, putting the local rabbit population to flight in the process, but never once disturbing sheep. At high level – and he climbed all the higher fells, most of them many times – he would be always ahead and would keep peering down at me as if to say, "Come on up, the view is great!"

But, big and strong tho' he was, he retained his great love for a piece of blanket! Whenever visitors arrived he would excitedly dash to his box and fetch the precious remnant, presenting it to them with wagging tail and a neck-bowed prance like a circus horse.

And so, through 14 years, he was a constant and remarkable companion, as warm and as loyal as any dog could be. Eventually, as is the nature of things, his allotted span came to an end, but he gave generously throughout his life, enriching mine in the process and leaving the fondest of memories, which will never fade.

Thank you, Simba, a 'Fine Feller', and this man's best friend.

62. Variation on a much-walked range

Extending in a north-westerly direction from a line drawn through Grey Knotts, Brandreth and Great Gable, lie three mountain ranges, stretching out like fingers trying desperately to grasp the Solway coast. Between the middle and lower fingers lies Ennerdale and between the middle and upper, lies the Buttermere Valley. Each range of mountains has a relatively smooth and featureless southern face and an infinitely more craggy and dramatic northern one. Facing Buttermere, the northern great buttresses of Red Pike, High Stile and High Crag, each falling steeply throughout with a deeply-serrated skyline and with two great combes between them. The most popular route on the range is the ridge track encompassing all three summits; it is a great walk – but there are others!

So, on this occasion we leave Buttermere, past the Fish Hotel and make our way along the southern side of the lake. Taking the upper path through the trees, we come to a fork; to the left goes the main track, while to the right we have no more than a footpath. This is, in fact, a traverse, which leads upwards and eastwards, gradually swinging to the right or in an increasingly southerly direction. It is the track rock climbers use to reach the favourite pitches of Grey Crags.

However, once we swing round to go straight up the fellside, we look out for a rather indistinct right turn – another traverse, in the opposite direction to the first, which takes us westwards towards the north-east ridge of High Stile.

By now we have reached a height of about 1,900 feet, with splendid views of Buttermere Valley and village, and on breasting the ridge we have the full length of Crummock Water before us, too. To our left stands the great buttress of High Crag and between the two tops is Burtness Combe (up through which is a far-from-easy scramble, in the right-hand corner, up unstable rock-and-earth, not without its hazards!).

Once we have reached the north-east ridge we turn straight up it and have a fine scramble of some 500 feet, followed by a further 200 feet of rough, but much less steep terrain, which includes a couple of the obligatory false tops before the true summit is reached. Overall, this route is by no means over-used and, as a result, it is not entirely clear all the way, but once the ridge is reached, the way ahead is virtually straight up and it is a matter of selecting whatever appears to be a sensible way, guided by the odd cairn and the sparse areas of boot-worn rock.

From the top we have the choice of circling Burtness Combe to the left or, as we did recently, going right and returning to Buttermere via Red Pike, Lingcomb Edge and Scale Force.

However, the high point of the walk is the ridge scramble on High Stile with its views, which include, perhaps surprisingly, Keswick and Derwentwater over Buttermere Moss. High Stile is a grand mountain in its own right and, standing at 2,644 feet, is some 200 feet higher than its two neighbours. The ascent by the ridge is a variation in a much-visited valley and on a much-walked range that is well worth exploring.

63. —an exhilarating mass of rock!

When viewed from Lorton, especially in the warm glow of a summer's evening, the towering peak of Hopegill Head is most impressive. Approaching it, however, may have its problems. To make the best of it, we really want to take in Swinside and Ladyside Pike as well and to do this we may either start from the Whinlatter Pass road, making our way along the track through Swinside Plantation and then sharp right up the side of the wall to the top, or alternatively we may start from the Hope Beck road and climb straight up the fellside from there, beside the wall. Either way is steep. If we want to miss out Swinside and Ladyside Pike, then we park just on the Whinlatter side of Hope Beck Farm, where there is a convenient pull-in, and the ascent may then be made along the side of Hope Beck to a pinnacle on the Swinside-Hopegill Head ridge, but below the final part of the climb.

The pinnacle stands at 2,300 feet and is reached whichever route is taken and, while it is a good walk thus far, the best is yet to come!

From a distance, Hopegill Head appears to present a massive vertical wall of rock, but like so many places of this nature, closer acquaintance reveals that it is by no means an impossible barrier. Nevertheless, it is an exhilarating mass of rock, which provides an excellent scramble to the summit.

Standing at 2,525 feet, Hopegill Head gives a great field of view, extensive in most directions, except for that shielded by Eel Crag and Grasmoor. Undoubtedly, the most dramatic is immediately to the east over Hobcarton Crag and its precipitous and craggy combe, which may, in fact, be scaled with care.

From the summit we turn west and make our way along the ridge to the east top of Whiteside, ie the penultimate top, and there turn right or north down a lengthy, bare and trackless fellside towards Dodd.

On approaching Dodd we have to descend into a strange and unexpected transverse gully known as Dodd Pass; an unusual feature, this, with Dodd itself guarding the side opposite. Clamber down into the gully and turn right or east and a track along the floor swings down and round, past a ruined sheepfold and all the way back to the car parked near Hope Beck farm.

And so we complete a fine circular walk, which includes the dramatic Hobcarton Crags, the fun of scrambling up the rock face of Hopegill Head and the unexpected appearance of Dodd Pass. Although the Whiteside to Hopegill Head part of the walk is inclined to be popular, especially in high season, the rest is usually relatively quiet and much less frequented. Any self-respecting pair of walking boots will find the route irresistible when viewed from Lorton!

64. 'Over the hills and far away—'

—which is surely one of the most evocative phrases in the English language! While the claim that walking is Man's natural means of locomotion is undoubtedly true, never was so clinical a definition more inadequate in describing so delightful an activity. Similarly, walking is said to be the best form of exercise, but this greatly understates the enormous pleasure and the great physical and mental benefits that are to be derived.

Mind you, we are concerned here with what might reasonably be described as 'real' walking, not that 20 yards to the pillar box or the stroll around the park! No – we are concerned primarily with the sort of walking that's measured in hours, miles and, hopefully, hundreds, if not thousands, of feet of ascent and descent; walking which calls for a little planning and the use of 'sensible' equipment.

Most fell-walkers agree that boots are by far the best footwear, providing good grip, sound support and ankle protection. Lightweight boots are alright for summer wear, but, in winter especially, there is nothing to compare with the comfort of good quality leather boots. Needless to say, wellingtons are most assuredly not the thing—not even the manufacturers would recommend them. They give little or no real grip, most of the tread is crossways, which means there is virtually no grip at all when traversing, there is no ankle support and, in fact, they are positively dangerous.

Old-fashioned, perhaps, but breeches and stockings are still my favourite form of leg wear, and for good reason. They are neat and compact, with nothing at all loose and flapping about to get caught by the heel or a jagged rock just at the wrong moment. We all know about the other basic requirements; the map and the compass and the mini first-aid kit and so on, but all this and waterproofs, too, can be carried in a bum-bag, thus relieving the neck and shoulders of an extra weight.

Once well-prepared, the call of the open air is there to be answered. The cool fresh air of early morning, the springy feel of dew-spangled turf beneath the feet, the scent of bracken, the song of the skylark overhead, the scramble over scree, the comforting clomp of boot on solid rock and that exhilarating moment as one emerges from the top of a gill onto a broad, expansive top or gaunt crag, beset with a panorama of breathtaking views. The initial shortage of breath and the first signs of aching muscles are soon overcome as the benefit of a 'second wind' asserts itself.

Any form of country walking is made a great deal more enjoyable if an interest is taken in wildlife, whether this is general or more specialised. An interest in plants, birds, animals or in a particular group, such as alpines, lichens or perhaps raptors, adds a further dimension and, since one is surrounded by wildlife in the country anyway, it does provide a great opportunity.

65. Kirk Fell

Kirk Fell was unfortunate enough to be born between two more imposing brother fells, Great Gable and Pillar and, as a result, it does receive rather less than its fair share of attention. Even at the very height of the season it may be virtually deserted, while each of its two neighbours is well sprinkled with walkers scaling their flanks from all directions. True, Kirk is not the most dramatic of fells, but it does rise to 2,630 feet and is not without its attractions, not least of which is the provision of a fine viewpoint from which to see many other fells from new and unaccustomed angles.

One way to approach it is from Honister – we take the usual well-worn track as if for Great Gable. As we round Brandreth and the track veers left, we move straight ahead to join Moses' Trod, which traverses the lower slopes below Green Gable, Windy Gap and Gable Crag at about 2,000 feet, to Beck Head.

While it is assumed that readers are familiar with the route, at least to this point, it would perhaps be churlish to ignore altogether the fine views that it provides, not least over the top of Haystacks and all that lies to the north and west.

Beck Head is the great col, which lies between Great Gable and Kirk Fell. We pass just over the rise and then fork right. The track – if indeed there is one – is indistinct at best, but we simply aim down to the floor of the col to our right and across it, past Beck Head Tarn, to where the track up Rib End to Kirk Fell itself is quite obvious. It is a loose, rough and rocky ascent in the early stages, but after a few hundred feet it becomes less steep and the going gets much easier. We climb some 600 feet from Beck Head to the summit, which is broad and rocky with no particular feature.

But it would be a shame to march straight up here without taking in the unfolding panorama. Perhaps the most dramatic sight appears behind us in the shape of Gable Crag; we turn round to look back over the col and there stands Gable in all its massive glory; the best, closest, uninterrupted view we can get, short of hovering in a helicopter. We can see Lingmell, the Scafells and the length of Wasdale; as we climb, Great End also comes into view. We can even see quite clearly the great gash that is Lord's Rake – a spot that holds strong memories of an unforgettable scramble in the past!

And so we move onto the summit, when a fresh vista appears; Pillar, Scoat Fell, Red Pike (west), High Stile, Grasmoor and many, many more. But on we go, over the top and look out for the line of old iron fence posts sloping off to the right. These we follow and very gradually descend about 300 feet; but, especially in adverse weather, it is important not to be lulled into a false sense of security by this relatively gentle terrain. Quite suddenly this easy descent changes totally in character. It is tempting to say, "the ground opens up beneath the feet" – but let's settle for, "it suddenly becomes very steep"!

Care must be taken from this point all the way down to Black Sail Pass. It is steep, rough, loose, and amongst it all is what is generally referred to as the 'awkward step' as well. And it *is* 'awkward'. 'Awkward' going up, even more 'awkward' going down and, indeed, those with a degree of shortness of the lower limbs may well find it difficult in the extreme. But, with care and a bit of luck, the Pass is duly reached. Here we turn right down to Black Sail.

Crossing the Liza by the footbridge, we take a breather here to admire this glorious dale head. Dominated by Great Gable, and with Brandreth, Kirk Fell and Pillar in attendance, this vast amphitheatre is carpeted with a fine array of moraines and divided by the embryonic Liza. And overall – silence – but for the occasional bleat of sheep and the ripple of water. Take time here; it is another special place of magic atmosphere which, once savoured, may forever be recalled.

Over the bridge, we turn right – although anyone who is that energetic may go left instead and take in Scarth Gap and Haystacks, too! But, for we lesser mortals, right it is, through the moraines, following the track and, where the beck forks, keep left and up the gill beside Loft Beck, with Seavy Knott on the left and Brin Crag on the right.

At 1,900 feet, this track forks. The right-hand fork goes to Brandreth, but we keep left for Honister and soon rejoin the main Honister–Gable route. A total of about eight miles, with about 2,600 feet of ascent in all – but worth every step of the way!

66. 'A rose by any other name—'

Publication of Dr Geoffrey Halliday's *Flora of Cumbria* marked a great advance for the study of plant life in the county. This massive work took 23 years to complete and lists the results of a detailed survey of the area, which was divided up into 10km squares for the purpose, every square being searched. It runs to over 600 pages and there is a location map for virtually every species. A truly mammoth task.

It is, of course, based upon the usual methods involved in systematic botany, namely on the appearance of plants and their parts, especially their flowers, and it is against this background that plants are classified. Systematic botany has been a recognised branch of science for many years, its great pioneer being the Swedish botanist, Carl Linnaeus, after whom the Linnaean Society was named. I well remember that my induction lecture as a Fellow, which must be some 30 years ago, was on the great need for more systematic botanists, a need that is still with us after all this time.

The sheer vastness of the subject is mind-boggling, even after all the work that has already been done. For example, of the vast storehouse of plant life in Amazonia, it is estimated that so far only 2% of plants there have been identified and classified. Bear in mind that this is by no means a merely academic pursuit; between 25 and 30% of our medicines are of plant origin. How many cures and for how many ailments might we yet find in the as-yet unknown plants of Amazonia?

But even that only scratches the surface of systematic botany and its application. Only recently it has been found that, in fact, the current system of identification and classification is flawed, and that relationships between plants cannot necessarily be determined with certainty by appearance alone. The study of plant DNA has revealed that while the stinging nettle and the rose, for example, are at present placed in widely separated families, they are actually very closely related indeed.

If we pursue the implications of this discovery, we very soon see that the task ahead may well be not only to identify and classify the unknown species, but to re-appraise all those studied since Linnaeus's work in the 18th century, and that of his successors, notably Brown and Darwin, in the 19th century.

The situation is made even worse in that species are being lost faster than they can be studied. It is currently estimated that we are losing plant species at the rate of 5.8% per decade, and that we shall lose 29% of all biodiversity within the next 50 years. And we must remember that extinction is forever.

Add to this the fact that we do not know how the loss of individual species is likely to affect the functions of ecosystems as a whole.

Much is being done. The Wellcome Trust and Orange plc are conserving no less than 25,000 species of wild flowering plants in a seed bank, for example. Just as well, since 300 of our native 1,442 flowering plants are threatened with extinction. And this is where we came in – we need a massive international botanical effort—and we need it to start years ago!

67. —the most handsome crag in Lakeland?

The mighty bulk of Pillar mountain stands four-square between Ennerdale and Wasdale, its broad and windswept summit soaring to 2,927 feet above sea level, only 22 feet less than Great Gable and one of a chain of fells which go to make up the western range. A fine fell, indeed, but one that is clearly named after a single feature more impressive even than the whole, namely Pillar Rock.

Pillar may be approached from a number of different directions, but the best way of all, which is certainly not the most popular, involves a long walk in and a long walk out. Starting from Bowness Knott, there is a stretch of four miles along the forestry road before it forks. Forking right takes us across the Liza by the concrete bridge, where there is a sign directing us right again. Now, at last, off the road and into dark, damp and dismal conifers, along a narrow and often slippery track, gradually gaining ground until emerging onto another spur of forestry road, only to cross it and dive into still more conifers; then, at last, at about 1,000 feet, out into daylight, over a stile and into open air.

Thus far there has been little to excite or even interest the walker, apart from the roadside flora – yes, there is *always* something to look at! Among many other species thus far are the carline thistle, butterwort, spearwort, burdock, coltsfoot and figwort. There is horsetail, too, that relic of the past, well-known to the dinosaurs.

However, on reaching the aforementioned stile, the mood changes entirely. Towering above is a steep stretch of boulder-strewn and beck-divided fell, totally dominated by the huge bulk of Pillar Rock, the magnificent northern buttress, its deeply-shadowed fissures starkly detailed in the morning light. Even at this distance, it is a dramatic and awe-inspiring sight, framed by the crenellated crest above and beyond.

The track zigzags upwards between Pillar Rock on the right and Raven Crag on the left, through grassy patches and, for a while, alongside a rushing beck with foaming falls and rushing rivulets. Great mounds of *Sphagnum* and *Polytrichum* mosses squelch beneath the boot, while brilliant jewels of pure white and carmine starry saxifrage appear. The track veers left above the falls; it is indistinct, but this matters not. Keep climbing, aiming just to the left of the Rock, and eventually the unmistakable High Level Traverse is reached. It is now possible either to go up to the right, behind the Rock, and so on up to the summit of Pillar mountain, or turn left along the traverse to the Robinson Cairn. This is a somewhat tortuous route, with many ups and downs, patches of scree, level stretches and mini-scrambles, until joining the main summit track from Wasdale Head, just above Looking Stead. Its way is punctuated by alpine ladies' mantle, spikes of yellow St John's wort emerging from rocky crevices, the fronds of hard fern and rock bracken or parsley fern. There is a sprinkling of the ubiquitous tormentil, the ink-black pearls of bleaberry and even the mauve-splashed white of eyebright.

The views are superb – across Ennerdale to the High Stile range, Robinson, Skiddaw, Helvellyn and, closer to hand, Kirk Fell, too. But most dramatic is Gable Crag. On rounding Pillar above Looking Stead, the southerly view emerges also, encompassing the southern Red Pike, Scoat Fell, Yewbarrow and Wasdale.

On down the track, now past a small tarn on the left, arriving at Black Sail Pass at some 1,800 feet. It's right for Wasdale, but this route takes us left down a rough, but easy descent, with only one rock step of any significance, below which stands, or perhaps more accurately, lies, what must surely be one of the oldest rowans in the district. Then, what a sight! An extensive moraine, a relic of the last Ice Age, consisting of over 100 mounds (– and he or she who wishes to check the precise number is welcome to the task!).

Over the footbridge, left past the Youth Hostel and stride off for Bowness Knott. However, to leave at once and at speed would be to deny oneself the enjoyment of a treasured spot; the peace, the serenity, the tranquillity should be savoured. This glorious dale head, surrounded by great fells, standing in silence, except for the occasional bleat of a lamb and perhaps the meouw of a buzzard. Off again, but not without a few backward glances at the valley head and the descent already made.

Overall, this walk includes eight miles on the forestry road, but with ample compensation through the central section, not least the approach to Pillar Rock, that bastion of the western fells – 'the most handsome crag in Lakeland'.

68. Napes

There are many fine walks and many fine scrambles to be savoured in the Lake District, some of which are regularly tackled and others rarely visited at all. It would be interesting to know, for example, what proportion of the tens of thousands of people who have reached the top of Great Gable and have peered down through the Napes, have ever considered climbing up that way! – and yet, in fact, the area of the Napes is most impressive and memorable.

We start in the old familiar way, parking at Honister Quarry, and make our way along the flank of Grey Knotts and on to Moses' Trod, passing beneath the towering north face of Gable Crag. We do this so often, in pursuit of one route or another, that we are inclined to take for granted all those superb views along the way, from Pillar to Skiddaw and taking in Buttermere, Crummock and Loweswater.

The well-worn track is easy enough to follow all the way to Beck Head, but thereafter a degree of caution is called for. From Beck Head the track descends to Wasdale, but we need to find the start of the south traverse of Great Gable on our left, about 100 feet below the level of Beck Head. This point is as clear as can be from the top of Kirk Fell, but not so easy to locate when on a level with it. However, once found, following it is not difficult. It is narrow, rough and often loose. The initial section goes due south, but then quite suddenly it turns sharp left and as the direction changes, so, too, does the terrain.

Thus far it has been of mostly small, loose rock, but now there is much more solid rock and more ups and downs; it runs at a height of just about 2,000 feet across the very steep face and the views are nothing if not spectacular. As we proceed we have some 1,000 feet of scree falling away sharply to our right; above and to our left, the scree continues upwards for yet another 1,000 feet, but standing starkly through the scree are the giant crags of Napes Needles, their gnarled fingers clawing at the sky. Three among them are especially dramatic: the extraordinary 'Cat Rock' – a seated 'cat' of solid rock, complete with tail; the Napes Needle itself, a spectacular column; and Sphinx Rock, a great boulder which provides the obvious silhouette against the sky above. Having once heard the names, they are instantly recognisable.

In addition to the endless interest in the immediate vicinity, there are breathtaking views of Great End, Lingmell, the Scafells and, of course, grand views of Wasdale and Wastwater. Among the Great Napes are a number of named spots worth seeking out, such as Eagle's Nest Gully, Needle Gully and Arrowhead Gully.

But, as usual, the summit is the goal, and so steps are retraced a little to Little Hell Gate, where one is faced with 1,000 feet of ascent up the right-hand edge of the scree chute where, thankfully, there is often the opportunity of hand and footholds in solid rock. This is a long, hard, very steep scramble, but, for those who enjoy scrambling, it is a really superb route. Care is necessary, not only because of the steepness, but because much of the scree is loose and caution must be exercised, especially if someone is climbing above. A dislodged boulder will go crashing and bouncing down for hundreds of feet and anyone in its path would be hard put to it to take evasive action.

The ascent was punctuated by three birds. First, while gazing up at Needle Rock, a peregrine falcon scythed across the sky at speed, the very picture of aerial mastery. Second, a deeply-croaking raven launched itself from a craggy outcrop, gliding out over the abyss, its finger-ended wings outstretched. And third, throughout the entire climb there was a glorious serenade by a ring ouzel, its silvery notes echoing around the gully from its vantage point on the very apex of White Napes; indeed, it was still singing its heart out when we had climbed right past it and were able to look down on it. A trio of real mountain birds.

At last, patience rewarded, and we emerge onto a ridge running from the top of the Napes towards the base of Westmorland Crags; a short detour round these and we have only some 400 feet to climb before the familiar summit cairn is reached. From here we follow the standard route to Windy Gap, Brandreth, Grey Knotts and Honister – but it is the quite exceptional area of the Napes and the climb from the south traverse that make this walk so memorable.

It is, on the one hand, the sheer grandeur of it all and, on the other, the detailed interest, the track changing direction, level and terrain so frequently, and there are surprises around each of its many corners. It is fascinating. And then there is the climb up Little Hell Gate, seeking finger holds and heaving tired limbs over and round a myriad of obstacles. Undoubtedly the area that put the 'Great' into Great Gable.

69. Two birds – one story!

In times like these, when we so frequently hear of species of bird, plant and animal around the world becoming endangered or even extinct, it is both encouraging and exciting to hear of instances in which the tide is turned and we have the opportunity of enjoying the company of wildlife saved from the brink. Two such instances have been in the news recently; one, of course, on our doorstep.

The osprey began to settle around Bassenthwaite Lake a few years ago, as it did further south at Rutland Water, giving us a chance to watch this magnificent creature in England again and to see its spectacular hunting technique.

The osprey, 'fish hawk' or 'fishing eagle' is a large bird; white underneath with a white head and large, yellow eyes and brown above. It has long wings, but is inclined to fly slowly, if not laboriously, and to glide when hunting. A fence post or tree branch is often used as a perch and from here it will take off, climb steadily over water and then glide or 'float', searching for fish of appropriate size near enough to the surface for a kill to be possible. Once a target is selected, wings are folded back, the head dips and there is a hurtling dive. Just before impact with the water, the talons are brought forward in readiness and there is a tremendous splash. The technique is successful in about 20% of attempts.

Once a fish is caught, the osprey struggles free of the water, clearly working very hard to gain height; meantime the prey is gripped tightly, often thrashing vigorously to and fro. The bird grips it with one foot behind the other, so that the body of the fish is roughly parallel to the line of flight, to reduce drag to a minimum.

On returning to the perch, it will stand on the fish, insert its hooked beak and tear pieces off by throwing back its head. Such morsels are then eaten or are fed to young in the nest.

Ospreys are with us only for the spring and summer months, before returning to the warmer climes of Africa. It is, without doubt, a magnificent bird and it is great news that, with Man's help and encouragement, it has begun to breed again in England after so long an absence.

The second story of success relates to the red kite, which at one time was common here and was even a common sight scavenging in the streets of Elizabethan London, but which was persecuted to such an extent that it became entirely absent from England and barely survived in Wales. Thanks to a reintroduction programme launched jointly by the RSPB and English Nature, however, it was reported recently that there are now 430 pairs nesting in the UK, mostly in Wales and southern England, but including also 16 pairs in the Midlands and three in the north of England.

The kite's plumage is basically a striking reddish-brown, but it has a brown-streaked white head and neck.

Its mastery of flight is supreme, partly due to its very long wings, but especially through its strongly-forked tail, quick flips of which serve to steer it this way and that.

Diet is quite varied. It will take fledgling birds, rats, mice and other small mammals; it will scavenge on carrion and will catch frogs and toads. But it is the colour, the markedly-forked tail and the mastery of the air that make the kite such an exciting bird to watch. In both cases, we have many hard-working people to thank for the return of these magnificent birds to our skies.

70. Red Pike again

It is nearly 30 years since Wainwright wrote *Book Seven* of his *Guides to the Lakeland Fells*, yet even then he referred to the ascent of the Buttermere Red Pike as 'the most trodden mountain track out of Buttermere, a ladder of stones'. So it was and, needless to say, it got progressively worse until recently, when the track was 'repaired' and indeed virtually re-built over much of its length. Such stretches are now solid underfoot, which is a great change from the shifting mass of loose soil and stones up which we trudged so many times.

It is still by no means an easy climb; the steepness remains and it is a long pull over the 2,150 feet of ascent to reach the summit, which stands 2,479 feet above sea level. But it's a good climb, with grand views over the Buttermere valley, Crummock Water and beyond, a view shared yesterday with a persistently-hovering kestrel. This bird's ability to hang motionless in mid-air, even when buffeted by strong gusty winds, is really quite incredible.

However, having started from Buttermere, we climb Red Pike over the long-established route, but this time, instead of following the usual course of High Stile and High Crag, we go over the top of the Pike and aim due west for Starling Dodd. After only a few hundred yards of descent we emerge from the rough and boulder-strewn terrain and have a fine stretch of uninterrupted walking over a distance of some 1¼ miles through something of a saucer, but one that holds no water to impede progress. There is water in the form of the odd mini-tarn, and there are areas in which, for some unknown reason, erosion is beginning to become only too apparent. Surely not due to walkers – this route is not that popular – but there it is; patches where the turf has gone and bare earth is there to allow the entry of water and a gradually increasing degree of damage from frost and wind.

The climb from the low point of the saucer to the top of Starling Dodd is a mere 240 feet, but it seems more and, in fact, this little hump looks much larger close to, than when viewed, as it so often is, from other tops.

Once on top, the next objective comes into view, namely, Great Borne – or Herdus, if you prefer; one of the two guardians of the entrance to Ennerdale, and rising to 2,019 feet. It is 1½ miles from Starling Dodd to Great Borne, on a virtually straight track until a fence comes into sight; look out for the stile and cross over to the right. The track becomes indistinct here, but it matters not; simply aim for the top, picking a convenient way through the rock-strewn slope.

On reaching the top there is another fence. Turn right along it, keeping the fence on the left, and in a matter of 50 yards or so we are over the top and starting the descent to Steel Brow. Caution is called for here. It is a very steep, grassy descent, with some areas of rock and a few places where it is necessary to zigzag in order to avoid the odd sheer drop.

When this walk was done recently we enjoyed a fine morning, but by the time we were on Great Borne, someone had switched the light out! It was as black as could be over Great Gable and the entire south side of Ennerdale disappeared from view! We knew just what was coming. Two or three massive spots of rain and – down it came! On went the waterproofs and by the time we began the descent, visibility was down to a matter of a very few yards. There was just one tremendous crack of thunder right overhead, for good measure.

Nevertheless, we made it safely to the bottom and splashed our way across to reach the Ennerdale-Floutern-Buttermere track. And, incidentally, I jumped one beck, skidded on landing on the soft and muddy bank and went full length in about three inches of water! But then, the human frame will only carry so much water, and having already passed that point long ago, it really didn't make much difference – except that the watery silence was broken by a good laugh!

71. Solway dawn

Six o'clock and already the sky was lightening from the east, exposing the glistening sands and mudflats of the Solway: wisps of early-morning mist hung over the sea in such a way that at times it was impossible to determine where water ended and sky began. A sort of universal blanket of grey, with an ever-increasing pinkish-orange tinge as the weak sun ascended. Cold, still, but far from silent. The lapping of the waves as the tide receded, slowly but surely exposing thousands of hectares of invertebrate-rich feeding grounds, to the excited cacophony of bird calls.

At first argumentative and aggressive, as flocks of feathered feeders compete with one another to pillage the small areas available, but gradually abating to a more contented 'conversation' as it became obvious that once again there would be plenty for all.

The distinctive, shrill, piping call of the oystercatchers echoed along the water's edge as they searched for their accustomed diet of tiny shellfish, opening them either by smashing them on the ground or by prising open their bivalve forms with the brilliant orange bill. A few suddenly took flight, for no apparent reason, and raced along low over the water to a fresh place, with that rapid display of strongly-contrasting black head, leading and trailing wing margins, with bold white between and beneath. Binoculars revealed also the deep pink legs and the shining black eye with red surround. Smart birds, indeed, to be counted in their thousands in the area.

Then there were flocks of knot, frantically searching for sustenance in the form of tiny crabs, molluscs and worms, packed tightly together in great numbers. But surely the most exciting aspect of this species of tide-hugging birds comes when they are in flight. Who gives the command that is so instantly and totally obeyed? The display is spectacular as they swoop and swerve. As they go in one direction there is a view of their grey-brown backs and then, as they turn, this is transformed into the flashing white undersides, only to revert to grey-brown as the direction changes again. The contrast is incredible, almost like switching a light on and off. No stragglers, no latecomers, no collisions; just fast-moving harmony and grace.

Also there are thousands of curlew, giving their springtime 'bubbling' call prior to setting off for the breeding grounds inland. Their progress across the sands is nothing if not stately on those long spindly legs; our largest wader, constantly probing with that long, downward-curved bill. Among them, but in far fewer number, are the redshanks, mottled grey-brown with darker brown in parts, with long, orange legs and straight red bills.

And, of course, there are many more – cormorant, heron, lesser black-backed gull, the godwits, even ruff, if luck is in. There are shelduck, our largest duck, with that striking black head with white and tan plumage – and a host of different calls and behaviour patterns.

A constantly-changing scene of birds, cloud formations and light, as the tides ebb and flow – an equally wonderful world of wide horizons, totally different, yet so close to the fells of Lakeland.

The weather plays an integral part in the appearance and atmosphere of both regions. Brilliantly illuminated, warm and calm, but in both, the clouds can appear from nowhere, the wind can spring up and an azure sky can quickly produce storm clouds to overtake the unwary. Whatever the weather, beauty is all around.

72. Springtime delights

Well, really! It's like coming out of a tunnel into broad daylight! Weeks and weeks through which every day, it seemed, was wet – and then we emerge into a spell of *dry*, warmer, bright, sunny weather, with cloudless skies! A treat for us all and not least for the animal world, in which there must have been many a back glad to feel the warmth of the sun, at last. And, of course, the early signs of spring are all around us; indeed, some, such as the snowdrops, have already been and gone. The odd celandine shone brightly on the otherwise seemingly-growthless banks and then, all of a sudden, they were there in great numbers, a veritable flush of gold; a botanical crash of cymbals! In Dorset, the celandine is known as 'spring messenger', which seems singularly appropriate, while perhaps the longest name for it comes from Somerset, namely, 'gentleman's cap-and-frills'! It has lots more in different counties, many of which reflect its use as a medicinal herb.

However, I suppose everybody's favourite spring flower is the primrose, or 'prime rose'. The primrose is somewhat under threat, having long been subjected to picking by all and sundry. It is reproduced by seed, but for seed to be produced there must be pollination between the two types of flower, the pin-eyed and the thrum-eyed. In the first, the stigma is situated at the top of the corolla tube, while the stamens only reach half that height, and in the second, the position is reversed. Clearly, too much picking reduces the chances of successful pollination.

Another spring favourite is the bluebell, or wild hyacinth, once much used for making glue, for any purpose from arrow-making to book-binding. English Nature have recently drawn attention to the fact that even the bluebell is not entirely safe, as 'unscrupulous bulb collectors seek out bluebells to plunder for sale', a practice which is illegal without a licence. Damaging bluebell leaves by walking on them, or by grazing, seriously jeopardises future flowering.

English Nature have also reminded us about the importance of the garden pond, especially for frogs. However, it is vital that the pond is in a sunny spot, has shallow margins with some sloping sides and with deeper areas in the middle, and a range of native pond plants. Heaps of logs or stones nearby will provide hiding places and some rough grass is also welcome. Needless to say, garden chemicals must be kept away from the site.

As for the birds, well, some of our spring visitors have already returned. The glorious call of the curlew is echoing across the countryside again, for example. One or two early wheatears have arrived – males that is, with their strongly-contrasting black, white and grey colouring; the females, which are more drab, follow a little later. Both must be delighted to achieve landfall in Cumbria after their long, long flight from Africa; another of nature's little miracles. Great crested grebes are in evidence on the lakes and those watchers who are especially fortunate may witness their unique and elaborate courting display, in which a pair swim towards each other, rear up and meet breast to breast while treading water, with their ruffs spread wide and with vigorous shaking of the head.

Meanwhile, this year's badger cubs are being safely reared underground and will not emerge for some time yet. Those setts being used as nurseries are easily distinguished by the abundance of discarded bedding around the entrance.

All signs that SPRING is here!

Many Happy Returns

Now underfoot lies tormentil,
Gold harbinger of spring,
And crosswort too
Its upright stance resumes.

Warm summer sun
The scent of aniseed proclaims,
As good sweet Cicely extends
Her graceful snow-white head.

And there, close by,
Fair Queen Anne's Lace
A ruff provides for campion's
Blushing hue.

Giant bellflowers in the hedgerow stand,
Their lilac blooms so proud
That soon methinks some goblin hand
Will ring them all out loud!

These and a hundred more fine blooms
Now deck our lonning ways,
And bring delight to one and all
On these, our summer days.

AJG

73. Winter walking

I suppose that, for many of us, the term, 'winter walking' conjures up a picture of striding out on a brilliant sunny morning, exhaling clouds of steam under a clear blue sky and with the sound of boots ringing against ground frozen like iron! A happy thought – such days create a wonderful glow and do us all a power of good. One in particular comes to mind, because it was recorded on film when I and a youthful Simba were to be seen tramping over pristine snow across the summit of Grasmoor. Brilliant, in more ways than one!

Sadly, such days seem to be rather rare. More common this winter have been grey skies, little or no sun, buckets of rain and the sound of boots sloshing through mud! However, in the words of the song, *Spring is in the air*.

Celandines are in flower, dog's mercury is already eight or nine inches high, the first coltsfoot is in bloom and even the odd dandelion has dared to show its head. If dandelion means 'lion's teeth', I reckon those teeth have been well and truly chattering lately! I can't help wondering if such early arrivals ever rue the day and wish they could tuck their heads back under cover for a while.

The frogs have emerged from hibernation and spawn already abounds in ditch, pond and puddle. Is the frog the only animal to enjoy two different methods of breathing, I wonder? The most important is, of course, gaseous exchange through the skin, the method adopted while hibernating, when the frog virtually switches off all other bodily functions and 'ticks over' during the worst of the winter.

Badger cubs will mostly have been born by now and adults will be busily feeding them as hard as they can go, in order to get them reared and toughened ready for next winter; they will be constantly changing their bedding, too, in the underground sett where they will remain for the next eight weeks or so before venturing out for the first time. Badgers are generally very good at selecting sites that are likely to stay dry, but this season's rainfall may well have tested some setts severely.

Incidentally, badgers are still under threat from diggers; one sett was dug in this very area only a week ago. If you do happen to come across this activity, *please* ring the police immediately and, if possible, give the number of any vehicle involved. Many of the diggers are well-known, but there is no substitute for catching them red-handed.

Peregrine falcons have paired now and, while some have remained in the vicinity of their preferred nesting sites all winter, others have wandered further afield, but have now returned. They provide us with some of the most exciting aerial displays to be seen in the wild anywhere in Britain, not least in the co-operative hunting by male and female and in the incredible phenomenon of the food pass, when the male, or tiercel, passes prey with his talons to those of the female in mid-air. This really is a breathtaking spectacle. Once rearing begins, the chances of witnessing such sights are much increased, as frequent hunting trips are essential to meet the constant demand for food for the ever-growing young.

We shall soon have the return of summer visitors, too; the feathered kind, I mean! The curlews will be back in earshot from where I sit, their unmistakable call echoing along with the bleat of spring lambs. The common sandpiper will once more be seen around the lakeshores and the wheatear will be calling along the lower slopes of the fells.

And so, even on the dreary days, there is much to look forward to, as things gradually warm up – and hopefully dry up, too! Enough to lighten the step while walking just now, because almost every day there is yet another sign of spring.

There is the old saying that, 'Hope springs eternal', but perhaps we might amend that at this time of year to 'Spring hopes are eternal'!

74. Lords and Ladies

Spring sees the arrival of a wide range of plant life, notably primroses and bluebells and, among the less common species, is *Arum maculatum*, better known as lords and ladies, cuckoo pint and nightingale – a corruption of 'knight in a galea', a galea being a helmet. In fact, it has, and has had, a host of names over the centuries and in different parts of the country, many of which could hardly be used in polite society, at least not before 9:00 pm! It was recently the subject of a rather unsatisfactory article in a local paper – unsatisfactory because it was claimed that (a) it is cross-pollinated by insects, and (b) that once inside the flowers insects cannot escape – something of a contradiction in terms! So, perhaps the record should be put straight. In passing, it might first be pointed out that the shiny, arrow-shaped and spotted leaves should not be nibbled; not that they are particularly poisonous, but rather because they contain microscopic and very sharp crystals, which painfully puncture the skin!

To clarify the story of pollination, we should first look at the structure of the flower. The flower stalk or spadix is enclosed in a pale green spathe, which is, in fact, a bract, and which hides the strange flower itself. Down within the spathe, the spadix is encircled by four whorls. The upper whorl is of downward-curling hairs. Next come the male flowers, then another whorl of hairs and finally the female flowers. Insects are attracted to the flowers by a nauseous odour, as if from carrion. (The flowers also have a temperature that is marginally, but measurably, a little above ambient, and are slightly luminous, but there is no evidence to suggest that either of these factors acts as an attractant to insects.)

When an insect enters the spathe it finds itself on a very slippery surface. It plunges past the first whorl of hairs and cannot get out again – at that time; but things change. Insects passing the hairs act as a stimulus and during the night following entry, the turgor pressure of the hairs falls; they therefore wilt and at the same time there is a change to the surface of the spathe, which becomes less slippery. This combination allows insects to escape, carrying with them the pollen grains to fertilise another flower to which they may be attracted, as before. Thus the 'imprisonment' of insects does occur, but it is temporary, ensuring that they are confined just long enough to become well dusted with pollen. Those that are confined fail to learn their lesson, promptly diving into the next spathe only to be 'caught' again.

The nature of the change in the surface of the spathe is less clear, but we do not have to look far for a reasonable hypothesis. If we look at the surface of a waxy leaf under an electron microscope, which is, of course, of a much higher magnification than an ordinary microscope, we can see the individual 'plates' of wax, laid like paving stones. Since the hairs wilt when stimulated, it may well be that the spathe wilts to a degree also – enough to make the 'plates' erupt, thus exposing their edges and providing a surface rough enough to allow small insects to obtain a grip.

When the spathe finally withers and falls away, it exposes the columns of first green and later scarlet berry-like fruits, which are highly poisonous, as are the tuberous roots. However, if the bitter juice of the roots is boiled out, dried out or fermented out, the poison is removed and the residue is starch, which used to be eaten in this country as Portland Sago, or Portland Arrowroot.

What a strange plant it is!

75. Mellbreak – by Pillar Rake

It is probably fair to assume that nine times out of ten the ascent of Mellbreak is made up the northern buttress; indeed, it might well be that this is the route used 99 times in every 100. But there is another way, namely up the eastern face to Pillar Rake.

We leave High Park and proceed along the well-worn track, as if to follow the lakeside, but shortly after leaving Green Wood on our right, we veer right and traverse to below a substantial rocky outcrop and then climb more steeply to skirt the rock itself and aim vertically towards the base of the right-hand or more northerly of the four pinnacles.

From the outcrop to the base of this pinnacle is only some 300 feet, but it is 300 feet of loose scree and heather. The easiest way to overcome this is to climb up where the two meet. The scree is very loose and the heather is deep, but where the two meet is a route that is relatively firm underfoot and where there are some handholds.

To seek an actual track is worthless, as this way is clearly not followed very often and, as a result, there is no sign at all to act as a guide. Simply aim roughly for the pinnacles and adjust direction along the way to make the best progress possible.

It is steep throughout, but some sections near the pinnacles are of almost vertical steps, three feet or so in height with few secure handholds or footholds, so, yes, care is needed. Once at the pinnacles, the object is to swing round southwards onto Pillar Rake, a clear traverse which runs along the very base of the summit and behind the four pinnacles themselves. This is a narrow, ledge-like track, which undulates for about 200 yards to emerge on the eastern rim of the saddle between the north and south tops of Mellbreak. Some might consider much of this climb arduous, but the reward is in the fascinating area of Pillar Rake, which is really quite dramatic.

Needless to say, on the way up there are fine views over to Rannerdale, Grasmoor, Whiteside, Lorton Vale, Low Fell, Loweswater and Crummock.

Once at the saddle we follow the edge of the heather due west straight across the top, and once on the western edge a wide grassy track appears. Follow this down to a small pointed cairn (there is only one) where the main track goes left and our less obvious one goes straight on for a few yards and then veers right across the very top edge of a small gill. This track, too, is narrow, but quite clear and provides a superb and easy traverse running half the length of Mellbreak, and an excellent panoramic view of Mosedale right up to Gale Fell and much more, to say nothing of the 'aerial' view of the meanderings of Mosedale Beck, while towering above on the right are the crags of Mellbreak's western face.

A walk which, although quite short, provides energetic scrambling, impressive scenery both near and far and fresh angles on many a well-known spot. Today it was enlivened by stonechats, ravens, buzzards, meadow pipits, a ring ouzel and others that could not be specified! A super little walk – and so close to home!

76. Times they are a'changing

How quickly the weeks and months fly by! Especially now that the differences between the seasons seem much less marked than in the days of yore. The era of roasting oxen on the frozen Thames in winter and the weeks of hot weather in summer seem to have come to an end; another case of levelling down, or is it up?

It's not long since we were avidly looking forward to spring and the joy of seeing the colour return to the woods and hedgerows, but already many plants have flowered, faded and seeded. Sweet Cicely, which decks the roadside verges with its lacy umbels, is now well past its best and its elongated dark-brown seeds are falling to the ground. Red campion, surely one of our most brilliant common species, holds its seeds in open-ended cups and, if nudged by a passing human, by stock, or even just by the wind, will scatter its tiny purple seeds like pepper from a pot.

These plants and many more depend on little more than gravity to distribute their seed, but others have developed a more positive approach. Cleavers, or 'goose-grass', bears seeds the surface of which may be likened to Velcro! Covered in minute hooks, they will stick to anything that brushes against them, be it a pair of trousers or the coat of a passing animal. When Toby returns from his statutory morning walk at this time of year, the number of cleavers seeds on and in his coat can be counted in dozens every day, and who is to say how many he has collected and deposited along the way, to give rise to another patch of the plant next year?

Some plants' seed pods 'explode' when ripe. Indian balsam, or 'policeman's helmet', is a case in point. Stand near a patch of that at the right time and the pods can be heard going off with a 'crack' as their seeds are expelled.

Wind is an important agent in the distribution of some seeds. A mature patch of willowherb will give rise to a veritable snowstorm of white-feathered seeds, which a gust of wind will carry far and wide. Similarly, the winged seeds of the sycamore, which rotate as they float earthwards, travel much further laterally if the wind is blowing.

But all this is as nothing compared with the distribution of fungal spores. Spores are single-celled and, unlike seeds, have no initial food supply attached. A field mushroom produces spores between the gills and they may be counted in tens of thousands. The giant puffball, which is something of a rarity and measures some 12–18 inches across, produces spores in billions! And they can be borne on the wind for many, many miles.

It goes without saying that not all seeds or spores survive; they face many hazards. The parent plant may be diseased and the pathogen may have passed to the seed, which may make it fail to germinate or produce an infected plant, and may even infest the soil, giving rise to further problems in the years to come.

There are disorders of seeds, too, which, although not infectious, may give rise to poor plants or even prevent germination altogether. The life of seeds, vital for the regeneration of so many plants, is complicated and beset with a host of problems; a fascinating world all of its own. In the wild, many of the problems go unnoticed but, of course, in agriculture and horticulture, performance of seeds and plants is monitored closely.

77. Never stand still

I suppose we could be forgiven for suspecting that, through the months of December, January and February, 'all nature sleeps and there awaits the dawn of spring'; but, of course, nature is just not like that or, at least, for the most part.

Very little in the natural world stands still. There are subtle changes going on all the time, except in the most extreme conditions, and some such changes serve to remind us that, even in the depths of winter, spring is on the way. Here we are, in darkest January, but already we have snowdrops in bloom! Snowdrops as we all know and love them, that is, not the green-veined, white fritillary which has, or had, 'snowdrop' as one of its 20-odd local names around the country.

To the surprise of many folk, the true snowdrop (*Galanthus nivalis*) may or may not be a true native of these islands; with the name-changing that has occurred over the years, it is difficult to be sure. The term itself was certainly not common until the middle of the 17th century.

Interestingly enough, they were called 'Candlemas bells' and, Candlemas being the 2nd February, brings to mind the subject of global warming, since they surely flower well before that date nowadays. Even in Somerset, where spring is markedly earlier than here in Cumbria, they were once known as the 'fair maids of February'! 'Times, they are a'changing'! Whatever their origin, it appears that snowdrops were not recorded here as 'wild flowers' until the late 18th century.

The very word 'spring' applies most markedly to northern climes, where activity is most slowed by low temperatures, for it is here that temperature rises at the fastest rate and life does indeed 'spring' into action. Just a day or two will turn an apparently lifeless alpine region into a veritable riot of colourful spring flowers.

Although a number of factors are vital for plant growth, from germination to the setting of seeds, it is temperature that provides the great 'starting gun' at the beginning of the year. Many seeds, especially the oily ones, may survive for long periods in the soil without taking harm, and germination will not take place until a certain level of 'accumulated heat units' has been reached. Once it has, and provided there is adequate moisture, imbibition will occur – the first step of germination, and the beginning of plant growth. Once started there is no standing still and certainly no going back. If a germinating seed once stops, it is lost.

Before long the migrant birds will be returning, at least, those which have survived the long and perilous journey from the south, while some which choose to winter on the coastal plain will be coming inland again to breed in our sheltered valleys. The call of the curlew, the flash of white of the wheatear, the rapid wingbeat of the sandpipers against a background of bursting greenery, and warmer days—SPRING!

78. Windy weather!

I suppose that to most walkers High Crag is simply that last top in the High Stile range – just something you need to pass over when going from Red Pike to Haystacks. And so it is most of the time but, like so many tops among the ridges, it *is* a fell in its own right and it can be climbed independently of the rest and from more than one direction.

So I thought it would be a good walk for the 'Mockerkin Mob' – the walking group – and it was duly arranged for the group's 70th walk, on 8th October 1995. It was a very small turnout; there were only five of us and one of those had limited time and was obliged to leave us after an hour or so.

However, we set off, but it was quite clear from the start that we had chosen a windy day and that, as it was blowing down below, it was going to be a bit rough on the tops. Off we went, having planned to climb High Crag and then walk the ridge to Scale Force and return round the bottom to Buttermere.

Round the lake end, fork right in the wood for Burtness Combe – that great corrie which lies between Crag Fell and High Stile. Across the jumbled mass of rocks and aiming for Sheepbone Rake, that broad and steeply-sloping shelf which leads up the face of the fell and at the end of which we turn right for the summit.

So far, so good. It was a dry and sunny day and, with the wind from the south, we were sheltered all the way up, but increasingly aware of the fact that there was a mass of cloud pouring over the ridge at considerable speed. Not only that, but it was swirling and soaring in a rather alarming manner, leaving us in no doubt at all that we were quite literally 'walking into trouble'. There was a conscious decision to press on and to deal with that when the time came!

As we climbed up over the rim we were met not just by strong wind, but by a singularly violent blow, not only exceedingly strong, but intermittent, which was much worse. Strong wind all the time, but amongst it were bursts of absolute ferocity. We were bending low and fighting to gain the ridge when suddenly I was hurled off my feet and finished prostrate on the ground, clinging on with fingertips. As the roar ebbed a little, I looked up to find that my three companions had been caught in exactly the same way – we were all flat on the deck!

The force of the wind was such that we realised at once that to attempt the length of the ridge would be impossible, and that the best course was to make for Gamlin End as fast as we could and retreat down the old wall track, make for the relative safety of the level of Gatesgarth and return to Buttermere from there. This we duly did, but throughout the descent of Gamlin End we were clinging on for all we were worth, frequently on all fours. I, at least, was spun round and thrown among the scree more than once.

Eventually we made it unharmed, apart from the odd bruise and scrape, but not without a considerable buffeting.

One of those walks during which you say, "What on earth am I doing up here?" – but equally one of those about which, once completed, you are likely to say, "*That* was a great day on the hill! You don't have to be mad – but it helps!"

79. 'The Spring has sprung'

Once more old Mother Nature's clock has turned full circle and, after the relatively short and drab days of winter, we are blessed with long days of riotous colour and magical rapidity of growth at every turn.

Bare hedgerows struggled to expose young leaves, a gentle greenish hue began to creep across the landscape and then, with the vigour of an explosion, the hawthorn bloomed. Mile upon mile of hedges bedecked with sumptuous, sweet-smelling blossom; a veritable arboreal snowdrift! Great swags of blooms, so tightly packed, edge-to-edge, each one craning to gain the greatest possible exposure to attract insects for pollination. A shower or two at just the right time – full flower – and we shall be able to look forward to a mass of berries in the autumn.

In fact, there is much white just now. The delicate flowers of hedge parsley, or Queen Anne's Lace, the much more solid blooms of the closely-related sweet Cicely, the upright stance of the 'route-lining' Jack-by-the-hedge and the bright displays of stitchwort, all brilliant white.

There's yellow in abundance, too, with celandine, buttercups, king cup, crosswort and the 200 sub-species of dandelion. Then there is wood avens, the flesh-coloured water avens and, if you're lucky, the hybrid version. Wood avens' flowers are yellow and small; water avens has larger flowers that are flesh-coloured, and the cross has large flowers that are yellow!

Then we have the pink of 'red' campion and herb Robert, to be followed later in damp places by ragged Robin. And the blues – carpets of bluebells at Rannerdale and in Holme Wood, the sky-blue of the speedwells and that spectacularly intense blue of alkanet, a dazzling blue, if ever there was one.

Occasionally there are the pink-and-white spikes of butterbur, short and heavy blooms that precede the appearance of the dinner-plate-sized leaves, which, in days long gone, were used by local farmers for wrapping pats of butter.

The grasses, too, are worth considering. The silver heads of meadow foxtail, the irregular and purple-tinged heads of cocksfoot and the firm, cylindrical heads of Timothy.

But, of course, spring is to be seen, not just in terms of flowers, but also in every branch of the natural world. The glory of the dawn chorus is enough to raise anyone's spirits; the sheer joy expressed in the ornithological symphony has to be heard to be believed. Perhaps even more touching is birdsong late in the evening, after a long day and just before roosting for the night. On a balmy evening, as shadows lengthen and a glow begins to creep across the sky, the serenade of a blackbird on the still, calm air is enough to melt the hardest heart, and to evoke memories of evenings long ago.

Spring: the time of new growth, the time of renewal and hope. And to think that we are fortunate enough to be in the very midst of nature's time of greatest excitement – while there are many millions elsewhere who seldom see so much as a green field. How grateful we should be to live among 'All things bright and beautiful'.

80. Switchback!

Due west from Wrynose Pass stands the famous Three Shire Stone, a landmark which may be used as a starting point for an excellent circular route through and over some of Lakeland's finest scenery.

Following the north-westerly track from the Stone to Red Tarn brings us to a col in which there is a 'crossroads'. It is left for the direct route to Crinkle Crags and right to Pike O'Blisco; but we go straight on over and down, across Oxendale Beck and then left along the floor of the superb valley of Mickleden. Pike O'Stickle towers above us on our right, where stone-age man produced some of his finest axes, while to the left there is an even older site of interest, namely a grand group of moraines deposited by the retreating ice.

The end of the valley is really quite dramatic, being steeply closed, and here we bear left for Rosset Gill. In passing it is worth noting that the track to the right at this point leads to another great walk – via Stake Pass and the full length of Langstrath Beck, all the way to Stonethwaite.

Rosset Gill was, in fact, one of the earliest 'popular' routes to become seriously eroded; it was worn down to a mere jumble of rocks and rubble even 30 years ago. Scramble up the gill and we reach Rosset Gill Pass, overlooking the forbidding waters of Angle Tarn, which we skirt and aim west to another 'crossroads'. Incidentally, this route from Langdale is said to have been in use for some 4,000 years, so no wonder it shows some signs of wear! Turning left here we approach Esk Pike and on up to Bowfell. This is one of the giant spurs or spokes radiating from Great End. From that spot Scafell and Scafell Pike run south-west, Allen Crags and Glaramara north-north-east, while Bowfell and Crinkle Crags are to the south-east. Bowfell stands just below 3,000 feet and is a very fine mountain of great bulk and character. As we climb, the going gets steadily rougher and rougher, but in fact Bowfell has so much to offer that it is well worth making a trip specifically to explore it thoroughly. It has many notable features, such as the Climber's Traverse, Cambridge Crag, Bowfell Buttress and many more, but on this occasion it is merely one of a series of tops, albeit the highest.

Still aiming roughly south, we drop down some 600 feet to Three Tarns and this sets the pattern for the remainder of the walk. To say that it is rough and a succession of 'ups and downs' would be a masterful understatement! Those who appreciate a constantly-changing scene with innumerable nooks and crannies, turrets and crags will love it. If, on the other hand, insufficient reserves of energy have been retained, or if one were to be expecting an easy run home, then this is not the place to be!

If prepared, it is great fun, with a score of hidden corners and unexpected viewpoints, but there is no escape from the fact that it is a hard and desolate stretch of terrain, covered in sharp and jagged rock. Each of the five 'crinkles' is around 2,700 feet in height, while the depressions between them are about 100 feet deep. The views are extensive on a good day: south to Coniston and north to Skiddaw; west to the Scafells and east to High Street; but perhaps the most dramatic is the 'aerial' view from the precipitous eastern edge across Mickleden and down Langdale.

Once we reach the final 'crinkle' we drop down once more to Red Tarn and the Three Shire Stone.

Simply to say that this walk is in the region of 11 miles may perhaps be misleading unless qualified by the reminder that it does involve an unusual amount of up-and-down and, equally important, that it is the second half that presents the tougher going. Provided it is tackled with these points in mind, it will be found to be a glorious round trip with a great deal of interest all the way, especially on a really good day when full advantage may be taken of all the views it has to offer, and preferably at some time other than in the height of the holiday season!

81. Blake Fell and its traverse

Nestling on the very western edge of the fells, about 2½ miles due south of Lamplugh Church, is a gathering of five or six houses known as Felldyke, where there is a small car park, the ideal starting point from which to explore this area. Follow the narrow track up to the gate where there is a track leading across a grass field, through a second gate and into a conifer plantation. This soon gives way to more open country. On the left is a line of mature beeches, a favourite haunt of mixed flocks of titmice – blue tits, coal tits and great tits, displaying much excitement and energy as they constantly change position from tree to tree and twig to twig in their unending search for food.

As we proceed there is a steep bank falling away to our left, at the bottom of which runs Rakegill Beck, which is now the outflow of Cogra reservoir. At one time this beck was a favourite spot for the dipper, that extraordinary white-breasted brown bird which bobs and dips and walks underwater along the stream bed in search of its prey. According to my diary, it was last seen here in October 1985, its disappearance no doubt being due to the increasing acidity of the water and the influence of this upon aquatic life on which it depends. Conifers regularly increase the acidity of waterways, especially when planted in close proximity to the water's edge, and this is known to result in a marked depletion of crustaceans and aquatic invertebrates. On one occasion the grassy bank on the right, just before the dam, was the site of an uncommon event – or at least, an event that is seldom observed. Broadly grouped with the mosses, among the seedless plants, are the liverworts; simple plant forms that thrive in damp situations, such as ditch sides. They reproduce by sporulation and, although clearly the process continues year after year, it is not commonly noticed. However, on this bank it was seen quite clearly, the mass of dewy, shining stalks glistening in the morning sun, each terminating in a tiny black or brown spore-holding capsule reminiscent of a cress seed. When temperature and humidity are just right, each capsule bursts and releases thousands of spores into the atmosphere, some, at least, of which will find a suitable substrate on which to germinate.

At this point we reach the dam and continue straight ahead along the water's edge. This reservoir was formed from what was once simply a marshy area, a sump into which a number of becks drained from the surrounding hills. It is no great expanse of water, but it is nevertheless popular with anglers and with a variety of water birds. One or two cormorants are often to be seen, as are small numbers of great crested grebes, tufted duck, pochard, heron, coot and even an occasional shoveller, so it is always worthwhile casting an eye across the water and around the perimeter before intruding too far into the open.

On approaching the one or two offshore islands along this southern shore there is water lobelia to be seen, the white or very pale blue flowers of which are in full view rising above the surface of the water in July and August. This aquatic perennial forms a dense green carpet on the bottom in the shallows, and has simple, erect, flowering stems which stand six or eight inches out of the water.

And so virtually to the northern end of the water, where a right fork leads upwards and, at about 1,000 feet, reaches a forestry road. Crossing this half-right and then turning left along a post-and-wire fence leads us up Middle Fell to High Pen, from which there is a fine view of the reservoir and the surrounding fells, notably Blake Fell, which rises to 1,878 feet. From here, too, may be seen the Blake Traverse, a very narrow little track which crosses the screes on the flank of Blake from east to west, and which may be used as an alternative to climbing to the summit. Either way, the aim is to regain the forestry road at its northern end by descending from the col, which lies between Blake Fell and Sharp Knott, a steep descent to the very highest edge of the conifer plantation.

The traverse is good fun, although it has to be said that by taking that route fine views are missed. The summit of Blake provides an excellent panorama in all directions from, on a good day, the Isle of Man to the hills of Scotland and right round to Skiddaw, Helvellyn, the Scafells and many in between, to say nothing of the waters of the Solway, Crummock, Buttermere and Ennerdale.

So, from either Blake or the col at the end of the traverse, it's down to the forestry road, following it a few hundred yards to a T-junction and then turning right. This track then leads all the way down to the northern edge of the reservoir and to a track along the western edge and over the rim of the dam itself. Once again, on emerging from the trees it is worth scanning the water to see what birds are around. The northern area bordering the water is a good hunting ground for both plants and insects, an area that is described more fully elsewhere.

82. 'May time'

So comes and goes another spring! And what an extraordinary time of year it is. For most of the time 'hedges is hedges' to most folk, but then, 'of a sudden', it's *May time*! Mile upon mile of hedge explodes into exquisite white – the wedding ribbons of spring and summer! Great swags of blossom, arching boughs borne down by the sheer weight of blooms packed together so tightly that there's hardly room for a pin between them. Surely one of the greatest concentrations of flowers in nature and, if we have a shower at just the right time, to be followed by the formation of millions of berries to nourish the incoming flocks of redwings and fieldfares in the autumn months to come.

Roadside verges, too, are packed with white flowers; the delicate tracery of hedge parsley or Queen Anne's lace and the denser heads of sweet Cicely, but – a sobering thought – much of their seed is already set in readiness for producing next year's crop. How short a season can seem!

Meantime, the birds have been working themselves to a standstill, trying their best to cope with the constant demand from all those frantic gapes, amid such frantic flutterings. Still coming in to roost past ten o'clock at night and yet back on duty for the dawn chorus shortly after 3:00 am. Long days, indeed. Small wonder they appreciate the nourishing titbits we put out for them. Sunflower seed is great, but another star turn is the niger. Tiny seeds they may be, but for the genuine seed-eaters, they are magnetic. Strange, isn't it? No niger seed, no goldfinches – but put some out and they are there in minutes! Do the ever-present sparrows call 'em on their mobiles? Is their sense of smell so acute they catch the scent of the seeds on the wind? Or are they really keeping watch from nearby trees in anticipation? I do not know – but their response is utterly reliable and *fast*! (They'd clearly never qualify as plumbers!)

Oddly enough, we do not seem to see goldfinch fledglings, despite the fact that this is a species that breeds throughout the summer and into the autumn. Mind you, we are lucky to have goldfinches at all, when we consider how many were caught and caged and used on ladies' hats at one time. 130,000 a year on the South Downs alone. Thank goodness those days are long gone, at least in this country.

83. In search of small but welcome holds!

Although it was still only early March, we were lucky enough to set off from Honister on a dry and bright morning. Up to the Drum House, left along the well-worn track almost due south towards Great Gable, past Grey Knotts on our left, along the way admiring all the familiar views down the length of Crummock and later Ennerdale, over the tops of Haystacks to Mellbreak, Red Pike, High Stile, Pillar and many more, reaching for the sky on what promised to be a good day on the hill.

Beneath Brandreth we left the main Great Gable track and followed Moses' Trod, the ancient legendary route for southbound slate – and not a little contraband to boot! An easy-going route; old Moses knew a thing or two about contours!

Below Windy Gap and, with Gable Crag towering above us, to Beck Head; just over the top and we swing right, leaving the tarn on our left and aiming for two cairns which signal the start of the Kirk Fell south traverse. This takes us gradually downwards some 300 feet, beneath the quite dramatic skyline of Boat How Crags and on to the even more dramatic source of Sail Beck, a notable ravine, but one which is easily crossed by cutting back into it and out again. Straight on from here and upward now, and we bisect the track leading from Black Sail Hut to Black Sail Pass.

On nearing the latter there are choices to be made. The 'standard' route is straight up the rocky ridge, which is fine; rather easier is to swing right of the ridge, which gives a much softer approach; but our aim was left of the ridge. From here one can see a clear and reasonably gentle gill climb straight ahead, which is distinctly red. Not difficult, and a good way up. However, on our right is another boulder-strewn gill which rises towards the ridge and, having followed this part-way, yet another 'off-shoot' gill comes into view on the left and this provides what is probably the best scramble on the mountain. It is certainly steep

196

Cormorant

Peregrine falcon at the nest

Common sandpiper

Buzzard soaring

Mountain yellow saxifrage

Starry saxifrage

Butterwort

Grass of Parnassus

and for much of the time one is among solid rock; there are pitches where arms and legs are at full stretch in search of small finger- and toe-holds, but with a little determination and a lot of care it can be done. It is quite an energetic exercise, hauling the human frame up its tortuous crags. It is a place that once more reinforces the old rule – no eating until you're on top!

It must be said that there are loose rocks and that, obviously, they do present a hazard – in fact a few spots of blood were spilled on the day in question! Nothing serious, but the first aid kit was in use, which, thankfully, is rare. The sudden dislodging of a rock, which plummets downwards at an alarming rate, *is* dangerous for those below.

On one occasion, up we went, hands and feet working well and thoroughly enjoying ourselves – for a time. Suddenly there was a shout and I looked down just in time to see that a lump of rock had come adrift and was flying straight for a member's head. In the nick of time, she threw an arm across her face as the rock struck. The result was a bruised and cut arm, but without the presence of mind to throw up that guard, she would have been struck in the face and would almost certainly have been tipped backwards off the crag. A close call indeed!

On reaching the top of the gill the way opens up and the old iron fence posts are followed until the north top can be seen off to the left. Swing towards this and follow a zigzag track towards the left-hand side of the south top, from which there is a steep and rough descent with lots of rubble, down to Beck Head. From the south top, below and to the right can be seen the start of the Great Gable south traverse, which is much more easily seen from here than when on a level with it in the region of Beck Head. Thence to Honister. A great day, a super walk and challenging scramble among some of Lakeland's finest scenery.

84. Sheepbone Rake

Of the three tops rising to over 2,000 feet and towering south-west of Buttermere, High Crag is in some ways the most striking and, while its neighbours provide good walking, scrambling and climbing, they have nothing equivalent to Sheepbone Rake.

This very steeply-slanting slash across the face of the mountain may easily be seen from Buttermere. To reach it, it is necessary to take the rather indistinct and grassy right fork off what is now the higher of the two tracks from Buttermere through Burtness Wood. This leads over a stile and onto the fellside, traversing south-east and all the way up to Burtness Combe.

The combe is vast and dramatic, with a craggy and turreted skyline, a floor strewn with a host of boulders, a great bowl of a place, surrounded on three sides by High Crag, High Stile and the 'curtain wall' ridge connecting the two. In the far western corner is a gill by means of which it is possible to reach the ridge, but it is hard going and much of the surface is insecure.

Cutting diagonally across the combe towards High Crag and aiming for a rocky 'gateway' to the left of a large rock buttress – Sheepbone Buttress, in fact – brings us to the foot of the rake. The going thus far is not entirely easy, but it is at this point that the hard work starts, all 1,000 feet of it! The rake is a steeply-sloping ledge, but, although it may look very narrow from Buttermere, it is in fact wide enough to drive a bus up (now, that *would* be a clever trick!). It is steep, rough and composed of an unhappy mix of grass, heather, scree, rock and soil, much of which cannot be trusted to stay put under the boot – but the worst may be avoided by keeping left, where the going is much more solid. Whichever way it is tackled, it is the steepness that sticks in the mind. There is a solid wall of rock on the right, but it is of little help.

While it undoubtedly provides a great walk, I must admit that I am always a little disappointed at the flora. There is alpine ladies' mantle, alpine clubmoss and fir clubmoss, it is true, but the habitat and aspect are such that I feel there should be something more exciting. If there is, I have yet to find it!

On reaching the top of the rake the route veers right and there is then a couple of hundred feet to go to reach the fell top, a very good scramble to a fine viewpoint from which may be seen a host of fells as well as Crummock Water, Buttermere and Ennerdale Water.

There are a number of alternative return routes, such as via High Stile and Red Pike; or on to Scale Force as well; to Scarth Gap and Buttermere from there; or Scarth Gap, Haystacks and Warnscale Bottom, depending on just how long a walk is required; but whichever way is chosen, the achievement of Sheepbone Rake will long remain in the mind as having been 'a great day on the hill'.

85. Welcome back

Once again the seasons' wheels have turned and spring has come. Subtle and unsure at first, but then a multitude of happenings in the countryside which herald another awakening. Already snowdrops have bloomed and faded, coltsfoot is in flower – one of the few plants which flower first and produce leaves later. There are primroses and dog's mercury, violets and celandines and many, many more.

The curlews have returned to the fields around Mockerkin, their unmistakable trilling calls echoing across the green slopes as, with arched wings and their long, curved bills, they float across the sky in search of that special place wherein to form a scrape, to lay their eggs and raise their young, as they have done for many a long year past.

The peregrines are busy, too, and, thankfully, the population is now thriving after its near extinction a few years ago; egg thieves are obviously having an easier time of it now that it is no longer considered necessary to guard the falcon's nests. Twenty peregrine nests were robbed in 1998, eight of them in the Lake District.

The other morning I was returning from my daily post-breakfast walk with the dog when a buzzard wafted up and away from a treetop only yards ahead. What a wonderful, effortless movement is appears to be! But happily, among all sorts of conservation doom and gloom, in this area we can no longer take it for granted that every large airborne predator in the sky is a buzzard. *Is it* a buzzard? Or has it, perhaps, a reddish hue and a forked, rather than a fan-shaped tail? Yes, we have at least one red kite in the district! Let's hope it finds a mate and that this glorious bird becomes established here. Not that we are likely to have it scavenging in the streets of London again, as was the case in the Middle Ages, but to have some around would be an exciting development. One such happening is already a fact of life, in that the otter is with us once more; another return from the brink. Very largely nocturnal, we must not expect to see much of them, but we can at least be sure of their presence by the signs they leave, such as the droppings, or 'spraint', characteristically placed in strategic spots, with their special appearance and oily scent. One of our most engaging and playful mammals, the otter is, of course, in its element in the water, where its under-fur serves as waterproofing and covers the body in a silver sheath of air. At one otter sanctuary in the west, there is a glass-sided tunnel, from which otters may be watched and photographed underwater. The wedge-shaped head, lithe body, five-toed, webbed feet and muscular tail make their swimming prowess unrivalled—which is as well, since fish is the prime diet.

Frogspawn is around in plenty, in large and shapeless masses, while the double-row 'necklace' of 'toadspawn' will doubtless soon follow; then we shall see thousands of tadpoles – some, at least, of which will survive – dark brown for 'frogpoles' and black for 'toadpoles'.

It's all happening – the spring has sprung!

86. Return to Ennerdale

The eight-mile circuit of Ennerdale Water provides a walk with countless opportunities for seeing wildlife in many forms – plants, animals, birds—as long as we really *look*!

The northern shore-side path has earthnut, water parsnip, spearwort – which is one of the buttercup family – wild thyme, water lobelia, valerian and lousewort, to name but a few. It is also an area frequented by reed buntings; pochard shelter there during the winter months and dippers are not unknown. Pied wagtails skim the surface of the water and just now there is the occasional flotilla of mallard and their ducklings setting out bravely into the vastness of the lake, only to return as soon as the coast is clear. The odd sandpiper perches on an off-shore rock with its bobbing movement, its dark eyestripe and its all-too-obvious wing markings flashing away as it loops out over the water.

There are red-breasted mergansers, so low in the water that they seem almost awash, with their white flanks and collar, their green head and down-turned orange bill, while out on the island there are cormorants and gulls.

The southern side sports common sundew and butterwort, currently in full flower, in the wet and boggy areas where a number of small becks emerge from the lower slopes of the towering fells above. From the centre of the butterwort rosette of leaves protrudes a single tall and wiry stem, topped with a single and rather beautiful violet-coloured flower—hence its other name of 'bog violet'. Where groups are in flower together, they make a fine display. The white tufts of cotton grass wave in the breeze like so many rabbits' tails.

This is a favourite haunt of the wheatear, too; that delightful summer visitor with its dove-grey back, prominent eyestripe and buff breast, with the unmistakable white flash as it drops from rock or wall. Happily, the lizards, which were reported here last year, have survived the winter and are once more to be found basking on sunny days, a warming-up process which aids their digestion. One particular fragment of tree stump was a favoured spot last year, and, sure enough, it is in use again now! One member of the 'community' only just made it, it would seem, now having lost the last inch-and-a-half of its tail. A safety mechanism, this; invaluable when attacked by a predator— jettison the tail, live to fight another day—and grow a new tail!

There is always the chance of seeing something special here— the flash of a swooping kestrel; the spectacular food-pass of the falcons; the massive sailing-past of the raven. Perhaps the most extraordinary occurrence witnessed here, which may stand re-telling, was to see a deer enter the water below Angler's Crag and swim across to the old Angler's Inn car park site: the very widest part of the lake. Just as it approached a car drew in, so the deer turned round and swam all the way back, only to crawl out on the shore exhausted and, after some wearisome minutes of catching breath, wander back up Crag Fell. But *what* a swim, with only those very thin, spindly legs with which to gain any purchase. Ennerdale – always a place of interest!

The ancient oak woods were once a 'chase' for wild boar and deer, but are also well endowed with a wide range of species of lichen, fern and moss. There is no track through here and the going is tough in the extreme, being a jumble of rock and undergrowth, which is almost impenetrable. As the new wilderness site matures, this whole area should become an increasingly fine habitat, a genuine sanctuary for wildlife for generations to come.

87. Highlights of summer

Like so many people, I am sure, my first sighting of osprey was long ago at Loch Garten, to which these magnificent birds had returned after an absence of some 50 years. The Loch Garten site became famous and was well tended and guarded. Slowly the population of ospreys grew and eventually some moved south to Cumbria.

For some time now there have been ospreys at Bassenthwaite and there were two memorable visits to the hide this year. On the first occasion one of the two suddenly appeared over some scrub and flew right over the hide – but not before I had managed two shots in quick succession with the camera, one, at least, of which was not bad, in the circumstances.

The other time one bird was perched on a post on the opposite side of the lake; too far off for photography, but near enough for good viewing with binoculars. After some time of inactivity it took off, lumbering aloft with its cumbersome flight, and began to quarter the water in search of prey. Suddenly it slowed and began to hover; then, lowering its head and folding back its wings it plummeted towards the shimmering lake, talons outstretched, and then – SPLASH!

Flap, flap, flap, and it climbed away again, well and truly saturated, but with no fish. This was witnessed three times more without a catch, but nevertheless highly spectacular. The osprey, or fish-hawk, is well adapted for its way of life. Not only does it have the most fearsome curved talons with which to catch its slippery prey, but its foot pads, too, have small spines to enhance its grip. Not that it feeds on fish alone; its diet extends to amphibians, invertebrates and even to birds and small mammals.

However, it is for its dramatic hurtling dive at, and into, the water that it is best known, and rightly so.

In July I was told of a flush of particularly pretty flowers on the top of one of our lowest fells, so went to investigate. What a picture! Hundreds of wild pansies, or 'heartsease', to use two of the more common of its 38 different names, otherwise known as *'Viola tricolor'*. While the most prominent colour is deep violet, some blooms display white and yellow, hence the 'tricolor' appellation. Needless to say, it is from this delightful wild flower that our garden pansies are derived. The name 'pansy' is from the French 'pensée', or 'thought', and for centuries the pansy has been associated with remembrance, love and romance. Shakespeare, for example, has Ophelia say in her lovelorn wanderings, "There's pansies, that's for thoughts", while in *Midsummer Night's Dream*, the Queen of the Fairies says:

"Yet mark'd I where the bolt of Cupid fell,
It fell upon a little western flower,
Before milk white, now purple with Love's wound,
And maidens call it 'Love in Idleness'."

Again, 'Love in Idleness' is one of the many synonyms for wild pansy, as are 'kiss and look up', 'kiss me love at the garden gate', 'love in vain' and, especially descriptive, 'pussy face'! There are many more, depending both upon time in history and place, too; names varying from county to county.

However, by whichever of its many and curious names it is known, it is singularly beautiful and a joy to behold, particularly en masse.

Osprey and wild pansy; two summer sightings to quicken the pulse and delight the eye!

88. The Coledale Round

On the morning of Sunday 10th October 1999, six members of the now famous 'Mockerkin Mob' met with a view to completing the Coledale Round. Starting at Braithwaite, there is an immediate and unremitting slog to the first objective, Grisedale Pike. It is three miles of constant and increasingly-steep uphill grind, with little or no respite. Steep steps from the little car park, a lengthy period on steep grass, then onto scree and slate. On this occasion, the landscape was somewhat softened by autumnal bracken, the delicate fronds contrasting starkly with blue sky and scant cloud, at least at first!

But that was not to last. As height was gained the wind grew stronger and, at around 1,500 feet, darker and darker clouds were scudding over the top of the Pike and drizzle became so intense that waterproofs were reluctantly donned. This ascent of Grisedale Pike marks the north-western side of Coledale, a valley of some three miles containing little of interest except for the road which leads to the formidable cliffs of Force Crag, blocking the head of the valley below Coledale Hause, where stands the site of the Force Crag barytes mines.

The summit of Grisedale is indeed a 'Pike', or peak, with room for not very many walkers on top at any one time. However, by the time we arrived, lingering was not a comfortable option. It was cold, damp and windy, while the climbs ahead of us were frequently obscured by driving mist and drizzle. Still the wind strengthened as we made our way across the Hause towards Scar Crags; clearly it was being funnelled up Gasgale Gill, but once across the Hause we managed to find a hollow in which to escape the worst of the blow and have a bite to eat. Unkind, 'tis true, but we couldn't help but laugh as some poor soul tried desperately to consult a map in the teeth of the gale! The gale won!

The plan had been to climb Scar Crags, but the strength of the wind was such that that was obviously unwise. Instead, we pressed on up the valley, with Grasmoor on our right, to the 'cross-roads', turning left over the wide expanse of Eel Crag – a much safer way. Down Eel Crag and on over Sail, picking our way along the narrow ridge and over and between the rocky outcrops. Fine views in all directions now, the weather having relented at last; or so we thought. Half-way down Sail we were taken completely by surprise by a sudden and very strong gust of wind, which came down behind us. So strong was it that it caused momentary chaos—indeed, two of us were flat on our backs in no time. Down to Sail Pass and left here for Outerside, Stile End and High Coledale, but over this stretch the weather closed in with a vengeance. This was serious rain, but having already suffered the cumbersome indignity of donning and removing waterproof trousers in a howling gale, it was decided that it was 'only water' and we pressed on as we were.

A great walk, although one of our number did remark that 20 years before he had vowed never to climb Grisedale Pike from Braithwaite again! When asked for his verdict on that route today, he had no hesitation in saying that his original decision had been right! And so the seven of us returned to the car and – bliss – hot tea! Seven, did I say? But we started with six, I hear you cry! Yes, but one additional member, who has a little knee trouble just now, had struggled up to meet us near Outerside – a feat of endurance and determination well beyond the call even of Mob duty!

89. A naturalist's natterings – part one

Hindsight, they say, is a wonderful thing! There is, of course, no doubt that the widespread use of persistent pesticides caused havoc among many species in the long term, but we must remember that these materials also provided enormous benefits worldwide in agriculture and human health. The adverse effects could not have been foretold, although it must be admitted that, while the agricultural research made rapid and numerous advances, toxicology seems to have lagged a long way behind.

There is no denying that the effect on some species was bordering on the disastrous, greatly reducing numbers. The otter, for example, became a rarity, but happily our waterways are now much improved and these delightful animals are returning to their traditional haunts. Largely nocturnal, we must not expect to see much of them, but their distinctive footprints and spraint prove their presence. While otter numbers were so reduced, mink escaped from captivity and multiplied along our rivers. There still is a population of mink today, but numbers are falling, which is more good news.

Sadly, the position with some animals is not so rosy. We have a substantial population of badgers, which are protected by law and monitored by the Badger Groups, and yet the disturbance of setts and the capturing of badgers for the barbaric 'sport' of badger-baiting continues. The government at one time reversed its policy and carried out the culling of 10,000–12,000 badgers in the west country 'as an experiment', despite outright condemnation from conservationists nationwide, because this so-called experiment was basically flawed and because, by the time it was completed, there was every hope of a vaccine to protect cattle against the TB which some badgers transmit.

The story of the red squirrel is well known; it has a number of serious disadvantages when faced with competition from the grey and, while it is currently greatly reduced and localised, it would seem that eventually it may disappear. Once again, the importation and escape of a foreign species is proving disastrous.

Similarly, our native species of crayfish, which inhabits some of our local becks, is under threat from the imported and escaped species, which is a carrier of crayfish plague, against which our species is defenceless. The stories of mink, grey squirrel and crayfish are an object lesson, and it is to be hoped it has been learnt well.

Of all our local birds, the peregrine is the most spectacular. Its complete mastery of flight and its outstanding speed of 150–180mph in its 'stoop', or dive, combined with its beautiful appearance, make it unique among British birds. Yet it, too, was driven to the brink of extinction by the combination of persistent pesticides, by egg thieves and by deliberate persecution. At one time the population was down to 10–12 pairs in Cumbria, but now it is back to normal, due to withdrawal of the pesticides concerned, increased protection and harsher penalties.

The sparrowhawk, too, was decimated by pesticides, but has now largely recovered. There are sometimes complaints that there are too many sparrowhawks, and that they are responsible for the falling numbers of some species of small birds but, in fact, the sparrowhawk population has done no more than return to its pre-pesticide level. The balance of nature will do the rest.

90. A naturalist's natterings – part two

There is good news, too, in regard to two other species of raptor. We have the osprey, or 'fish hawk', on Bassenthwaite Lake, which may be seen making that dramatic dive into the water to catch its prey and, if it is in luck, we can see the ponderous take-off thereafter. And then we have at least one or two red kites, whose rufous plumage and clearly-forked tail were absent from England for 150 years.

While we do have recovery of some native species, the picture is also bright regarding the arrival of species new to our shores; some 40 species are now breeding here which were not doing so 100 years ago, and this trend is likely to continue. So, on the one hand we have a reduction in numbers of some of our accustomed inhabitants, in fact, over 50% reduction of seven common species over 25 years; at the same time we have a considerable number of fresh species, a case of checks and balances once again.

Not all species are popular with everyone. Anglers have little time for the cormorant although, in fact, only 7,000 pairs breed in this country. Those who have grouse moors complain about the peregrine and the sparrowhawk, despite the fact that it has been conclusively shown that good management of heather has a far greater effect than predators. Things are not always quite what they seem, and nature seldom presents a picture that is pure black and white. What appears obvious must be carefully checked by thorough research, professionally conducted. It is not so very long ago that folk believed an eagle would carry off a baby!

The greatest event in the local plant world was undoubtedly the publication of Dr Geoffrey Halliday's *Flora of Cumbria*, after 23 years of study by him and his team of helpers, which provides an invaluable index of plants growing in the county and their location. Unwelcome plants are also imported, such as Indian balsam, which is spreading fast. Giant hogweed was first imported as a spectacular species for the gardener, but, of course, it has escaped and is becoming widespread. Not only is it a massive plant, but exposed skin brushed against it soon displays severe blistering when exposed to sunlight and hospital treatment is often necessary; a plant to be eradicated whenever possible.

Brief though these notes obviously are, they may serve to illustrate that many aspects of our wildlife are constantly changing. Some species are threatened; some that were threatened now return from the brink to thrive, while others appear which pose threats for the future. In the light of experience, constant vigilance and care are the key to avoiding unnecessary contamination and to conserving and encouraging native species in the interests of biodiversity.

Apart from all other considerations, the maintenance of biodiversity is important because so many species are inter-dependent; the loss of one influencing the survival of another, often totally unrelated. And again, it must be admitted that we still know very, very little about many of our species, and among them there are likely to be those which will prove valuable in the years ahead. We are merely the stewards of our wildlife, and should aim to pass it on to future generations in no worse state than when we inherited it.

91. Two special species

1. The Pine Marten

Despite considerable efforts over the years, a degree of mystery still surrounds the true status in Cumbria of one of our most elusive mammals. The pine marten (*Martes martes*), is a member of the *Mustelidae*, a family which also includes the weasel, stoat, polecat, otter and badger. It is intermediate in size between polecat and badger and is likened to the size of a slim cat measuring 25 to 32 inches from nose to tail tip. It has glossy, brown fur, with a distinctive straw-coloured 'bib' and ear edges and a bushy tail. 'Marts' have always been shy creatures which were never very numerous in England, though more so in Scotland. They were prized for their pelts, but classed as vermin and were trapped, poisoned and shot by gamekeepers for many years. However, since 1988 they have been protected against killing and disturbance at their places of rest. In Cumbria their traditional haunts were the open fells, especially where there were vertical rock faces and, perhaps in particular, where the upper edges of forests meet open fellside. They were reported as being quite common in the Lake District in the late 1930s. They are very agile and are fast enough to hunt red squirrels through the treetops.

Surveys of varying degrees of reliability in recent years have reached different conclusions, not least because any population there may be is certainly sparse, and searching for mart droppings over great expanses of boulder-strewn fellside cannot be expected to provide a very accurate picture. However, three sightings of marts reported in Ennerdale last year gave grounds for optimism. Members of the staff of the Vincent Wildlife Trust, which specialises in the study of British mammals, were immediately despatched, armed with night sights, but failed to confirm the presence of marts.

Nevertheless, there are clearly grounds for suspecting that we may still have a small residual population and any sighting should be recorded. If you do see a pine marten, or know of someone who has seen one, please let me know and I will pass the information on to the Trust. The collection of such data will lead to the consideration of a plan to encourage and conserve this elusive inhabitant of the fells and crags.

2. The Peregrine Falcon

It was recently claimed in an article in a local paper that, "A peregrine will eat a pigeon a day" and intimated that this meant 365 racing pigeons per falcon per year! – and therefore a cull was justified. This is, of course, utter nonsense.

First, a pigeon will last a peregrine for two days, not one. Second, as far as the peregrine is concerned, the 'pigeon' is likely to be a wood pigeon or dove. Third, peregrines do not, in any case, live on pigeons alone. The exaggeration was thus one of probably 800%; but a further aspect of the matter was totally ignored, namely, whose air space is it, anyway?

The peregrine is a *native* of the crags, fells and cliffs of Cumbria and was established long, long before Man raced his first pigeon. It is an integral part of our wildlife heritage and is without doubt one of the most spectacular and most beautiful of our native species. Persistent agricultural chemicals resulted in dramatic losses and, indeed, the species only just survived. It has now recovered and is fully protected by law, and anyone caught disturbing or harming peregrines may expect very severe penalties indeed. There is no chance that the culling of so outstanding a species would be entertained for the benefit of a minority sport, let alone on the basis of the arguments put forward.

92. 'The flowers that bloom in the spring'

Recent weeks have once again seen the annual 'explosion' of vegetation in the countryside – the incredible rate of growth of plant life, rapidly turning the drab tinctures of winter into scores of shades of green and a veritable cornucopia of wild flowers. The technicalities are all very well and, indeed, are essential, but they should never be allowed to prevent us from admiring the sheer beauty and wonder of the natural world. Has May blossom ever been more prolific? Great swags of blooms, branches weighed down with flowers so tightly packed there was hardly room to put a needle between them. Rich cream, sometimes tinged with pink, and with that wonderful scent, too. And then there were the wood anemones – one of the earliest harbingers of spring, best seen in woodland on a sunny day:

> 'When earth, exulting from her wintry tomb,
> Breaks forth with flowers.'

Violets, too, bedeck the hedgerows and the woodland glades, their deep purple hue another sure delight, which moved Tennyson to write:

> 'The smell of violets hidden in the grass
> Poureth back into my empty soul and frame,
> The times when I remember to have been
> Joyful and free from blame.'

The whin, or gorse, is yet another glory of spring; flowering all year, but the spring 'performance' is especially welcome. Its seed pods are already formed, their cracking in the sun prompting Cowper to proclaim:

'The common, overgrown with fern, and rough
With prickly gorse, that shapeless and deformed
And dangerous to touch, has yet its bloom,
And decks itself with ornaments of gold—
Yields no unpleasing ramble.'

Then again, the hedgerow roses now appear, the field rose and the dog, long since used as heraldic emblems, not least by York and Lancaster. Shakespeare used them well, when Warwick says to Plantagenet:

'—this brawl to-day,
Grown to this faction, in the Temple Garden,
Shall send, between the Red Rose and the White,
A thousand sons to death and deadly night.'

Not that springtime development is confined to the plant world. Tadpoles abound in ponds and ditches, but populations of amphibians are being depleted worldwide; sometimes due to pollution, loss of habitat or disease, but it is being closely monitored. Similarly, the population of dragonflies and demoiselles is being closely studied. Areas such as Cogra Moss still support large numbers, such as the golden-ringed dragonfly and the 'chasers'. When dragonflies alight, they rest their wings at right angles to the body, but demoiselles fold theirs along the back.

The heavy vegetation helps conceal stoats and weasels, the two most widespread carnivores among our native mammals. The stoat is the larger of the two and has a black tip to the tail. A singularly unhelpful comment on the problem of identification is that, "While one is weasely identified, the other is stoatally different"!

215

93. Combes and coves

It began in a very routine way by three of us meeting at Bowness Knott and setting off along the forestry road towards Gillerthwaite, taking the first turn right over the new Irishman's bridge spanning the Liza. Through the gate at the top, turning left and, after a few hundred yards, turning right up the broad drove road between the trees. A steep, grassy section to the next gate and then even steeper and rougher going, quite a usual way to make for Steeple. But, having traversed Lingmell and crossed Low Beck, we continued on the long traverse of the bottom edge of Steeple at a height of some 1,200–1,300 feet and up into the vast arena bordered by Pillar to the east and by Steeple to the west.

This is an enormous combe, a great saucer a mile or more across, the sides of which increase in steepness as height is gained. Seen from the air it describes an 'M'; the left 'leg' is Pillar, the right, Steeple and the central 'intrusion' is Black Crag. To the left of Black Crag is Wind Gap Cove and to the right is Mirk Cove. The basin is largely boulder-strewn and the surroundings are nothing if not awe-inspiring. The west face of Pillar is the least daunting, while Black Crag and the east face of Steeple consist of spectacular rock faces with craggy fingers reaching upwards against the skyline. It is a place of atmosphere, especially in winter, but we were blessed with a bright and dry day, not too hot and with a gentle breeze – ideal.

Our route was through Wind Gap Cove to Wind Gap itself, an arête between Pillar and Scoat Fell, and to reach this we crossed the entire cove, selecting a way to avoid the worst of the jumble of rocks. Higher and steeper until at about 2,400 feet we came over the lip of Wind Gap and – what a view! A vast panorama came immediately into sight – from Kirk Fell and Great Gable all the way to Windermere.

From here we turned right and made the good rock-scramble to the top of Scoat Fell. Now veering due west, walking the ridge for some two miles, with dramatic views back over Mirk Cove, Steeple and Mirklin Cove, which lies below Steeple's western flank. At first sight the ridge looks easy but, although there are good stretches of springy turf, there are also depressions and rocky outcrops to negotiate. This is great walking country – sheer space and vastness, which makes a never-to-be-forgotten impression. A stone wall runs along the length of the ridge and we kept this on our left until we reached the top of a spur ridge running down to the north, bordered by Deep Gill to the east and by Silvercove Beck to the west. We made our way down this long descent, over grass and through heather, where we found the track, such as it was, clearly acted as a waterway at times and was thus deeply eroded. We eventually reached the forestry road and made our way down in the welcome shade to the footbridge over Silvercove Beck. This is a delightful spot, with rushing and foaming waters cascading towards the Liza and the lake.

And so back to the valley floor, the return down the dusty forestry road and to Bowness Knott. We had left the cars at 10:00 am and we returned at 5:20 pm, after a most enjoyable and memorable day, in which we covered some 12 miles with 2,730 feet of ascent.

Another great day!

94. Cogra Moss

After the many wet and dreary days, some of the recent improvements have been much appreciated! A visit to Cogra Moss took place on one of those days, the sort that is a real promise of spring and a tonic to us all. Clear and crisp, a 'wall-to-wall' cloudless azure sky and brilliant sunshine.

On approaching the reservoir, Blake Fell and its western partners, Sharp Knott and High Hows, were brilliantly lit by the morning sun, while the Knock Murton side was deep in shadow; similarly, the well-lit northern half was frozen – tho' only just. A stone thrown horizontally would skid across the ice for hundreds of yards, but one pitched a little higher would land with a plop and penetrate the thin skin.

There were 30 or 40 birds out on the water, including mallard and tufted duck, pochard and coot. I suppose no duck is better known than the mallard; the drake with its magnificent green head, and the drabber duck who has that cackling 'quack', like raucous avian laughter. The tufted duck only began breeding here a couple of centuries ago and, while some now remain here all the year, others are visitors from Iceland and the Continent. For much of the time the drake is particularly striking; its dark plumage contrasting strongly with its pure white flanks, and with its distinct crest flowing from the back of the head.

The pochard drake is also striking, having body plumage of a soft and somewhat mottled grey, but with a chestnut head. It is largely a winter visitor, breeding mostly in eastern Europe. Both are diving ducks, feeding on aquatic plants, insects and their larvae and also on some of the amphibians. Their diving habit makes them difficult to count accurately. One group at Cogra, however, appeared to stay on the surface and to keep very close together, suggesting the presence of a predator, perhaps a bird of prey in the vicinity or a pike?

There were coots, too; those rather bad-tempered, almost-black water birds with the striking white facial mask. They, too, have a mixed diet of aquatic plant and animal life.

This tranquil scene was suddenly interrupted by the arrival of a small skein of greylag geese. Three circuits of the reservoir to decide details of the descent, and then down they came, wings arched as they began the braking sequence, then tails down and webbed feet forward to 'ski' to a standstill. This routine was followed by much conversation and the customary ruffling of feathers into their accustomed places after the turbulence of the recent flight. Thereafter – a stately progression around their new abode.

On retracing steps along the water's edge and reaching the beech trees, there was a sudden commotion down the steep bank towards the beck and a pair of red squirrels came bounding up through the fallen leaves. They dashed straight for one of the old beech trunks, which, though smooth to our eyes, afforded no problems for their needle-like claws. Up and up they flew, high into the branches and then, with no hesitation and clearly on a well-accustomed route, they sped along branch and twig like lightning, right across the roadway and into the conifers on the other side! For sheer speed, nerve and agility, our little rufous friends really do take some beating!

95. All change!

While history is littered with the remnants of forecasts and predictions of events and phenomena which have failed to materialise, those relating to global warming are apparently already coming to pass. Just how far this process will go, only time will tell, but most meteorologists agree that against the background of the mass of data collected over many years, there is a clear trend towards increasing temperature. 'Most meteorologists' – the view is not entirely universal because there are many trends of one sort and another, some of which are genuine trends, but which turn out to be short-lived. However, it does seem that, unless we take unpopular, and therefore politically risky, decisions drastically to reduce the emission of greenhouse gases, real problems lie ahead.

The impact on wildlife is likely to vary between subjects, those which are distributed widely are expected to survive, while more specialised species will suffer. Our own common hedgerow plants, for example, will probably feel little impact, whereas our already-struggling sub-alpines in the high fells will be under greater threat.

The life cycles of many plants and animals are governed quite precisely by temperature, and changes in temperature will doubtless result in changes in seed-germination and egg-hatching times. The emergence of even so humble an animal as a midge is directly related to temperature. There are animals that emerge as a particular temperature is reached because that temperature also triggers the appearance of their main food supply. But if temperature change affects different species to different degrees, clearly the necessary synchronisation may not occur, with fatal consequences.

One example of the change taking place is that of the snowdrop, a change no doubt we have all observed, but few of us perhaps will have realised its extent. In fact, over the last 50 years the flowering date of snowdrops has receded by some three weeks – a significant change, indeed.

Similarly, some birds, notably blackcap and chiffchaff, are now overwintering here, rather than migrating south. Even the human activity of grass-cutting is taking place at times unheard of years ago.

Changes in the flowering dates of plants may have marked effects, and the effects may be quite different according to whether the plants are pollinated by wind or insects. Again, plants whose flowering dates coincide may perhaps hybridise, whereas those whose dates do not coincide cannot do so. Changes are taking place in the leafing times of trees and the reproduction of amphibians – there have been some shifts of up to a month in 50 years, despite the fact that the temperature change to date is a modest one degree.

For as long as we can remember we have referred to 'the balance of nature' – that delicate mechanism by which the intricate relationship between organisms is maintained – a balancing act of the first order, involving synchrony, breeding, feeding, migration, germination, flowering, predation and many, many other factors, and a balancing act which is steadily being upset. Some species will adapt; some will be lost; few will be unaffected.

Many scientists are working on phenology, the reaction of wildlife to the changing seasons, and its impact; one sometimes wonders if more people are working to observe disaster than to avoid it!

96. 'When autumn leaves—'

The subtle onset of autumn, like each of the other seasons, brings with it sights, sounds, feelings and even smells to many of which we pay little heed – accepting the inevitable changes around us as an overall pattern, without noting the detail.

I suppose the sights are perhaps the most obvious. The dulling of the foliage, the changes in the trees from green to gold and brown and, when the wind blows, the fall of leaves. Small wonder the Americans refer to it as 'the fall'. Some trees shed their leaves very reluctantly, while others, such as the ash, seem to make a sudden decision and deposit great showers all at once. The relatively short-lived bracken fronds provide a dramatic change, too, to varying shades of yellow, brown and bronze.

Among the birds, we see great gatherings of some species as they mass in readiness for that long trek southwards. Thousands of birds, hopefully well fed, in preparation for the most dangerous flight of their lives, chattering in eager anticipation of warmer and sunnier days to come.

Again, among the sights of autumn, there are aspects of the weather that come to mind. This is the outstanding time for mists to gather across the lakes and in the valley bottoms, presenting beautiful, if somewhat eerie, changes to the views, markedly in the early mornings. Half-hidden trees, valleys deep in mist, but with felltops protruding and bathed in sunlight.

One of the most evocative sounds in nature's locker is the distant honking of geese as it floats towards us when they make their way down the coast in vast numbers, an arrowhead of pencil thinness away to the west, but emitting a sound that carries for miles. While we are well-used to the meouw of the buzzard, at this time of year we can still hear the weak call of the young, as the adults play and feint with them, teaching them those vital hunting skills so essential if they are to survive their first winter.

Even some flowers emit sounds of autumn! The much-despised Himalayan balsam 'explodes' with a 'crack' to distribute seeds as widely as possible from their pods. Yellow rattle emits a sound, too, as the loose seeds in its pods rattle when the wind blows.

Then there are feelings of autumn. The gradual drop in temperature, the shortening days, the lowering of the sun and eventually that fresh, keen nip in the air. And how many of us cannot recall the feeling of gathering blackberries? Sticky, purple fingers, with the odd scratch and thorn! Who can forget that wonderful smooth, waxy feeling of a conker, freshly removed from its prickly home?

Then there are the smells of autumn; garden bonfires, for example and, again, the smell of autumn leaves. The smells of fungi, especially in the woods, where the stinkhorn, in particular, gives off an odour that can be detected yards away.

All these sights, sounds, feelings and smells and many more, right on our doorstep. Aren't we *lucky* to live where we do?

We all know our area is one of the most beautiful in England, with a thousand-and-one delights to capture the imagination of young and old, locals, 'grockles' and visitors alike, but those of us who live here must not miss these magic moments, these fleeting glimpses of beauty and fascination which make this such a special place. Familiarity must not be allowed to breed contempt, or even indifference. Let's LOOK, ADMIRE AND PROTECT!

Autumn

When mountain ash its scarlet fruits does show
And hedges ripe with hips and haws do glow,
When conkers glisten on the ground
And squirrels dash with beech nuts newly found.

When fellsides draw their bracken mantle tight
And each day has a little less of light,
When strengthening winds through rustling leaves do sigh
And skeins of honking geese do southwards fly.

AJG

97. Grasmoor then and now

Rising to 2,700 feet above Lanthwaite Green, Grasmoor presents a dramatic spectacle and one of the finest scrambles in the district. The 'direct route' up the western ridge of its craggy face offers steep grass, scree, exposed solid rock, gully and pinnacle. The name derives not from 'grass', but from 'grise', or wild boar, although it's a long time now since wild boar roamed, grazed and rooted over its windswept flanks.

A population of wild boar was only too apparent in this country for thousands of years; indeed, they were being hunted 9,000 years ago. In their usual efficient manner, the Normans introduced game laws to retain the best hunting for the king and nobility, and poaching was a capital offence. Wild boar was avidly hunted on horseback with hounds, spear and sword, and it was probably among the beasts hunted in such 'chases' as that which borders the south-east shore of Ennerdale Water. Small wonder the population diminished over the years, since Edward III's Christmas feast in 1251 included no less than 300 wild boar! There were attempts at reintroduction in the 16th and 17th centuries, but without much success.

In 1997, however, we experienced another twist in this very long saga, in that trees felled by the mighty storms served to bring down fences, breach the security of wild boar farms in the south of England and release some of their stock into the surrounding countryside.

Wild boar meat has become increasingly popular in recent years, due to its superior flavour and low fat content. Escapees have apparently thrived, and it is estimated that there is now a population of around 300 running wild in Sussex, Kent and, to a lesser extent, in Dorset. One beneficial effect is the restoration of biodiversity, while in addition, wild boar help the regeneration of woodland through rooting and the burying of seeds and effect some control of bracken. There is also the opportunity for stalking, which can help to fill the big gap between public demand for wild boar meat and the supply from farms. On the debit side, the wild boar is officially classed as a dangerous animal, having a reputation for bad temper, its speed, its weight and its tusks. However, a considerable population on the Continent presents no threat to humans, not least because the animals tend to be shy and secretive.

Impact on agriculture is perhaps another matter, and against the background of instances in the past in which introduced animals have caused havoc, caution is called for; one has only to think of the grey squirrel and the mink. Parts of some farm crops could be rooted up, for example, but it would seem that judicious culling and perhaps the use of sacrificial crop strips could minimise this.

A potentially more seriously threat could be in maintaining a reservoir of foot and mouth disease, or swine fever, although it appears that such cases as have been investigated have shown that such diseases in wild boar have come from infected swill or their having contact with infected domestic pigs, rather than the other way around, a situation reminiscent of the conviction of many in relation to the badger and TB. Thus, there are pros and cons. It is to be hoped that research is in full swing, while the wild boar population remains small and in a relatively confined area.

However, to return to Grasmoor; since diet of the wild boar consists primarily of coarse grass, roots, fruits, berries and the occasional small bird, eggs, young rodents and carrion, and in the autumn, beech and oak mast, Grasmoor no longer presents a very tempting habitat. If they return – do let me know!

98. Seed

Walking along the sheltered lonnings always provides interest, even at this time of year; there is always something to see to set off a train of thought. A glance at the hedge bottoms now reveals a host of seedlings, for example.

Seeds scattered in the previous autumn lie dormant. Some will rot, some will be eaten by birds and rodents – and some will survive. Seeds of each species have a 'base temperature' below which no development occurs. Once that temperature is reached, and provided moisture is present (no problem this year!), and when a certain number of degrees above that have accumulated, growth will begin.

Imbibition is the first stage; the uptake of moisture by the seed through a tiny pore, the micropile. This causes the seed to swell and, after a few days, the root or 'radicle' will emerge and grow downwards (geotropism) in the soil. Once germination has begun, it must be a continuous process; if the seed dries out it cannot be restarted. Some days later, the shoot, or 'plumule' will emerge and grow upwards, towards the light (phototropism).

The proportion of seeds sown which germinate and produce plants is clearly of great importance to the grower, especially in crops grown for processing, where all produce must be ready to harvest at the same time. Much emphasis used to be placed upon seed rate, and it was not until the 1960s and '70s that the full light of research was brought to bear on the relationship between seed rate and spatial arrangement, ie the number of plants per unit area. It is this latter factor that greatly influences yield and profitability.

Extensive studies revealed that the pea crop, for example, from which all our frozen, canned and dried peas come, yields highest when sown four inches apart in rows also four inches apart. But this was by no means the end of the story. Field experiments revealed wide variations in the number of plants surviving from different seed lots, even when their laboratory germination was the same. The lab test was missing something. This 'missing link' was dubbed 'seed vigour'.

A programme of research was devised jointly by three bodies, Processors and Growers Research Organisation, the National Vegetable Research Station and the Scottish Horticultural Research Institute, to study the problem. We found that seeds soaked overnight lose salts into the water at different rates. Seed lots that lose much are of low vigour, while those that lose less are of higher vigour. This led to the development of a laboratory test for this factor, which is now used routinely in addition to the standard germination test, the two reflecting well the prospective field performance. Seed lots of high vigour are sown early, since they can withstand tough conditions, while those of lower vigour are perfectly satisfactory for later showing in kinder conditions. Bearing in mind the importance of achieving target plant populations in the field, this has provided a major advance in efficient crop production.

No doubt the seeds of wild flowers have varying degrees of vigour, too, so next time you catch sight of those seedlings struggling manfully in the hedgerow in a howling gale, or poking their heads through a layer of frost—give a thought to the story of seed vigour!

99. Ravens over Rosthwaite Fell

Glaramara, our first target for the day, stood there before us and, like me, was decidedly grey on top! But off we set along that lovely bracken and tree-lined track and up along that superb, rushing beck at the lower end of Combe Gill. Alright viewing it from there, but we knew we would have to *cross* it on our return later in the day – a sobering thought!

Onward and upward, over Thornthwaite Fell, the twisting and turning trail meandering along its stony way until eventually we came over a brow and the full extent of the climb was in sight. I am increasingly convinced that there is a conspiracy afoot – these fells are higher than they used to be! Needless to say, we paused a few times, not only to get our breath, but also to look back and savour the view over Seatoller, Derwentwater to Ullock Pike, Skiddaw and Blencathra.

Finally we reached the massive summit crag and decided that here was the place to halt and feed. There was a cold wind, it was damp and there was scudding cloud. What chance to get home dry? Suitably refreshed, we scaled the crag, breathless but unbowed, and again surveyed the panorama to all points of the compass. Wainwright lists no less than 70 tops that may be seen from here!

Circling east and then north is the track to Rosthwaite Fell, at times poorly defined; on to Rosthwaite Cam and Bessyboot, but this is splendid country and one could spend a day exploring its nooks and crannies. The earlier grey having lifted, we were blessed with powder-puff clouds in an azure sky, sunshine and clear views in all directions, from the Langdales to Great Gable, Honister Crag to Grasmoor, right round to Watendlath, and we could even see Dock Tarn. The going underfoot was very varied; pronounced tussocks giving way to sundew-speckled bog, buttresses festooned with prostrate juniper, between which were framed the distant glimpses of far-off felltops.

And then we had a further treat; a guttural croak announced the arrival of a pair of ravens overhead. Then the huge forms were floating high above, effortlessly soaring on their great wings. Curiosity overcoming suspicion, they descended and passed over; then, as the ground fell away as they glided across the ridge, they performed that glorious tumbling act for which they are renowned. A sudden 'flip' of the wings and, in a flash, the bird is upside-down, wings closed and falling fast; another 'flip' and it is upright and floating away once more with wings outstretched. Magic moments!

The track along the ridge is undulating and, on reaching one crest, the sight of Tarn at Leaves below us comes as a surprise. Then on to Bessyboot, veering left for a long descent through steep grassy slopes and rock fields to regain Combe Gill. On the way, looking back towards Glaramara, there was the great cliff of Raven Crag, with its enormous 'chimney' running from top to bottom, and on which we could just make out two specks – climbers on their way up. Selecting what we hoped was a safe place to cross the rushing beck, we regained the track down to the valley floor, having completed some seven miles of excellent walking. Another unforgettable day on the hill.

A walk which really has everything: a good climb, a good scramble, varied terrain, superb views – including not a few surprises – some wildlife interest and, on this occasion anyway, perfect weather. There is no denying just how lucky we are to have such country right here on our doorstep!

100. Walks and talks

Oddly enough, it seems that a little group of three 'anniversaries' came together one spring. The 100th edition of *Walkers' Way*, the 150th walk of the 'Mockerkin Mob' and my having given 100 talks around the county, mostly on various aspects of Lakeland and its wildlife.

Public awareness of the need for conservation of our natural heritage and historic artefacts, for ourselves and for future generations, has steadily risen over the last 20 years or so, a fact that is reflected in the membership of our leading conservation bodies. Membership for the National Trust now exceeds three million; that of the RSPB exceeds one million, while that of the Wildlife Trusts is approaching half a million. While that is the national picture, it is sad that the local branch of the Wildlife Trust and the National Trust North Cumbrian Club have both closed due to lack of support, despite valiant efforts by the respective committees. A great pity, especially as the North Cumbrian Club raised many thousands of pounds for the National Trust. We are fortunate enough to have a substantial number of nature reserves in the county, many of which afford excellent opportunities for observing plants, birds and animals in the wild. It is now some years since the National Trust designated part of Kinniside, Ennerdale, a wilderness area, completing the mammoth task of walling the area to exclude sheep and allow natural regeneration. Unfortunately, the fire that swept up the fellside recently will have disrupted this process, but it will recover in time. If, as one would hope, the area is subjected to regular surveys to monitor the regeneration process, the results will be complicated by the fire and, very probably, by global warming, too. Some species are far more resilient and resistant than others, and the changing patterns and populations will be of immense interest.

Without doubt, the most significant contribution to the botany of Lakeland has been the publication of Geoffrey Halliday's *Flora of Cumbria*. For this colossal task the county was divided into 84 x 10km squares, each square being meticulously surveyed, the plants in each being both identified and mapped. The flora runs to some 600 x A4 pages and is quite invaluable to anyone with an interest in plants and their distribution.

In addition, *Flora of the Fells* was published in 2003 as part of the Flora of the Fells project being carried out jointly by English Nature and the Friends of the Lake District; the object being to increase awareness of the flora of the region. As with so many aspects of wildlife, it is believed that increasing awareness promotes interest, enjoyment, concern and responsible attitudes.

Needless to say, farming has changed, is changing; and this in turn will influence biodiversity. And there's a word! Twenty years ago it was a word used by biologists and few others, but now there are surely few folk who are unaware of it, its meaning and its importance to us all. We have been losing species from the world at a faster rate than they could be studied and named; the brake has been applied, tho' not yet hard enough. In this county we very nearly lost the magnificent peregrine falcon, as a result of the use of persistent agricultural chemicals, predation by egg thieves and general persecution, but happily this position has now been reversed.

101. One hundred, not out

Anniversaries, fell walks, conservation, nature reserves, research, biodiversity – the list of viewpoints is endless – and in addition to all that, we have only to look at any stretch of hedgerow, wood, field or fell to find something of interest, from the very large to the minute.

Within 100 yards of my front door there are docks – *Rumex obtusifolius*, that is – growing on the verge. Nothing remarkable about that, but the leaves of some of them are peppered with holes to such an extent that in some cases there is little left but veins and midrib. This is the work of the dock beetle (*Gastrophysa viridula*). The dock beetle is a bright bluish green, with gold/bronze and green wing cases or elytra. The female is about ¼ inch in length, while the male is somewhat smaller and they are to be found on the leaves, sometimes above and sometimes below. On the lower surface of the leaves are clusters of their tiny bright orange cylindrical eggs, in groups of 20 to 50 or, at a later stage, groups of their tiny black larvae. Occasionally, there are a few white eggs among the orange ones, which have been laid by a particular species of hoverfly (*Parasyrphus nigritarsis*), with the intention of their larvae being provided with immediate access to eggs or larvae of the beetle, as soon as they hatch (fast food, in fact!). The dock beetle is specific to docks and the hoverfly larvae are specific to dock beetle eggs and larvae. Thus mere holes in the leaves of a common plant remind us of the interdependence of species, which in turn reflects the importance of biodiversity. Many areas of the natural world may be likened to the proverbial 'house of cards' – remove one and who knows how many more will fall? And, of course, there must be a host of such relationships of which we are as yet blissfully unaware.

One of my nest boxes is once again nursery to a brood of blue tits and I have a constant flight of weary parents ferrying caterpillars to the hungry inmates. The average blue tit brood is of just over 11 chicks, so bringing them up is no mean task. Not that they will all survive the many hazards along the way; in fact, only a quarter will make it. If all progeny of one pair survived for five years, they would number over 15,000! But in countries where a much higher proportion do survive, the clutch size is much reduced – another of nature's remarkable balancing acts!

But then again, if we leave all the planning, the politics and the science on one side, we are still left with the sheer beauty of it all – and right on our doorstep. Just to take one simple and very close example: Holme Wood, Loweswater, from across the lake or from the Coffin Route, early on a spring morning or late in the evening. The apple green of the beech, the yellow green of the oak, the bronze of the sycamore, the blue-green of the pine reflected in the motionless water. Or a partly-wooded and boulder-strewn fellside, such as that between Surprise View and Watendlath. This striking scene is not just the product of colour alone, but also of the dappled sunlight and the shadows thrown by tree, shrub and rock, imparting a magical '3D' effect, which gives immense depth in every sense of the word. Long may the beauty of this glorious corner of England be protected, for us and for those who follow.

102. South of Ennerdale

South of Ennerdale lies a vast sprawling area of rolling moorland hills, interspersed by gills, becks and rivers which, compared with most other parts of the National Park, is largely featureless and is therefore to be penetrated with care, especially in poor weather. A brief taste of this wilderness may be obtained by starting from Scarney Brow, due south of Ennerdale Bridge, and walking up the forestry road that begins by the cattle grid.

Those who have not done so for some time are in for something of a surprise, because whereas the road was once closely confined by dense arrays of conifers, it has now been opened up by much felling. Clearing to the right has exposed a view of Blakeley Raise, not seen for many a long day, while there is now an extensive view to the north and west as well. As always in these circumstances, there is also a tract of the utmost devastation – an impenetrable jungle of tree stumps, roots and brash.

The road twists, turns and climbs until eventually passing Grike and Crag Fell, to both of which diversions may be made if required. As Crag Fell rises to the left the road descends a little and, where it bears left there is a fork, a distinct but less worn track veering off down to the right. Taking this, the next 100 yards or so is inclined to be wet and boggy, but this improves on approach to a stile. Once over that there is a particularly fine stone wall, which runs some way up the fell and then turns sharp left. At this point, by leaving the wall and carrying straight on up, although there is no clear path, a 'two-wheel' track is soon bisected. Turning right onto this takes the walker along the ridge to the end of Whoap, but as soon as the ground on the left slopes down, turn left and after only a few yards there is a 'single' track running across at right angles. Turning left onto this brings one down Long Grain to Worm Ghyll – a large cleft between Long Grain and Lank Rigg.

On a recent occasion, by the time the first stile was reached, the cloud was well down and visibility was very poor, but nevertheless the route was clear enough to follow, even in these conditions. On descending Long Grain we dropped out of the cloud and had a good view of Lank Rigg, directly ahead, and of the Whoap Ghyll valley down to our right.

Worm Ghyll runs off to the left southwards for some distance, then turns right towards the Calder. It can be walked, a circuit of Lank Rigg thus being completed, but it is a mighty wet trudge! Alternatively, it is possible to climb Lank Rigg and make a way down to the Calder from there, but again, the going is very wet. Turning right at Worm Ghyll and going down to the Whoap Beck 'hidden' valley presents a much easier and dryer option. There are one or two wet spots, easily negotiated, one of which on the recent walk was bedecked with sundew and common spearwort – even in September. The track crosses an especially delightful gill with a lively rushing beck, well worth exploring, which dashes down from the right, ie from Whoap, but it must be said that crossing it is not so easy when in spate.

The track is clear all the way to a ford over the Calder, up the slope beyond, veering right and all the way back via the stone circle to Scarney Brow. All in all, a good, open, short but invigorating walk, with great views on a good day and enough 'markers' to follow in cloud or mist. A 'humble' route, but 'different', and with a charm of its own.

103. Autumn

Well, a glorious summer was swiftly followed by an equally glorious autumn! I guess we all agree that it was probably the most colourful we have ever seen, both for sheer brilliance and for the range of colours. It was quite exceptional.

Leaves of pale yellow, medium yellow, deep gold, orange and red, light brown, tan, dark brown, plum-coloured, bronze, bronze-green – and so the list went on. Quite a challenge to identify them all – and even more so to find them in a paint box!

Mind you, hot, dry weather doesn't suit everything. The badgers, having at last been proved innocent of being solely responsible for the rapid advance of bovine TB, have a tough time when the ground is hard, since the earthworm is their staple diet. Poor old Brock; one of our most ancient and harmless native wild animals and, just when persecution and misguided slaughter have been outlawed, he's faced with a food shortage! It's not just a matter of having to find enough alternative foods, but the problem of rearing the young well enough and strong enough to survive their most testing time, their first winter.

Once again we were treated to that lovely sight and sound of skeins of geese flying south. Just the faintest and most distant 'honk' at first, and then way up, very, very high, the unmistakable arrowhead formations. A singularly beautiful marking of the passage of the seasons.

Then there was another primeval sound to witness – the sound of the rut. On one occasion I was deep in a wood and could hear stags in the distance for some time, only to have one roar very, very close to me! Completely hidden in undergrowth, I never did see it, but it was mighty close and I had the full benefit of a strong pair of lungs! Talking of 'wildlife close by', we have recently had a very bold heron; odd, for this is usually a timid bird. However, it has carried out a number of fishing trips to more than one pond in Mockerkin, so is not the most popular of visitors! One has been seen by the roadside on Fangs, and on the verge near the tarn, but whether or not it's the same one, who can tell? Also strange was a recent experience with starlings. Walking down a lonning, I saw a veritable mass of them in a field on my right. Nothing odd about that at this time of year, but then they started to move. Although there were clearly hundreds of them, they took off in a thin but constant stream, in a band three or four deep, and took minutes to clear the field and settle in another across the road. The 'ribbon' or 'plume' effect was extraordinary. If they wanted to move, why did they not all go at once, as is usual? Who gave the command, 'Advance in column of fours'?

It was reported in the English Nature magazine that – at last – the naming of fungi is being tackled to try to provide rather more memorable names than the Latin ones used by those who work with such organisms all the time. (Anthracnose is a lot easier to call to mind than *Colletotrichum lindemuthianum*!) Latin names often turn people off, which is a pity, because the world of the fungi is totally fascinating. Lots of the 'common' names being devised are imaginative and descriptive, such as 'toughshank', 'candlesnuff', 'honey waxcap', 'elfcap', 'slimecap', and so on. The naming process was undertaken by mycologist, Elizabeth Holden, and she has produced a book listing all the new – and some old – names for this interesting group.

Lakeland Autumn

On lower slopes, each hill
Rich bracken draws, as t'wer a scarf,
Around itself in readiness cold blasts
To ward away.

Each mountain dons a purple hue
As heather mirror'd mists lull
Ragged rocks to sleep,
Snug from coming winter's icy snows.

While way aloft, so high
The eye is sorely taxed,
Tho' keen ears catch the eerie notes,
As geese, in formal majesty, fly south.

Rest well, great Fells,
As storm and tempest roar,
Sleep on, 'til Spring
Bursts open new life's door.

AJG

104. Watendlath wanderings

Watendlath must be a place well-loved by countless thousands of locals and visitors alike. What a spot it is! A tiny hamlet at the end of a beautiful valley, its name derived from the old Norse, 'vatns endi' – the head of the lake. Well known as the centre of Hugh Walpole's *Herries Chronicles*, too.

Approached by car along the narrow lonning, or on foot alongside Watendlath Beck, the valley is especially steep-sided to the west. It is home to kestrel, buzzard, peregrine, roe deer – and even the occasional red deer, too, together with a wide range of plants. To the east stands an extensive ridge, recently the focus of a search for one particular plant. The climb due east from Watendlath to High Tove is quite steep and is now stepped with stone; the zigzag track has little to commend it, other than the excellent views to the west which improve with every step (always a good excuse for a breather!). On approaching the top, the going gets steadily wetter, but this is a mere hint of what is to come. The route planned was not just to High Tove (1,665 feet), but from there on to High Seat (1,996 feet), which stands due north. There is a fence just before reaching High Tove, which runs all the way to High Seat, on either side of which the terrain is similar. Suffice it to say it is WET! A walk best done after some weeks of dry weather and, contrariwise, best avoided after some weeks of rain; at no time is it good underfoot. There are great peat hags, bogs, tussocks and plain swamp, and a direct route is difficult, if not impossible. As for vegetation, well, there is ample heather and all the acid-loving plants one would expect – sundew, bog asphodel, cotton grass, sphagnum moss and so on.

High Raise is not exactly a dramatic 'top', but it is a superb viewpoint. Wainwright lists no less than 60 tops that may be seen from here (try naming them!) – and the views make what some would consider a dreary climb finally worthwhile. From here, too, one can appreciate the extensive area through which the approach has been made – its wetness glistening in the sun! The return route chosen was a diagonal one towards the top of Raise Gill and the stepped track where we began.

To the west of Watendlath there are a number of modest walks of interest, including the gentle climb to Dock Tarn, resplendent with its raft of water lilies in their season. A nicely-rugged area, this; all sorts of humps and hollows to explore. Mini-gills, pools, protruding rocks and hidden corners abound.

Gale or bog myrtle grows in profusion in the vicinity, especially in the lower areas; a plant with many a name and many a use in days gone by. *Myrica gale* L., to give it its classical name, is a resinous shrub associated with wet land – indeed, it was common in the Lincolnshire Fens until reclamation. It was burned for its aromatic properties; it was used as bedding because its aroma repelled fleas and moths; in fact, in Northumberland it was known as 'flea wood', and it was used in brewing, to heighten the potency of beer.

Watendlath: an interesting area (is there an area of English countryside without interest?), and one that sports an excellent café, too!

PS   My visit to High Tove was in search of a particular plant. I didn't find it – but you can't win 'em all!

105. 'The Weasel is weasely recognised – the stoat is stoatally different!'

May blossom is a joy to see every year, heralding the arrival of spring. It was unusually prolific this year, splendidly decking out the hedgerows for mile on snowy mile, and it is now apparent that not only was there a profusion of flowers, but they were blessed with some showers at just the right time, because the set of berries, too, is phenomenal. Surely, there has seldom been a heavier crop. It is due, of course, to the combination of 'flowering and showering'; this is what achieves the 'set' of fruit, not the threat of a hard winter, as was once believed!

The hawthorn, whitethorn or May tree has a host of alternative names; one old Lakeland name was 'hip-haw'. In fact, there are two native species, but it is the midland hawthorn (*Crataegus laevigata*) we see here. However, the haw crop will certainly be welcomed by our annual invasion of fieldfares and redwings, which will have a memorable feast as they 'fold' their way across country from east to west very shortly.

While the display of berries in our hedgerows is one unmistakable sign of the arrival of autumn, the current activity of the buzzards is another. Frequently seen in most western and northern parts of England, it is the most common of our larger birds of prey. Pairs usually produce two or maybe three chocolate-brown eggs in April or May.

Like so many birds and animals, however, surviving their first winter is an enormous challenge and to this end parents feed their young as well as they can to give them the best possible chance in the lean days ahead, while at the same time teaching them to hunt and forage for themselves. That done, the young are discouraged from staying 'at home' and are persuaded to leave and look after themselves.

It is, therefore, quite a common sight at this time of year to see adult buzzards displaying dramatically with two or three juveniles; climbing high, stooping on their young; initially to make them discover their own aerobatic skills and later to make it quite clear that their departure to a life of their own would be appreciated.

Unexpectedly, I recently came face-to-face with a wild animal at close quarters! A ferocious beast, only three or four yards from me. It reared up on its hind legs and fixed me with a menacing stare; it drew itself up to its full height – all seven inches of it! Yes, it was a weasel! Almost certainly a female – the male is much larger – and indeed the difference in size is such that, for a very long time, it was thought they were two separate species. The weasel is markedly smaller than the stoat, has a much shorter tail and lacks the black tail tip of the stoat, too. Despite its size, it is agile and ferocious, being quite prepared to tackle prey far bigger than itself. A carnivore, it will prey on mice, voles, rats, ground-nesting birds and rabbits. Often destroyed by gamekeepers, in fact, the weasel does much more good than harm, like so many of our persecuted wild animals.

They have been here for a long time – some 10,000 years, in fact, and they are notorious for disappearing in a flash into crevices of stone walls or undergrowth.

Mine was no exception: now you see it – now you don't!

106. Ups and downs

The day before had been one of those very wet and dreary ones; you know the sort, we do get one or two now and again in Cumbria! But the morning in question was bright and still, with a cloudless sky, and it was mild. A wan sun was struggling to penetrate the mist, and the water had barely a ripple.

A small group of members of the 'Mockerkin Mob' met at the 'phone box car park', below Miresyke. We set off up the footpath towards the Mosser road, turned right for a few yards and then left over the stile, aiming for Darling Fell. Immediately on leaving the road we learnt two facts about the forthcoming walk. First, the stile was treacherously slippery and, second, it was very wet and muddy underfoot.

Having rapidly gained height, the view behind us over Loweswater and towards Mellbreak was such that cameras soon emerged from rucksacks. Mellbreak presented a somewhat ghostly sight, heavily shrouded as it was, while the indistinct sun was dazzlingly bright. In the foreground was the skeletal silhouette of a large tree, black against the glaring white beyond.

Scaling Darling Fell first thing in the morning comes as something of a shock to the system. No gentle walk-in to warm up the muscles, just a good old-fashioned flog straight uphill, an unremitting and steep ascent, albeit only to a height of some 1,300 feet. But the route is even less kind than that, because, having reached the first top there is an immediate descent to Crabtree Beck, only to be faced at once with the return to 1,350 feet on Low Fell! A good start to any day!

Crabtree Beck was easily crossed, but we are reminded of the tragedy in 1828, when a dam burst and resulted in loss of life and the destruction of buildings down below.

These hills to the north of Loweswater saw some of the first changes to the local landscape early in the 13th century, when farm holdings, fields and lonnings were first marked out, facts which are clearly stated in a charter granted by Richard de Lucy to Adam de Mosser in 1202, when much of the area was still forest.

The ascent of Low Fell is also steep, but on a morning such as this, it is highly rewarding. It may not be a great or dramatic fell, but it offers superb views of Loweswater, Crummock and Lorton valleys and the surrounding hills, from Lord's Seat via Whiteside, Grasmoor and Rannerdale, all the way to Great Gable and back along the Red Pike range.

While we had set out in rather damp and misty conditions, on Low Fell we were in full sunshine, tho' the mist still hung heavily below us in places. Having admired the views, we made for Fellbarrow; easy walking, which could be described as little more than undulating. Views were good all the way and, having passed the summit, we veered right down to the ruins of Hatteringill, over the slippery (and wobbly!) stile and along the track that leads all the way to the Mosser-Lorton (or Whinfell) road. Once on this little-used road, we turned right and made for Lorton and the Wheatsheaf Inn! As we descended, we dropped gradually into thicker and thicker mist, and such clothing as had been removed while in the sunshine on top was soon replaced to ward off the increasing damp and chill.

A good autumn walk on a good autumn day, rosy cheeks all round and a thirst efficiently quenched, by a roaring fire in a welcoming hostelry. Great!

107. Changing times

Keeping a diary is one of those activities that many of us will have tried – it can become a bit of a chore – but it can also be useful. For example, reference to my own diaries of years ago reveals that 'first snowdrops' were recorded on the 8th March, 1985, 23rd February, 1986, 13th February, 1989, while this year it was the 9th January. If only the universal tackling of global warming matched the number of observations on the subject! And three celandines appeared on the 24th January, too!

One of the great many effects of warming is that in some cases it disrupts essential synchronisation between the young of some species and the prey upon which they depend. The golden plover is in danger, because warming is resulting in earlier egg-laying, but the larvae of the crane fly, or 'daddy-long-legs', the leatherjacket, on which the young depend, are not reacting to warming in the same way. The newly-hatched chicks are thus deprived of their prime source of food.

Other changes wrought by man also greatly affect wildlife. Seventy years ago, one could expect to see cirl bunting, a small bird closely related to the yellowhammer, anywhere below a line roughly from North Wales to the Thames estuary; but the cirl bunting is a seed-eater and relies heavily on stubble for winter feeding. The introduction of profitable varieties of autumn-sown cereals resulted in less and less stubble over winter, with the result that, by the 1980s, the bird's territory had been reduced to a very small stretch of the South Devon coast, around Prawle Point. Happily, the RSPB and Countryside Stewardship Scheme have worked on this problem and, by compensating farmers for sowing more spring cereals, have succeeded in raising the number of cirl bunting territories from 100 to 700.

Another success reported is that in Yorkshire 19 pairs of red kites raised 44 young in 2004. Sadly, the story is not repeated in

Scotland, where persecution persists. Long the target of gamekeepers, kites are still being shot and poisoned, despite the fact that they are purely scavengers and offer no threat to grouse whatsoever.

Such messages do take a long time to get through. Only recently there was yet another cry to 'cull the badgers' despite the fact that it is now known that culling can make matters worse, because it promotes much movement of badger populations and thus spreads any TB present; and despite the fact that before any such cull could be completed, there is every reason to suppose that a vaccine will be available. Hold the line and save both cattle and wildlife. To cull now smacks more of misguided 'revenge' than science.

108. Spring sightings

One of the eagerly-awaited signs of spring each year is the arrival of frogs and toads at ponds, pools and tarns. 'Arrival' is a term selected with deliberation, because it is often erroneously supposed that these amphibians 'return' to such sites, a myth perpetuated by elderly married ladies (ie an old wives' tale!).

While some may indeed 'return', most of the invasion is merely by those that happen to be in the vicinity at the time. Any shallow and well-lit area of static water is likely to be colonised by algae; these are single-celled, non-vascular and rootless microscopic plants − of which there are some 25,000 known species. Where there are algae, there is the production of glycolic acid, and it is the smell of this that acts as an irresistible attractant for amphibians. Instinct tells them that where there is glycolic acid, there is a site suitable for spawning.

Each female frog may lay some 3,000 eggs in an amorphous mass (unlike toad spawn, which is in long strings), and the spawn of a number of females is often lumped together. The spawn is fertilised externally by the male as it is laid. Only a small proportion of eggs result in adults as, at all stages, as eggs, tadpoles and juveniles, they are constantly heavily preyed upon by numerous species of birds and animals. Frogs normally start to spawn earlier than toads, but there is a degree of overlap, since toad spawning often coincides with the second spawning of frogs.

Bird activity also quickens at this time of year, of course. The 'mobbing' or 'harrying' of birds of prey is not an uncommon sight, but is worth watching. It involves one or more birds diving and swooping at a bird of prey, usually with the object of driving it away from a feeding or nesting area. The relatively ponderous buzzard is especially prone to this nuisance.

On one occasion recently I noticed a buzzard was harried by a crow eight times, and that each time the crow gave eight violent wingbeats to gain enough momentum to mount an attack. Sixty-four strong wingbeats, in response to which the buzzard merely 'floated' and soared, with an occasional dip of the wings, but not a single beat. Only once did it roll and register its annoyance by presenting its talons to its tormentor, as if to say, "Do that just once more and—"!

A few days ago I was asked to identify some bird pellets. Not all that difficult – its a matter of measuring their length and width, taking note of their shape and, sometimes, noting also the colour and contents. This time they were the product of a tawny owl.

The site concerned was merely a perch, not a roost, and was clearly given away, as is so often the case, by a brilliant splash of birdlime high up, and the pellets on the ground beneath.

There's always *something*—!

109. This and that

While forest clearing has been going on since Man first began to grow crops rather than hunter-gathering, the rate of actual deforestation has steadily accelerated, and continues to do so. The sheer scale of forest loss in Amazonia, Siberia, the American West, Australia and Mediterranean Europe is difficult to comprehend, but suffice it to say that in the time it takes you to read this page, an area about the size of one sixth of Wales will have been felled in Amazonia alone. The effects of such massive clearances on wildlife are catastrophic, while in addition there is more flooding, loss of topsoil and silting of river deltas. Forests are often looked upon as the lungs of the world, and the combination of their loss and pollution rings alarm bells, but the lemming-like destruction continues. Too great a subject for this page, but it has been studied in depth by Michael Williams (*Deforesting the Earth: From Prehistory to Global Crisis*, Chicago, January 2003).

It was reported in the Journal of the Institute of Biology (March 2005) by a 26-year-old who was on Ton Pai, an island off the coast of Thailand, that while swimming early on Boxing Day, "—the fish were acting strangely". So much so that the swim was abandoned. Within ten or fifteen minutes, the tidal wave could be seen out to sea, thundering towards the shore. It would seem that sound or shock waves, which travel faster through water than through air, had alerted the fish to impending disaster. Needless to say, this potentially vital observation has been passed on to those in seismology in the hope that appropriate detecting devices might be installed in areas at high risk. How many lives might have been saved, given ten minutes in which to reach higher ground last Boxing Day?

Now, much closer to home, I recently took the opportunity to renew acquaintance with a wild flower last seen some 30 years ago! The bee orchid. Common on the Continent; not uncommon in the south of England. With 19 known sites in south Cumbria, the bee orchid is only known to be at one site in the whole of the northern half of the county (and even then, I only found ONE!). The lower lip of the flower does resemble a bee, but while this 'lure' tempts bees to alight and pollinate continental species, they are wasting their time with ours, which is self-pollinating anyway! Appearances of this orchid vary greatly from year to year, there being far more in some years than in others, but where they do occur, grass-cutting should be delayed, if possible, until they have seeded. Let's hope that this beautiful species will not be among those we lose. It is estimated that there are somewhere between 5 and 30 million species of organism in the world, of which we have so far managed to identify only two million; so little time – so much to do! A race between identification and extinction.

However, it is not all 'doom and gloom'. An experiment carried out by the National Trust suggested that flowering plants and birds can recover by as much as 78% soon after the introduction of organic and wildlife-friendly farming practices, so there's hope, if we all pull together – HARD!

While we must all be aware that it is against the law to disturb bats in any way, circumstances can, in some instances, dictate that it is felt necessary to move a bat. I once awoke in the small hours to find a bat on my pillow within inches of my right ear, and moving such an intruder is unlikely to result in prosecution! However, some bats carry rabies. *If* you have to move one, wear gloves and if bitten or scratched, report to hospital – fast.

110. It's an ill gill that impresses no walker!

In August the 'Mockerkin Mob' walk took us to Irton Fell, Whin Rigg and Illgill Head, returning via Burnmoor Tarn and Miterdale. By no means a difficult walk, but a steady climb all the way to Illgill Head with a few undulations, the lower parts of which are notoriously wet, and amounting to some 11 miles in all.

Whin Rigg, or Gorse Ridge, if you prefer that interpretation, has little gorse today, but it provides superb views to both west and east; the former being the most dramatic. It was some years since last I was there, and I had forgotten just how good they are. So much so that I returned only a week later, armed with camera.

The approach to Whin Rigg is not particularly inspiring, but the rewards on reaching it make it well worthwhile.

There is a fine view of the whole of Wastwater, showing off our deepest lake to perfection. Given a reasonable day, the vista extends southwards to Black Combe and north-north-east to Skiddaw, an overall distance of some 28 miles and with a host of other fells in sight, including Great Gable and the Scafells. However, there can be no doubt that the great excitement of this walk is not so much the distant views, as the fact that for much of its length the preferred track follows close to the rim of the famous Wastwater Screes. Observing the screes from below, from the lakeshore or the road, is dramatic enough, showing their vast fans plunging to the water, but looking down from above is something else.

About 400 feet before reaching the summit of Whin Rigg is the top of Greathaw Gill, a massive gouge out of the escarpment, as if by some gigantic claw, while just past the summit is Great Gully, a similar ravine. Both show breathtaking glimpses of the screes and the lake far below, but for me there is one place which is even more dramatic, and which comes as quite a shock when first seen. Just past Great Gully there are two small tarns and, shortly after them, a peak right on the edge. This is an excellent viewpoint, but the true spectacle of its shape and position cannot be appreciated until looking back after a further 50 yards towards Illgill Head. Then all is revealed. The eastern side of the peak is a gentle climb, but the western side is vertical! Incidentally, this peak may clearly be seen from the lakeshore road. It does surprise me that it has no name of its own. It is such a feature that it warrants 'Whin Rigg Crag', or something of the sort.

From there it is a case of 'onward and upward' to Illgill Head and its cairn which, although another good viewpoint, is less of note than earlier elements. From there it is possible, but not advisable, to descend directly down the eastern flank to Burnmoor Tarn; not advisable because it is a long, steep and tortuous way. Better to stick to the track running north-east and reach the tarn by the Corpse Road. The return along Miterdale is pleasantly varied and not without interest. We did see some mountain yellow saxifrage there.

PS I was watching a vehicle in Mockerkin the other day and calculated its speed to be 60! "Sixty?" I hear you gasp! "In Mockerkin? The perpetrator must be mad!" Well, in fact it was quite safe – 60 inches per hour, not miles! A small snail chugging up a window pane! Steady, but sure – 'You can be sure of Shell'!

111. Go fly a kite!

The media seem to have been paying a great deal of attention lately to that glorious bird, the red kite: a piece in the Daily Telegraph about one seen and photographed in Lower Clapton, East London; a piece in the RSPB magazine, 'Birds'; and a substantial part of a wildlife programme on 'the box' all appeared in the same week. The overall story of the near-extinction (down to four pairs in Wales), its reintroduction from Sweden and its subsequent protection and conservation by RSPB and others is one of the great success stories of the last century.

Although the story is now well-known, it might be worth giving a few pointers to identification, for reasons that will become obvious a little later.

First, the kite is *big*, with a wingspan of five to six feet. The plumage is *red* – brick-red. The head is pale *cream*. Wing tips are *black*; but above all, it has a very clearly *forked tail*, as opposed to the rounded, or 'fan'-shaped tail of the buzzard. It has a habit of flicking its tail to adjust its flight path and it loves to swoop. It is, of course, no threat to other birds or livestock; it is a scavenger.

Near habitation, it can develop a naughty habit of stealing, as jackdaws often do; indeed, reference to Shakespeare's *Winter's Tale* is mentioned in the Telegraph article: 'When the kite builds, look to lesser linen.' In other words, a kite is not above pinching a handkerchief or two from a nearby clothesline with which to line its nest! But above all, this is a spectacular bird.

Why am I labouring the point again? Well, there have been sightings within this county; one was seen recently at Caldbeck, but better still, there was a positive sighting recently within our parish – on the western flank of Low Fell. This was at close quarters, and by an experienced observer. These two may have been of the same bird passing through, who knows? But the fact remains, there is an increasing chance of seeing one. I await your call!

Still on birds of prey, it is interesting how the habits of buzzards change with the seasons. Through summer they are mostly lazily soaring up in the thermals, with seldom a wingbeat. Then, as the young fledge, we see them being 'trained' by their parents, feinting, swooping, rolling with them, exercising their wings and building reaction times and other hunting skills in readiness for the hard months to come. Whereas now, in midwinter, when the leaves have fallen and trees adopt their skeletal form, they are to be seen silhouetted, sitting hunched and vulture-like, clearly hoping some form of prey will appear to stem the pangs of hunger. This is a very good time to see them; the view is seldom obstructed as they perch on a branch, and with steady movement they will often stay put until a close-up view is obtained.

A shade smaller than the red kite – although this is not something one could detect in the field. Both have light patches under their wings and both have golden talons with which they stand on their food to steady it while they deftly insert the hooked beak and tear pieces off by throwing back the head.

Both birds are superb, but it must be said that the red kite has that little extra panache – so keep looking!

112. 'Aliens!'

Having specialised in pulses all my working life, with the final 25 years as director of PGRO (the curious may care to log on to www.PGRO.org), the move to Cumbria gave me the opportunity to spread my biological wings once more and take an interest in 'living things' in general. Walking, wildlife and photography – what a super combination of interests, and what a glorious part of England in which to indulge them! If a little of the pleasure such pursuits have given me has rubbed off on readers – GREAT! Incidentally, you do know the definition of a 'specialist', don't you? 'One who gets to know more and more about less and less!'

Walkers' Way began as a series of descriptions of mostly local walks with, I suppose, the odd wildlife observation thrown in. Indeed some may recall that the first 25 were combined into a booklet – long since out of print. However, over the years, and there have been a lot of them, the wildlife content has steadily increased, I suppose in tandem with a considerable reduction in what I would call 'real' walking. Some people say the fells gradually shrink through erosion, but in my experience, they get higher and steeper each year!

At this time of year we all see welcome signs of approaching spring. The snowdrops appear, birds are courting and inspecting likely nest sites, and we reckon to see frog and toad spawn, often in the most unlikely places. The amphibians are an important group in the overall scheme of things, but all is not well. Recently a Global Amphibian Assessment was carried out which showed that, while one in eight bird species is threatened with extinction and one in four mammals faces the same fate, in the case of amphibians, it is one in three. I have mentioned before their highly sensitive and permeable skin; this makes them especially vulnerable to pollution, which is one of the factors responsible, as are habitat loss and climate change, plus the fact that there is a 'new' fungal disease. Luckily, research is in progress on the subject and there is a chance that the tide may still be turned.

I was interested to read a letter in a spring magazine of the National Trust, which extols the virtue of, believe it or not, the grey squirrel! Well, yes, I do understand that if it comes to the stark choice between greys or no squirrels at all, many folk would vote for the grey. However, to suggest that 'species substitution is evolution' is going too far. This is not 'evolution', but the sheer irresponsibility of Man. How many more times are we going to allow the introduction of harmful alien species at the expense of our own natives? The grey squirrel, the coypu, the mink, the American bullfrog, the signal crayfish and many more, including, of course, the rabbit, each of which have inevitably escaped and caused havoc in the countryside. A pity the NFU cannot sue the Normans for bringing rabbits over from the continent. I wonder what *they* have cost British agriculture over the centuries?

Ah, well! Whatever the problems, whatever the weather now, spring really *is* on the way, so ENJOY, have Happy Days and always remember, it's the second mouse that gets the cheese!

113. Falco peregrinus

Twenty-odd years ago, those of us who were involved in guarding peregrine nest sites spent many a night under the stars to ensure that our magnificent feathered friends could rest in peace, without fear of their eggs being stolen. It was a lonely watch, finally ended by the welcome sight of approaching headlights heralding the arrival of the morning relief.

Watchers during the day had great compensations, of course, with superb sightings of the peregrines and other species, too. The great highlight was, and is, the food pass, when the tiercel meets the falcon head-on and the two rear up, passing the prey from the talons of the male to those of the female. This is a breathtaking and never-to-be-forgotten spectacle.

We put a caravan there once, with a view to offering telescopic sightings to interested parties – but the birds decided to change nest sites that year, so it was of no avail. Watching from the picnic table by the small car park at Bowness Knott a week or two ago, it was possible to see peregrines, ravens and a barn owl, all at the same time! What a spot!

Peregrines are much more numerous now, of course; indeed, we are said to have the greatest concentration in the world. While the peregrine is spectacular, and probably the most spectacular of all our birds, the raven comes a good second. Very large – it is the largest member of the crow family we have – jet black and with a massive bill. Spring is the best time to witness its aerial display, when it rolls over in flight, tumbling downwards and even flying upside-down for short periods. All this, plus that very, very deep croak.

Unlike the peregrine, however, the raven creates little excitement over feeding, since it will eat almost anything on offer, but mostly carrion, using both beak and claw to tear pieces off.

The raven has its place in legend, too, since it is said that, if the ravens leave the Tower of London, England will fall; in the same way that it is said that, if the Dymoke Lion Crest above the stone entrance archway at Scrivelsby Court, home of the Champion of England, lowers its paw, then too, England will fall.

And so this is a great place to sit and watch: always the possibility of peregrines and ravens, whilst kestrels have also nested. Plenty of small birds around; there have been hedgehogs and even a reported sighting of pine marten, but then, that is another story.

PS   Fear not for England – the ravens at the Tower have their wings clipped – so they cannot fly away and the Dymoke Lion rests its paw on a *very* stout iron post!

114. 'Flights of fancy'

Identification is a fascinating aspect of bird watching, involving many factors, each important in their own way. The extremes of size are such that nobody is likely to confuse, say, a wren with a goose, but then, there are a lot of 'SBJs', or 'small brown jobs', where the recognition of features other than size alone are essential elements.

Colour can be very distinctive, such as in the 'topknot' of the goldcrest, the grey, black and pink of the long-tailed tit, or the electric blue of the kingfisher.

Then again, many birds have very distinctive flight patterns, a factor which can be especially useful when observing birds in poor light or silhouetted against the sky. For example, the broad-winged and laborious flight of the heron, or the 'whirring' zigzag flight of the snipe. The curlew has what might be described as an extravagant flight, its wings describing an extensive arc. Then there is the unmistakable muscular flight of the pigeon, immediately recognisable.

The flights of birds of prey are distinctive, too. The near-stalling flight of the marsh harrier, the 'soft and gentle' flight of the barn owl, quartering a meadow in the evening light, as opposed to the violent dash of the sparrowhawk as it races along the hedge top in the hope of disturbing prey.

Only yesterday I heard the familiar 'meow' and looked up to see what is, in fact, a common sight at this time of year – a parent buzzard 'training' a couple of youngsters. The adult was soaring, apparently aimlessly, but would then suddenly side-slip and feint at one of its young, forcing it to take evasive action. All part of the vital lessons in 'flight-craft', so necessary if the young are to find sufficient food to survive their prime test – the coming winter.

259

The red kite is one of the foremost 'swoopers'. Its apparently lazy flight suddenly transformed by the famous flick of the tail, which sends it plummeting downwards to snatch a morsel from the ground as it sweeps past.

Then there is the speed merchant supreme, the peregrine, the fastest living thing. Just how fast it really is is a matter of debate, but whatever it is, it is breathtaking. Perched high on a rock, or even a windowsill in town or city, on spotting prey it will launch itself into the air, close its wings and streak downwards at such a ferocious speed that it can decapitate a pigeon as it rushes by. Not only is its speed phenomenal, but also its manoeuvrability is unsurpassed.

There are other great 'plummeters', too. The osprey, for example, searches high above the surface of the water to spot its prey, then partially closes its wings, plummets and swoops, catching its fish with those enormous talons, assisted by the highly roughened feet. The gannet uses another approach; again spotting its fishy prey from high above, steering its descent with partially-closed wings and then, at the last moment before striking the water, thrusts forward its sharp beak, closes its wings entirely and, with total streamlining, enters the water in the shape of little more than a pencil, to gain maximum depth.

115. Plants

The uses to which Man has put plants over the centuries are, of course, legion. The great herbalist, Nicholas Culpepper, found innumerable species to cure all manner of ills, while plants have been, and still are, used as food, for clothing, for decoration and even for industrial purposes. In fact, a country walk does not have to proceed very far before one or other 'useful' plants may be identified.

Alexanders, the teasel, the bluebell, angelica—the list is endless and, needless to say, all our modern crop plants have been developed from wild ones, too, tho' much modified by plant breeding and selection to improve yield, disease resistance, quality and reliability. At PGRO, for example, my old research station, we produced Progreta in the eighties which, with its stiff straw and upright habit, soon became the most widely-grown pea variety for processing throughout western Europe.

And the process continues. One of our best-known 'weeds', the common nettle, is the subject of current research, despite the fact that we mostly associate it with the discomfort of the rash it causes and the fact that it can be a nuisance in the garden. It has been used before, both as food and for the production of cloth from its fibre. It is still used today for the production of 'ramie', a fine fibre used by the fashion houses.

The nettle is well-known for its stinging properties, which are due to the injection of a toxin by the 'needles' or trichomes, the points of which break off on contact. However, commercial production of nettles for fibre, or for future production for medicinal use, does have its problems. Methods of cultivation and mechanical harvesting are being studied, but while protection of hands is easy, by the use of gloves, the needles and hairs become detached as they dry and, once airborne, may be inhaled by workers and may well be carcinogenic, as are the fibres of asbestos, necessitating the use of masks and maybe goggles.

So, next time you go for a walk, spare a thought for the common nettle, its many uses and its defence mechanism! Common it may be, but our 'friend', the nettle, is not to be ignored, either in terms of its value to Man or in terms of its ability to dissuade us from too casual contact. As for the future, well, watch this space!

Reverting to the subject of plants and their uses, we must not forget the tobacco plant, which has made millions of pounds both for individuals and for governments, in the form of taxes. It has also resulted in untold suffering as a health hazard, as we all now know.

Which reminds me of a notice I saw recently in a local hospital. It read: 'Stop Smoking Clinic'. I always thought it was tobacco we were being urged to stop smoking!!

FOX AT DAWN

Sweet smells the morning air
As cool deep draughts are drawn
While yet the rolling mists
To ghostlike fellsides cling.
Each footstep falls upon
The luscious turf and scatters o'er
A thousand sparkling diamonds
Of the glistening dew.

And there, ears pricked,
The watchful vixen lays
Alert to slightest scent or sound
While warming in the rising sun.
Around her play her tiny cubs
Which skip and scamper, jump and run
Before descending for the day
Within the tunnelled mound.

AJG

116. 'Every Picture—'

The old adage that 'every picture tells a story' is very apt in relation to photographing wildlife. While a certain amount of equipment is required, the first essential is patience! I once rose at 4:00 am to visit a fox earth. Day one – nothing. Day two – nothing. Day three – a very close close-up of a fox cub looking straight down the lens! Success!

Initial interest in wildlife is usually from the point of view of recognition. What's that flower? What's that bird? Or, what's that animal? But if interest is maintained, it deepens and the fascination of behaviour comes into play.

The badger and its behaviour make a good subject for such study, and a sequence of pictures does tell quite a story.

1. The entrance to the sett illustrates both size and cleanliness.
2. When the badger introduces fresh bedding, it bundles it up under its chin and waddles backwards to the sett. Effective, but not very efficient, as it leaves a trail of dropped bedding all the way.
3. The badger's sight is poor, but its senses of smell and hearing are acute. When the first one appears above ground, usually the boar, it will often incline its head and sniff the air carefully.
4. If there is no hint of untoward intruders, he will venture further and the sow will follow.
5. After a good look around, they may be seen to groom each other, as many animals and birds do.
6. Such preliminaries then give way to the need to feed, and they can be seen 'hoovering' nearby grassland for earthworms – of which a single badger may consume 200 in a night.

7. They may also be seen relaxing, when they often adopt a very bear-like stance, which no doubt gave rise to the old name of 'little English bear'.
8. Provided the watcher is downwind, or if watching becomes so established that they accept the watcher's presence, they may come very close indeed, giving the opportunity to see clearly the black and white head, the grey coat, the strong paws and sturdy claws.
9. At the appropriate time of year, there is also the spectacle of the emergence of the cubs and the sheer delight of seeing them playing together.

Many hours cold, cramped, midge-bitten – all is forgotten and forgiven!

Not that all wildlife photography is 'planned'; many good shots are achieved by pure chance, but if a particular subject is to be studied in depth, then planning and fieldcraft are essential.

117. The beck

Way up in the high fell lies a col – a shallow feature, nestling between two massive hills; part grass, part scree and part jagged rock – a scene we all know so well. The col is silent and of no especial note, giving no hint whatsoever that it harbours the birthplace of something quite magical.

Within it is a patch of sparsely-covered ground, a patch that is barely more than damp, yet it is a start. Follow it for a few yards and, rather than just a dampness, there is a positive seeping, which in turn becomes a trickle and the grass-free strip through which it now passes is gradually broadening. It becomes a rivulet of water, bravely ambling its way over increasingly steep terrain, coursing its way around such rocks as lie in its path. Steadily gathering speed, it deepens all the while as it is joined by others from each side. Onwards and downwards, past bracken and bilberry, saxifrage and the myriad of brilliant emerald-green mosses which deck its banks.

Positively pouring now, dashing – not just round rocks, but over them and slithering down over solid rock faces too, deeply grooved, smoothed by centuries of non-stop cascading, every hour of every day and every night without respite.

Cool and refreshing in summer, ice cold in winter, its rocky bed an ever-present slippery trap for the unwary walker who dares to trust a boot thereon to cross the gurgling torrent.

Now passing through a deep, deep gully, whose precipitous sides are punctuated by a mountain ash, clinging on in some impossible crevice as, despite its precarious hold on life, it manages to develop to a reasonable size and bear its orange berries in defiance of all logic.

Once in spate, the surge overshoots and strikes a lower rock head-on, sending up a shower of droplets and a mist of sufficient density to create a rainbow in the sunlight, while a sudden updraught sends a plume of white water skywards, back from whence it came, only to descend once more in the maelstrom.

At last, the system broadens, slows and presents a calm and gentle visage.

Through the lower reaches there is every chance of seeing a dipper – that remarkable bird of deepest chestnut hue, with its winking false eyelid and creamy breast – bobbing and dipping before plopping into the water in search of a meal on the stony bottom.

Once the water slows, the heron, too, will glide into the little valley on its broad and arched wings, silently to bounce to a standstill before stepping silently into the shallows in search of unwary prey.

The whole, a familiar story of hustle and bustle, a myriad of experiences and, at last, peace and serenity. Life!

118. Shades of opinion

Looking back over hundreds of walks and the array of memories that come to mind, one aspect that looms large is that of outstanding splashes of colour. The brilliant gold of a peregrine's talons as it swooped overhead on Grasmoor; the dazzling yellow of a tuft of mountain yellow saxifrage in the dawn light on Pillar; the glorious deep red of a young fox in Ennerdale and the stark contrasts of the black-and-white mask of badgers as they emerged at dusk. The purest white of grass of Parnassus above Watendlath and the white and cerise of starry saxifrage below Maiden Moor.

However, within the plant kingdom – indeed, within the natural world as a whole – there are few more spectacular displays of colour than that provided by trees in autumn. Every shade of yellow, orange, brown, red and purple; a fine technicolour production.

And yet, all is not quite what it seems, nor are things quite as we were told as students, years ago. We were told that leaves fall in autumn because, to remain *in situ* exposes them to severe winter weather, and that the ensuing physical damage would render the tree prone to invasion by pathogens. The tree, therefore, sheds leaves and adopts a safer dormant pose for the winter months. At that time observers seemed to miss the fact that some trees retain most of their leaves – like the conifers. We were told leaves fall because of the formation of the abscission layer between stem and leaf stalk, thus cutting off vital supplies, but we now know that there are plants, the leaves of which fall without an abscission layer being formed.

All plants shed some component parts at some time or other; and it has now been observed that many of these are rich, not just in pigments, but in heavy metals, too. Even the common duckweed (*Lemna minor*) can concentrate lead and cadmium in this way (J. Inst. Biol. December 2007).

While the ability to eliminate waste material is one of the essential elements in the standard definition of living things, the fact that trees appeared to be an exception was given scant attention.

It is now postulated that leaf-fall in the tree is its means of disposing of waste accumulated from all the normal activities, such as photosynthesis, respiration, transpiration and so on; a new light on autumn colours, in fact, as the author of a recent paper puts it, "We shall never look at autumn colours in the same way again".

As we all know only too well, the fells themselves continually change colour, due to differing intensities of light, cloud formation, time of day, time of year and so on. We sometimes see them as dark, almost black silhouettes, with no detail showing at all. At another time, especially in bright sunshine after a shower, all the true colour is exposed and every detail is sharp. There are occasions when some fells seem to glow, as if lit from within, usually in evening light. Grasmoor is one such.

And, of course, there are the colours of dawn and dusk. Dawn, beginning as a mere hint of 'lesser darkness' along the horizon, leading to an explosion of blazing light as the sun itself finally appears. And sunset, especially over the sea, when a blaze of deepest orange extends as far north and south as the eye can see. These are grand colours, on a grand scale.

Conversely, there are combinations of colour that amuse us. What about the goldfinch and the puffin – two of nature's clowns – both of which look rather as though they've been let loose in the make-up box backstage!

Colour – what a joy it all is!

119. Identity parade

Each year the arrival of spring reignites interest in wild plants in general and wild flowers in particular. Banks of star-spangled celandines, the welcome cushions of primroses, the serried ranks of Jack-by-the-hedge – the list is long and summons up the annual delight of winter's end and summer's promise.

Identification of wild flowers is, of course, merely the beginning; the first window into a botanical wonderland full of interest from innumerable perspectives.

Without the great facility of classical or Latin names, identification soon dissolves into the utmost confusion, partly because most plants have many names, according to district and to make things worse, the same name is, or was, often applied to quite different species in different parts of the country. For example, lesser celandine (*Ranunculus ficaria L.*) has been known as figwort – a name more usually attributed to *Scrophularia nodosa L.*, as well as having some 26 other names! Similarly, both water avens (*Geum nivale L.*) and the ox-eye daisy (*Chrysanthemum leucanthemum L.*) share the name, 'Billy's button', despite the fact that their appearances are vastly different. The primrose (*Primula vulgaris*) has quite a few names, too, including butter rose, darling of April, early rose, Easter rose, golden rose, golden stars, Lent rose, May flower and May spink! The common dandelion (*Taraxacum officinalis L.*) has in excess of 50 local names, dandelion itself being perhaps the most intriguing. In mediæval Latin it was 'dens leonis' and in French 'dents de leon' – 'tooth of lion', presumably after the yellow and serrated petals. Many old names were fanciful indeed, and the origin of many has been lost over the years.

The wild pansy (*Viola tricolour L*), most commonly known as heartsease now, was a symbol of remembrance, and has been known as 'call me to you', 'heart-pansy', 'Jack-behind-the-garden-gate', 'kiss-and-look-up', 'kiss-her-in-the-buttery' and many more.

Similarly, a host of plants or 'herbs' have been used as cures for all manner of maladies, and the names of many have been chosen because of their appearance, too. For example, that especially beautiful flower, viper's bugloss (*Echium vulgare L.*) has seeds which resemble the head of a snake; not only was it, therefore, named viper's bugloss, but, because of its appearance, it was assumed to be a cure for snake bite! A common philosophy among the herbalists of the past being—'Like cures like'!

There is, of course, no doubt whatsoever that hosts of plants have been used, as indeed many are used today, as cures for many maladies. Many such were purely imaginary; for example, viper's bugloss as a cure for snake bite, and many were used to fend off witches and evil spirits.

A thousand attributes: a rose, or any plant, by any other name, would cure, or fail to cure, just the same.

repeatedly and obviously very concerned about something. Only after a careful search was the object of their concern discovered. There among the stones and the sand was a chick—long, ungainly legs, remarkably camouflaged and, yes, it promptly had its picture taken before rapidly being left for parents to reclaim.

Just a few of the 380 photos of birds considered good enough to be retained in the main collection—with, of course, the additional great many which are not quite so good, where the subject proved to be a bit too far off, or was inconsiderate enough to move at just the wrong moment! Next time, 'Six of the best – plants'. At least they are polite enough to stand still when a picture is to be taken, although even then the wind can sometimes play unhelpful tricks!

'God gave us memories
That we might enjoy roses in December.'

120. 'Six of the best' – animals

Walking and photography are good companions! While walking there is often the opportunity to capture good views, there is always the possibility of a chance encounter with wildlife and there are times when sites of wildlife may be noted and returned to at a later date.

Two of my most memorable meetings with red squirrels come to mind. First, a pair, either courting or two males fighting for territory, chasing spirally up and down a tree trunk at break-neck speed. Second, and conversely, a squirrel, quite close, hunched under its bushy tail and sitting motionless on a branch, silhouetted against the sky. Photographically, in the first case – no chance! But in the second – click – and I still have the picture!

To be sure of seeing, studying and snapping badgers, it is wise to be in the right place, settled and still in the evening, often with a good supply of patience. On one of the many occasions I recall, I had taken a few shots, I was cramped, damp, well-'midged' and about to call it a day (or night), when a couple turned and walked straight towards me and trotted past within three or four feet. It was rather dark by then, but not too dark and, yes, I still have that pic, too.

As for foxes, well, I have both 'planned' and 'fortuitous' pictures. Probably the best 'lucky' one is of a fox nonchalantly strolling home across a field at 6:00 am after a night's foraging. At some distance, this, but nevertheless atmospheric. The best 'planned' one came on the third consecutive early-morning watch, when suddenly there was a cub looking straight at the lens, and close, too. Another time I was well hidden when a cub walked past, again only a few feet away. There was no clear shot, but within seconds he turned away and I had a picture of head and shoulders from behind, with ears pricked!

In hiding on one early morning, I had a roe deer doe wander into view – followed closely by a very young fawn, only 18 inches or so tall. There they were in dappled sunlight, as peaceful a scene as one could wish for.

The stoat is notoriously difficult to photograph: nervous, very fast, seldom still – but just once I had the opportunity. Three pictures resulted – in swift succession! None perfect, in that in each one, one or other part of the animal is obscured by foliage, but together – not bad!

The adder, our only native poisonous reptile, is by no means rare, but is seldom seen – unless you know of a regular haunt. One such is at the RSPB reserve at Geltsdale and, armed with this knowledge, I once went with the express intention of getting pictures. Soon after arrival on a suitably sunny day, there it was, coiled and basking. An immediate telephoto shot, to at least get something 'in the can', and then, after some careful stalking, more shots close to.

All great fun—but the abiding memory is that of the quiet and the stillness of dawn and dusk.

121. 'Six of the best' – birds

It was the buzzard on which I cut my birdwatching teeth. I remember vividly the thrill of watching them through my grandfather's stalking 'scope, when I marvelled at their easy flight, coupled with a great turn of speed when after prey.

Then there is the peregrine, the 'feathered bullet', the fastest living thing. I once saw a heron stray into a peregrine's airspace, only to be attacked immediately; heron in total disarray, legs and wings in all directions and – 'click' – another shot for the collection!

At one time a little owl was to be seen frequently atop a stone wall between Lamplugh and Ennerdale, a little hunched bundle of feathers topped with enormous eyes, which became the object a telephoto shot. But then it disappeared; its nest had been rob and it left, never to return.

The stonechat is most often seen perched on a gorse b similar vantage point. Near the shore below Mellbreak there he was. A slow and cautious approach resulted, not as one might expect, but rather retreat within the bush, close-up to be taken as it stood on a branch, quite unc

There have been many shots of geese: an arrowh geese overhead in full sunlight; a pair of greylag water to land on Ennerdale; a single greylag in Highnook Tarn, and so on. On one winter's day of greylags. As the camera was brought to be delayed, there could be a shot of them with as backdrop and, sure enough, 'click' – and the can'.

The common sandpiper may well devoid of bright colours, but how w shores in spring! A pair were on the day, very, very agitated; dashin

122. Still more plants

While I cut my birdwatching teeth on the buzzard, I cut my plant-hunting teeth on the round-leaved sundew (*Drosera rotundifolia*). I first heard about insectivorous plants in biology class at Taunton School and heard, too, that examples could be found on the Blackdown Hills to the south. The Blackdowns were within cycling distance and, after a number of fruitless searches, patience was doubly rewarded in that I found, in the same location, both sundew and butterwort (*Pinguicular vulgaris*). Many, many years later, I was to find another sundew (*D. anglica*) at Drumburgh Moss. As is so often the case, it was surrounded by sphagnum moss and obtaining a picture necessitated kneeling in inches of water. Wet – but worth it! *D. rotundifolia* has round leaves, as the name suggests, whereas *D. anglica* has pear-shaped leaves.

Sometimes the thought of a plant recalls seeing it in a stunning situation. My most memorable sighting of mountain yellow saxifrage (*Saxifrage azoides*) was soon after dawn on the northern face of Pillar. This had meant leaving Mockerkin at 4:00 am but, like so very many early forays, it was well worth leaving a warm bed and venturing out in the dark!

For sheer strangeness, lords and ladies (*Arum masculatum*) takes a bit of beating. Not only is it strange in appearance, but it has a strange smell; it maintains its own temperature – a little above ambient, and it is slightly luminous! As if that were not enough, it traps insects within its spathe, or sheath, only to release them once they have effected pollination. Strange indeed!

Then there is sea campion (*Silene maritime*), which closely resembles bladder campion (*S. vulgaris*). Although primarily associated with the gravelly foreshore, it also grows high up on the western face of Grasmoor, apparently quite content in this harsh sub-alpine habitat. However, of all the hundreds of species to be found in the district, I suppose tormentil (*Potentilla erecta*) is among the most common, its beautiful little golden flowers adorning thousands of acres of fell. Apart from its sheer delight, it has had many uses in the past, including as a medicinal herb, a dye and in tanning.

From a purely personal point of view, the golden flower of gorse (*Ulex europaeus*) and the very rare Cheddar pink (*Dianthus caesius*), which is confined to the Cheddar Gorge, are of particular significance to me, being one of those 'odd bods' with a coat of arms. Canting arms have been used since the inception of heraldry in the 12th century and, since gorse is synonymous with whin and win is synonymous with gain (or Gane), it's hardly surprising that a pair of gorse flowers feature in the Gane arms. In addition, since gorse may be found in flower on every day of the year, it stands for constancy. The Cheddar pink features in the crest because of a long association of the family with the Cheddar area of Somerset. Thus botany is one of the many aspects of heraldry – the ramifications of which make it such a fascinating subject.

123. 'If you go down in the woods today—'

Well, if you *do* go down in the woods today, you'll find they present a rather drab and colourless picture. Gaunt, skeletal trees, decaying leaves beneath the feet, the autumn colours gone and spring not yet apparent. And yet, we know full well that in a matter of weeks there will appear a rash of woodland flowers, making full use of all available sunlight, before the canopy closes in. An explosion of bright young greenery to delight the eye, lift the spirit and freshen the atmosphere around us.

Each 100-year-old beech will draw up some 20 tons of water in the year by means of the suction created by transpiration through its 250,000 leaves. The mighty oak will be working away in similar fashion, while at the same time playing host to some 152 species of insect.

The wood, or forest on a larger scale – a wonderful, beautiful, invaluable and complex ecosystem.

Only recently there was yet another programme 'on the box' about the destruction of the rainforest, almost as if this ongoing tragedy was 'news' when in fact we have all known about it for years, but it still goes on. The size of the problem is unimaginable: two million hectares of rainforest are destroyed annually – an area the size of Belgium, Denmark and Switzerland combined. Where rainforest is lost, it is usually replaced with monoculture on a vast scale, which is of little or no use to wildlife and of little benefit to the local community. Of the 30 million species so far identified in the world, 20% are found in these forests, together with an unknown number of species yet to be discovered. The loss is vast and irreplaceable. In addition, although 50% of the oxygen produced in the world comes from marine plants, the forests play a vital part in this field and are important components in the global warming scenario.

It has been declared by some that global warming is nothing new—it has all happened before and is nothing to worry about! But the situation *is* unique. For example, in Roman times the world population was 250 million. By 1810 it was one billion, 1930 – two billion, 1975 – four billion and today, six billion. By 2050? An estimated nine billion.

Add to that the rise and rise of industry, motor cars and aircraft and it is easy enough to see how the impact of Man has tipped the delicate balance.

All this is, or should be, well known – yet, despite all the conferences, agreements, statements, intentions and promises, we are still on a very slippery slope and, whatever brakes have been applied, the reduction in speed is inadequate.

And so, if you *do* go down in the woods today, you will visit a very tiny, but nevertheless important link in the safety net of nature. Enjoy it, marvel at its complexity, do what you can to help and protect it and pray that those who have the power to do the same thing on the global scale will do likewise, with success— and quickly.

Report on Man's efforts so far? *'Could do better – must try harder'*.

124. Badgers and TB – the conclusion

At last, the Select Committee has reported on the problem of bovine TB. I say, 'at last', not at all in a critical way. The problem is a most serious one, costing hundreds of millions of pounds, but it is complex and has called for prolonged and intensive research and the most careful consideration of the results. Of course, the recommendations will not please everyone. At one end of the spectrum we have the 'badgers can do no harm' group, and at the other we have the 'cull 'em all, guilty or not' bunch. Both attitudes are illogical and are well-known to anyone who works in research. 'Why let the truth spoil a good argument?' and 'We'll draw the conclusions now and do the research later'!

The recommendations made together form the best possible advance until vaccine becomes available. That is the ultimate goal, but again, let's be fair; research takes time as well as effort and there is always a point at which throwing in additional effort or money speeds the outcome not one jot.

There are four main recommendations in relation to cattle testing, cattle movement, biosecurity, the use of vaccine a.s.a.p. and last, that culling of badgers *could* help in hot spot areas. Even then, culling would be allowed only in such areas (a) under licence, (b) in accordance with strict rules and (c) under the supervision of DEFRA. The 'hang 'em and flog 'em' brigade must take note that the badger remains a species protected by law and it is still illegal to disturb them, let alone kill them.

Thus the research shows that culling may be appropriate in certain cases, but that the badger is not the prime villain of the piece. It must also be remembered that it has been demonstrated that, in some cases, culling can make matters worse.

Overall, the problem of TB is a desperate one; the cost in terms simply of money, to say nothing of the loss of herds which have been built up over many years, is enormous and the farmers concerned warrant every possible sympathy and support – but it is upon the science that progress must be based.

Changing the subject altogether, full marks to the management of the Trout Hotel, who now advertise the fact that they are using no less than 29 local suppliers of produce and services, thus supporting the community and minimising food miles. What a shame the supermarkets can't do the same.

Sitting minding my own business recently when a slight sound attracted my attention. On looking up I found that there, standing on its hind legs, forefeet on the windowsill watching me was a fox! I've heard of 'role reversal'—but, really!

Well, spring is on the way in the usual hesitant fashion we come to expect this far south. Not for us the sudden burst of alpines associated with the extreme northern climes, but rather a day or two of spring followed by a return to winter. However, we had primroses in January and celandines in February, so something is happening.

At midday on 2nd March there was a skein of some 200 geese, high over Mockerkin flying north – another good sign, and we have also witnessed rolling flocks of fieldfares, clearly gradually returning to their summer haunts. Yes, there's hope!

125. Mostly flowers

It seems no time at all since we began to see the first signs of spring – and yet already many flowers have had their allotted time and have set their seeds in readiness for next year. The extensive roadside ribbons of white have come and gone; mostly of hedge parsley, but with a goodly sprinkling of other members of the same family, the *Umbelliferae*. Being closely related, they have many similarities, of course, but they have their points of difference, too. Probably the most frequently-occurring 'other member' is sweet Cicely, the flowering heads of which are much more dense than hedge parsley. Indeed, once you have 'got your eye in' it is possible to spot the difference at 20 paces! Once flowering is over, other differences appear. The seed pods of sweet Cicely are three times the size of those of hedge parsley and, when crushed between finger and thumb, they smell strongly of aniseed.

Within a few hundred yards of where I write there is also hemlock (green stems splashed and spotted with purple), earth nut (only eight to twelve inches high) and angelica (later-flowering with a purplish hue to flowers and stems) – but all members of the same family.

Once again this year, nature has played one of its little tricks down the lonning, one that I have probably mentioned before. On the verges there is wood avens, and in one particular spot there is water avens. Occasionally these two plants cross, the result being various forms of flower, which are similar to – but not the same as – the two parents, in terms of both size and colour.

As usual, broad-leaved dock is in abundance and is peppered with holes. Turn the leaves over and there are the tiny yellow eggs and the black larvae of the dock beetle and, with luck, the adult beetle itself, about a quarter of an inch in length and a brilliant iridescent green. Meadowsweet is just coming into flower, but some of it has been having a hard time, being infected with powdery mildew (*Erysiphe spp.*), a white mould, forms of which attack many wild, garden and farm plants, reducing yields and spoiling produce, and which is associated with hot, dry conditions.

The lonning from Mockerkin to Black Beck bridge on the Pardshaw road is generally unremarkable, but in early spring and summer it is home to over 50 species of wild flowers. Giant bellflower will appear there soon, while at the other end of the scale, the minute yellow flowers of crosswort are virtually over, while the equally tiny white flowers of cleavers are in full bloom.

As for the grasses – often overlooked as wild flowers – meadow foxtail predominates early in the season, but is now largely overshadowed by cocksfoot. The soft mauve tassels of Yorkshire fog are plentiful now; there is some crested dogstail, some ryegrass and, as far as I can see, just one plant of soft brome!

Just back from the road is a buzzard's nest in an oak and, needless to say, the parents may often be seen floating around in the vicinity, a peaceful, domestic scene. Sudden pandemonium the other day, when a sparrowhawk dashed into the airspace – an immediate acceleration all round, as screaming parents left the visitor in no doubt that he was not welcome!

On another occasion, a dispute arose for some unknown reason when a redstart landed on the fence by a field being coursed for insects by a pair of swallows. The redstart was promptly mobbed and driven off. There's always something—

126. Plants and their names

Late summer prompts another 'botanising' piece since, before long, wild flowers will be little more than a memory – until next year! While the great annual flush has subsided, there are still plenty of flowers about; indeed, a greater diversity than we might think. My local lonning may look a bit drab, but a walk of little more than 20 minutes revealed the following – even now: angelica, herb Robert, red campion, meadow cranesbill, nipplewort, wood avens, great willowherb, broad-leaved willowherb, rosebay willowherb, tufted vetch, Jack-by-the-hedge, great burnet, St John's wort, hedge cleavers, corn buttercup, creeping buttercup, hawkbit, broad-leaved plantain, ribwort plantain, white clover, bramble, broad-leaved dock, valerian, foxglove, nettle, earth nut, silverweed, spearwort, germander trefoil and meadow vetchling – to name but a few!

In addition, for those who are really keen(!), it is worth remembering that wild plants may be recognised by their leaves (and seeds), as well as by their flowers, so one can still find plants of crosswort, hedge parsley, giant bellflower and many more. This is a good time to study leaves, because in many cases there are some plants still in flower and some not – a good time to test one's knowledge. Identification by seeds alone is rather more difficult, while identifying varieties of cereals from just two or three ears is even trickier – but essential for seed crop inspectors.

Flowers of the meadow cranesbill are violet in colour, but by now many have lost their petals and the sepals and some leaves are usually bright scarlet. A little poor this year; probably due to all the wet weather. Great burnet is perhaps unusual, in that its globular flowers are burgundy in colour, turning dark brown as they mature.

The many-awned seed heads of wood avens and the upright pods of sweet Cicely are brown, too. Indian balsam is, of course, something of a pest plant. Introduced in Victorian times, it is a strong grower, spread far and wide by 'exploding' seed pods, which scatter seeds in all directions. Willowherb seed is 'plumed' and as light as a feather; once mature, given a fair wind, it can be blown for considerable distances.

Needless to say, the majority of seeds do not survive – there would simply not be room for all the progeny. For example, I once took the trouble to count the number of seeds produced in one foxglove. The result? Five thousand!

While clearly the use of only 'common' names may cause confusion, because many species enjoy dozens of different names in different locations over the years, every effort is made to use the most common 'common' names. To give one example of just how complex the subject can be, the very common herb Robert (*Geranium robertianum*) has been accorded no less than 105 'common' names over the years in England and Scotland.

'Herb Robert' is probably the oldest, being recorded in a 13th century vocabulary: in old herbal lore, the appearance of a plant was thought to reflect its medicinal use. The red leaves of herb Robert were therefore thought to indicate that it is useful for the staunching of blood! The origins of some names, such as 'soldiers', are pretty clear, while in others it is not. Among the more fanciful names for herb Robert are: baby's pinafore, candlesticks, chatterboxes, cuckoo's victuals, death come quickly, dragons' blood, granny-thread-the-needle, hop-o'-my-thumb, Robin Hood, stinker bobs, and the longest of them all – from Buckinghamshire, kiss-me-love-at-the-garden-gate!

127. Never look back—!

Well, so they say, but once the trauma of the cessation of fell-walking has eased – which can take a very long time – there is much to be said for looking back on all those great days spent in 'the high country'.

Donning the boots, grabbing 'the sack' and setting off on yet another 'adventure'! What a host of features come to mind.

The Shamrock Traverse on Pillar where, soon after passing the Robinson cairn, the track drops steeply down and round to the left, then turns right and up to a great sloping slab, across that and left again up among the massive rocks to the summit!

Or the favourite route up the western edge of Grasmoor from Lanthwaite Green; a steep, grassy pull followed by scree, then heather and then, at last, solid rock! Part-way up there is that narrow traverse to the left before turning right up the gill or, for those confident enough to brave very exposed positions, and provided it is dry, there's that fine scramble up the rock ridge to the right of the gill. All good stuff, whichever route is taken, and at the top of that section there's a good platform on which to draw breath and admire the view across the road far below, over to Mellbreak and beyond.

And what about some of the superb cairns dotted about; on Thornthwaite Beacon, High Spy and Dale Head, for example, or the welcome 'shelters' on Scafell and Grasmoor? Rudimentary, they may be, but what joy to reach them on a bad day!

Then there are the steep and rough scrambles, such as Sheepbone Rake on High Crag, or the way up to the same ridge via Burtness Combe. Some good uncharted routes come to mind, too, such as from Gasgale Gill up the flank of Whiteside, starting off along one of the becks beyond the sheepfold. On Grasmoor again, what about the ascent of that from the Gasgale sheepfold, via Dove Crags? High up there is a great basin where one might expect to find water – but, no, it's as dry as a bone!

Great Gable, which is certainly one of the favourites for 'tourists'; great, whichever route is taken, and the view from the Westmorland Cairn is spectacular. But for those who revel in scrambles, what better way to gain the cairn than from the traverse? Now, that *is* a good pull!

Then there are the 'folded' rocks on the right of the track as you near the top of Whiteside, and the sloping slabs on the ridge, which can be a bit treacherous when wet. And, talking of 'treacherous' rock, what about crossing the boulder field towards the summit of Scafell? If ever an area was designed to test knees and ankles, it is surely this! Many balanced rocks, ready to tip this way or that as soon as the boot is applied! And what about that good old lump of rock at the top of Glaramara? Lovely little scramble – having flogged all the way up from the valley! Or the descent of Sharp Edge, Blencathra, where there is a stretch of smooth downward-sloping rock with an adverse camber, where the trick is to have faith, let go and slide a few feet to the next hold. Not far, 'tis true, but quite exciting!

'Never look back?' On the contrary, when fell-walking days are done, painful it may be to admit it, but there's much satisfaction in looking back at all those GREAT DAYS in the fells; the exertion, the fabulous scenery, the magic of dusk and dawn, those special sightings of wildlife – what price the call of the falcon? – to say nothing of the good company of kindred spirits. So, yes, look back and give thanks for some of the happiest days of my life.

128. Birds

Well, it wasn't actually raining – which was something of a novelty – but it was most certainly wet. Overnight rain had positively drenched the area. Every leaf was dripping, becks were rushing with a white froth and muddy brown and no field depression could escape being designated a temporary pond! However, all was not lost: the wind had abated and there really was some blue sky to be seen, albeit obliterated in parts by enormous billowing clouds, white around the edges, but a dark and menacing grey at the centre.

Nevertheless, at first, anyway, it was a peaceful scene that greeted me as I trudged off in the (relatively) early morn. I say, 'at first', because it didn't last. After little more than a quarter of a mile, I became aware of a noise; distant at first, a sound of agitated birds. It steadily got louder and it became obvious that 'it' was approaching me from over the trees at the bottom of a field that sloped up on my right.

In fact, it became so loud and frantic that I stopped in my tracks, awaiting I knew not what. By now it was a positive screaming of birds; desperate, continuous shrieks of alarm. Then 'it' came into view. It was an extraordinary flock of crows. Not just a flock, but a clearly-defined avian sphere of dashing, tumbling, rolling black feathers, moving quite rapidly across the sky, emitting this constant barrage of furious noise.

Suddenly, in an instant, I saw what 'it' was all about. Fleeing from the very centre, making all possible speed away from its tormentors, was the cause of all the trouble: a sparrowhawk! In no time at all the 'sphere' disintegrated, its component crows fell away in all directions, the caterwauling ceased and peace was restored. Somewhere, somewhat shaken and stirred, a sparrowhawk was tending its ruffled feathers and wounded pride and probably emitting a bird-like 'Phew!'

While there are, of course, many successful projects aimed at the protection, conservation and reintroduction of birds, it is a sad truth that, even in this day and age, there remains wanton persecution. It was recently reported in 'Birds', the journal of the RSPB, that the relentless killing of golden eagles is halting the recovery of the species in Scotland and thwarting its return to northern England; that 2009 was the worst on record for the poisoning of red kites; that peregrines are being deliberately caught in spring traps in the West Midlands and that, as a result, their young are being left to starve to death. In fact, bird crime reached an all-time high in 2007 – up by a third on the previous year – and how many more incidents went undetected? The penalties for those caught inflicting such suffering are severe, and rightly so, but clearly one of the problems is that birds such as peregrines and golden eagles are frequently to be found in relatively isolated places, where the activities of the perpetrators are difficult to monitor. While countless thousands of professionals and volunteers strive to help our wildlife, it seems there are still those bent on destruction.

129. Deposit account!

Ever since Man first started hunting for his food, the signs and tracks of birds and animals have been of importance as indicators of just what wildlife is in the vicinity.

Such indicators may also be of interest and concern in domestic situations to this day. Only recently, I was invited to identify some droppings (apologies for the indelicate subject!) in case they were those of rats. They had been found close to habitation – and few of us welcome rats around the house!

The ease with which droppings may be identified varies; sometimes it is easy, sometimes difficult, but seldom impossible. On this occasion they fell into the former category. They were clearly of animal, rather than bird origin and, that established, the four aspects to consider are size, shape, colour and, maybe, content.

The general appearance suggested a carnivore, while the markedly-twisted or spiral form, with a lengthy point at one end, indicated a member of the *Mustelidae*, a family which includes the otter, badger, pine marten, polecat, stoat and weasel. Purely from size, it was possible to exclude the first four of these and thereafter to measure diameter. The fact that they measured 5mm in diameter, rather than 2mm left no doubt. The animal responsible was a stoat.

It is sometimes necessary to tease out the contents of droppings, and in the case of carnivorous animals and birds of prey, it is often possible to identify bone fragments and so determine the diet of the 'depositor'.

It is not uncommon, especially in the spring, to come across animal remains in the form of small, white, gelatinous 'objects', which are in fact the ovaries of frogs. Buzzards will eat frogs, but will reject the ovaries. Similarly, where cleaned-out skin of a hedgehog is found, the culprit is invariably a badger, being one of the few animals with paws and jaws strong enough to unravel a curled-up hedgehog.

Food remains often give useful clues. The squirrel's anvil is a case in point. While the wood mouse, bank vole, great tit and nuthatch will all attack nuts, but in different ways, the size, shape and angle of the hole in the shell being distinctive in each case.

It is not only faeces that are 'dropped' by birds, but pellets, too, which are regurgitated indigestible remains of food. As in the case of faeces, size, shape, colour and content help to identify the depositor.

Then again, especially where there is soft mud or snow, the identification of tracks is a study in itself, involving not only the shape of feet, but often the gait as well. Each species of deer, for example, leaves a different shape of hoof print, or 'slot', as it is called. Ease of identification from tracks depends greatly on the surface on which the imprint occurs. An otter crossing firm snow may well leave paw prints, while on soft snow the underbelly will also leave its mark, between left and right paws.

Identification is not always easy, but it *is* always fascinating, and reaching a firm conclusion is very satisfying.

So, thank you, Mr Stoat—(or was it Mrs?) That we shall never know – but all this does underline the first three rules of nature study – Observation! Observation! Observation!

130. Stirrings of spring

As always at this time of year, bird activity is accelerating as we emerge from the dark tunnel of winter.

On the morning of 1st March there was a distant, but unmistakable 'honking' of geese and, minutes after the sound could first be heard, there they were, very, very, high and moving northwards – a welcome sign of the approach of spring. To count them accurately was, of course, impossible, but an estimate of some 200 would not be too wide of the mark. To hear their evocative calling is always emotive and to watch them closely is fascinating. This skein was displaying the usual behaviour, in that the leader was constantly changing. The bird at the forefront of the arrowhead formation leads for some minutes and is then replaced by another, presumably because being leader calls for maximum effort and, on tiring, another takes its place, while still more can be seen jockeying for position with a view to taking their turn.

Another welcome sight has been the growing excitement among the mixed flocks of fieldfares and redwings, in readiness for their departure for northern Europe. It is rare for them to nest in the UK.

But then, all birds are busy now, courting and frantically seeking out potential nest sites.

One pair of jackdaws provide interest on the parapet of Mockerkin Hall. Always together, they stand side by side, clearly discussing the news; they bill and coo, groom each other, shelter from the south-westerly winds and rain and occasionally have a tiff and stand back-to-back, beaks in the air.

Walks to and over Black Beck bridge are always accompanied by a brief peep over each side, despite the fact that there is seldom anything to see. One morning recently, however, there was a fine pair of dippers, with their glorious chestnut plumage and creamy-white breasts, quickly dashing away downstream only inches above the water. On another day a heron took off on approach, neck tucked well back and its long legs trailing behind, and emitting the well-known guttural 'kraak'. Its partner stood its ground rather longer, but then off it went with that almost-stalling flight. Male and female are often said to have the same appearance, but I suspect that, in fact, the male *is* a little slighter than the female, an observation only possible when the two are in close proximity.

Then again, Saturday 7th March was a red-letter day – the pulse quickened at the first warbling call of a curlew returning to the fells. Another encouraging sign!

Frogspawn has been appearing for some time now. Not renowned for their intelligence, frogs seem prepared to drop their spawn just as soon as they touch water, irrespective of its extent; as a result, spawn can often be found in little more than a puddle, in which survival is singularly unlikely. More than once I have collected such spawn and deposited it in a better spot nearby, where there is at least some hope of it hatching before the water dries up altogether. Oh, yes! It's all out there – good hunting!

131. This and that

I recently took a stroll through Lanthwaite Wood along the bank of the Cocker on a glorious sunny day with wall-to-wall blue skies and the surface of the lake like glass. Spring flowers were in profusion, among them the lesser celandine (*Ranunculus ficaria L*), or 'swallow herb', as it was once known, since it flowers as the swallows arrive in spring and withers as they leave in the autumn. There was wood anemone (*A. nemorosa L.*), whose hanging heads earned it the name of 'daughter of the wind'; wood sorrel, too, (*Oxalis acetosella L.*), which was once used in salads, also known as wood sour and in the 17th century as 'alleluia', since it appeared around Easter, when alleluia was sung.

On the river and lake there were mergansers, mallard and dippers. Oddly enough, they were all males – perhaps their wives were at home looking after the young ones!

One surprise was that the pond by the pumping station was devoid of tadpoles; strange, this, because at this time of year it is usually full of 'wrigglers'. Worrying, because ponds play such a vital part in our biodiversity, supporting about half the species of animals we have in the wild. Having lost some 80% of our ponds through pollution, agricultural 'improvement' and the building of roads and houses, we can afford to lose no more. Garden ponds are vital, too, in providing havens for wildlife, a great deal of interest and an invaluable educational resource. A sobering thought is that a recent survey revealed that 38% of 9 to 11-year-olds could not identify a frog. Similarly, in a way, it is strange that, despite all the publicity about the importance of our wildlife, there was recently a case in Shropshire in which a gamekeeper was prosecuted for having killed 102 buzzards, 40 ravens and 37 badgers.

The other day I saw a snipe and heard a woodpecker, which reminded me of two odd events some years ago. Only once have I heard the 'drumming' of the snipe – a remarkable humming noise created by the violent vibration of the tail feathers during a steep dive. The other event was a peculiar 'whittering' from way up a tree, with nothing to be seen. It transpired it came from young woodpeckers within the trunk, the sound emanating through the horizontal hole drilled by the parents.

One development that never ceases to amaze me at this time of year is the rapidity of plant growth – which was in fact the subject of my very first experiment in biology – a very long time ago! The combination of greater light intensity, greater day length, higher temperatures and adequate moisture results in unbelievable growth rates. The woodland canopy is now fast closing in, so we shall soon have more difficulty in seeing our red squirrels. Their food is now in the tree tops, so why take the risk of coming down to the ground, where most of the predators are? Down in the autumn, yes, to find and bury fallen nuts for future use, but not now. They do not, of course, 'remember' where they bury such items, but relocate them by smell. In reading scientific papers about animals, I am often intrigued and amused by apparent references to their 'thought processes'. One in front of me as I write is about hoverflies – those wasp-like, but harmless members of the Diptera, in which the author suggests that 'many of these brightly coloured insects look like bees or wasps – and they use this similarity to protect themselves'! Imagine a hoverfly getting up one morning and thinking to itself, 'I know, I'll put on a striped jumper – that'll fox 'em!'

132. Hedges

It is probably true to say that hedges are among the most overlooked of habitats for wildlife, despite the fact that we have many thousands of miles of them, providing 'corridors', nesting places and feeding grounds for a host of birds and animals. The largest group of earth's animals, the insects, are among those that abound in this situation.

Only the other day I was watching a golden-ringed dragonfly 'patrolling' a local hedge in search of prey. This very large insect – which has one of the longest bodies of any insect found in Europe – is a predator, catching a variety of insects in flight. To us it is a big dragonfly, but we know from fossils that it would be dwarfed by some dragonflies of the past, some of which sported wingspans of two feet!

Another renewed acquaintance recently was with a common green grasshopper, which seems to me to be much less common than in the days of my youth. It obligingly stood still long enough for me to have a really good look at it and then, inevitably, it hopped – or rather leapt – about two feet. Since it is only about one inch in length, this is roughly equivalent to me jumping some 144 feet from a standing start. A very clever trick, if I could do it!

Midges, too, often inhabit hedges, among them some of the gall midges, which are responsible for the spherical and 'spangle' galls to be found on the leaves of some trees and shrubs. These particular species appear to do no especial damage to their hosts, unlike some other midges. In the 'prairie' farming country of eastern England, for example, where tens of thousands of acres of peas are grown for the canning and quick-freezing industries, the pea midge can be a serious and costly pest. The larvae feed on the developing flower buds and can totally destroy them, so that a crop yields no produce at all.

'Cuckoo spit', that well-known white liquid found in 'blobs' on hedge and verge plants, is produced by the nymphs of the common froghopper. Examination of the 'froth' will soon reveal the nymph within, which later develops into the adult froghopper, a brownish yellow insect about a quarter of an inch in length. Commonly seen at rest on hedge leaves is the noon-fly, a shiny black fly, not dissimilar to the housefly, but with a striking tan-coloured area at the base of each wing. And, talking of flies, the yellow dung fly is always to be seen, usually around cow or sheep dung.

One of the most colourful results of insect activity is the 'robin's pincushion', a bright red and green 'hairy' ball two to three inches across, to be found on wild roses and which is especially noticeable at leaf-fall. The midge responsible is only about ¼ inch in length and is therefore seldom seen. Each ball contains a number of larvae, in separate compartments.

Hoverflies, of which there are a number of species, some much larger than others, are wasp-like in colouring; in fact, they are quite beautiful creatures and well worth observing closely. They are easily found; some, at least, favouring the flowers of hogweed.

And, of course, there are many, many more; a whole host of insects and other 'creepy-crawlies' which are not insects; all are little wonders in their own right – and every single one a masterpiece of design.

What a wonderful world!

133. 'Beetling along'

There are few subjects more fascinating than animal behaviour. Much of it is strange and as yet not understood. Not long ago a large snail began the totally unrewarding ascent of a drainpipe. A smooth surface, in full sun, with no apparent prospect of food, water or shelter throughout the considerable climb the height of a two-storey house! Why? Perhaps because, on realising that its surroundings were utterly alien, it 'thought' – if indeed snails do think – that the sooner it got off it, the better, and that to go on might be as good as to go back?

While in higher animals trying to separate 'thought' and 'instinct' is often difficult, if not impossible, trying to account for particular activities is an interesting exercise.

Earthworms, for example, may often be found crossing country roads. Why? On leaving the shade, moisture, comfort and relative security of a grass verge, they venture out onto a singularly rough, unyielding, inhospitable surface, fraught with danger. If the road is dry and wide, there is the problem of dehydration before the other side is reached, while in addition there are the hazards of exposure to predators and the wheels of passing traffic. Whatever the attraction across the road, is it really worth this gamble? Why not do an immediate right-about-turn and head back from whence they came?

Which brings to mind an incident witnessed only a few days ago while walking along the lonning towards Sossgill. A ground beetle set forth from the verge, travelling from east to west. Nothing remarkable about that, especially considering that a scuttling beetle travelling at top speed stands a better chance of survival than a wriggling earthworm.

So all was well – at first. What the beetle was unable to see at the start, because of the camber, was that running down the west side of the road was a rivulet of water, five or six inches wide. On reaching it, the beetle stopped in its tracks and one could imagine it thinking, 'Oh, dear, now what?' After some moments of apparent indecision, it came to the conclusion that the best way was 'head down and charge', and so, with a commendable degree of determination, off it went into the surging torrent. In the event, it made little headway, little legs thrashing away to no effect, and after being swept downstream for a yard or two, it was unceremoniously dumped back on the same 'shore' from which it started, no doubt embarrassed and decidedly damp.

Another brief pause and it set off back to its original starting point, on dry land, and tried again. The result was precisely the same – a speedy trip downstream and once more back on the same shore. Totally undaunted, the process was repeated yet again – back up the road followed by a re-launch, but this time, success – we have lift-off! Through some quirk of the 'waves', rather than any newly-found navigational skill on the part of the beetle, this massive effort was rewarded and our armoured friend disappeared among the welcoming grass, no doubt with a feeling of great satisfaction and a thrilling adventure story to relate for years to come. Two morals come to mind:

'If at first you don't succeed—' and also, 'You never know what you can do until you really try!'

134. Memories!

Not surprisingly, the completion of some 140 'Mob' walks brings back a few memories! Walks in high summer, when occasionally the waterproofs may be left at home with confidence – and *that's* a novelty! Days when the rock is warm to the touch, when dust covers the boots and when ample intake of liquid is essential. The long slog back, with the promise of ice cream and gallons of tea! Sizzling days, when the tired feet have been dangled in a rushing beck, beneath an azure, cloudless sky, to the 'meouw' of the buzzard and the kek-kek-kek call of the peregrine high above.

And walks in the autumn, renowned for a thousand shades of colour as the bright-green leaves of summer dull and start to dry, when foliage takes on every hue of green, yellow, orange and brown, more than could be found in any man-made paint box. Lower slopes, enwrapped in bracken's bronze, while heather's heady perfume fills the air. The pungent scent of the soft and rustling carpet of autumn leaves beneath the feet; once blows the wind and there – bare branches, stark and grim against an angry sky and yet, look closely and we find each has its buds, waiting patiently for far off spring.

Then winter bites, with walks on iron-hard, icy fells which take upon themselves a shivering shade of blue; when tracks, raised up by frost, crunch down beneath the feet like some new-baked crust; when snow piles up in the lea of hummocks and we are suddenly knee-deep and, with rising temperatures and increasing glow, we struggle free and stamp the powder from our limbs. When the views from the tops are at times of serried ranks of ever-diminishing fells, away into the distance; the nearest dark, and each succeeding ridge a lighter shade of grey. Lake margins, repeatedly sprayed with water by the wind, now inhabited by ice-encrusted grasses, shrubs and trees, each sprig entombed in

299

shining crystal. Then there is that unsurpassed magic of the low angle of winter sun, which streams across the landscape, brilliantly illuminating the southern aspect of every feature, while at the same time casting the northern aspect into deepest shadow. Thus appears a world in sharp relief. While on a dull day a fellside may appear a mere hulk, it now emerges as a scene of infinite detail; that which was plain silhouette, a scene of depth and sharpest clarity.

But then, once more, there dawns the spring; days lengthen and the scene begins to change. Sub-alpines bloom and raise the spirits of those who venture to the heights, with starry saxifrage bravely surviving in the crag-side runnels and the glowing cushions of mountain yellow saxifrage clinging on some northern face. The early-nesting ravens and falcons at their chosen sites, ready to lay just as soon as they dare, in the fight to have sufficient time to rear and train their young before the all-too-soon onset of the next winter. The first sightings of spring visitors, the sandpiper and wheatear and the curlew returning to upper slopes.

Through these and many more such scenes, the 'Mob' has walked and scrambled, with many a good 'crack' and many a laugh and leg-pull along the countless miles.

135. Favourite things

No doubt the vast majority of the thousands of folk who walk the fells have their favourites – favourite fells, favourite views, favourite sights and sounds. As we all know, 'AW's' favourite was Haystacks, while mine is Grasmoor, by the direct route from Lanthwaite green, which, for me, has everything. A superb scramble, involving grass, heather, scree, solid rock, gullies and viewpoints, emerging at Grasmoor End and finishing with that final windswept push to the summit cairn.

I daresay we all have our favourite birds, too. The blackbird, for its song – unless of course we are lucky enough to hear the song of the mountain blackbird, or ring ouzel – which is increasingly rare – surely the purest note of all, sheer musical silver! The call of the curlew across the fells, heralding spring; the 'meouw' of the buzzard for its effortless floating across the heavens, the kek-kek-kek of the peregrine for its incomparable speed and manoeuvrability, down to the excited chattering of the wren as it darts back to its brood in the undergrowth.

And favourite wildflowers, too. The grass of Parnassus, for sheer purity; the saxifrages in the high fells and, for me, sundew and butterwort, the first plants to catch my imagination some 65 years ago, leading me into a career primarily concerned with plants and their problems.

As regards wild animals – it is tempting to say that the favourite is the one you happen to be watching at the time! The roe deer, for its deep, limpid eyes and its delicate prancing through the wood; the joyous scampering of badger cubs at dusk; that glorious red coat of a young fox; the antics of red squirrels as they chase through the branches. Each in its way quite extraordinary, and each enriching our countryside.

When it comes to times of day, for me there is no contest. High noon may be delightful, late afternoon may be restful, sunset may be spectacular, but daybreak is magic. Which is sad, in a way, because it is witnessed by so few – which conversely is part of its charm. The breathtaking scene in the late night chill as the first hint of light creeps onto the horizon, slowly spreading until with a visual crescendo, the sun itself peeps above the rim, sending a blazing shaft across the hills. The stillness; the silence, broken only by the occasional bleat of a distant lamb or the throaty chuckle of a cock pheasant; the mist hanging over the valley, with odd wisps rising heavenwards. The earth seems to hold its breath for a while. Diamonds of dew or frost upon the ground, glistening brighter by the minute.

The sheer beauty of it all. A time to pause, to stand and stare and to reflect upon just how blessed we are to live in such a glorious corner of England in peace, harmony and security. A time to give thanks, indeed.

It is magical anywhere: by a lake, where there may be a heron gliding silently over the mirror-like waters; from the Coffin Route, as duck or geese float down to the water far below; from Mellbreak, as the sun emerges down Gasgale Ghyll, or from Robinson, as Helvellyn is illuminated from the east. From any vantage point, in fact: Magic.

136. More memories!

Recent preparation for another talk on Lakeland and its wildlife, for the benefit of UNICEF got me thinking of memories, sparked off by some of my (thousands of) slides.

There's that one of the perky little fox cub in close-up, ears pricked and head on one side, looking at the camera as if to say, "I'm sure that wasn't there last night!" This came as a result of rising at 4:00 am on three days in succession and getting in position close to the earth; nothing at all for two days, but on the third day – bingo!

Then there is the close-up of an adder, coiled and ready to strike. A trip to Geltsdale brought this about – a walk-and-search specifically for adders, basking on a warm and sunny day (remember them?); quite a few were around, and a number of pictures taken, but this one clearly illustrates the threatening pose of our one and only venomous snake.

One of my favourite birds is the peregrine, a magnificent falcon, if ever there was one, and again this features in the collection. Telephoto shots of falcons at the nest with their young, some of adults in flight and one in particular as it dashed downwards while I was on the face of Grasmoor, dark against a deep blue sky, but with its talons shining like gold. What a sighting that was!

Enlarged and hanging on the wall is a photo of Wastwater, taken at 5:00 am, with Great Gable and adjoining fells black against a beautiful red dawn sky. From there I did the Pillar traverse, just for good measure, and got a good shot of mountain yellow saxifrage on the face of Pillar rock in the horizontal morning light.

There is a very close close-up of a damsel fly – which surprised me, because as a rule they dash off before the approach is close enough. But then I noticed that this particular damsel fly had a gnat in its jaws! It was obviously more interested in its meal than in my activity!

And, of course, there are hundreds of pictures of walks, details of which come flooding back as they are viewed.

All weather conditions: from baking sun down the never-ending length of Langstrath; deep snow on Coledale Hause and Maiden Moor; pack-ice, which I clearly remember creaking and groaning as it compacted on Buttermere; Dale Head, where once the wind reduced us to all-fours, and Sheepbone Rake, where four of us were once swept off our feet and dumped in a heap by a mighty gust.

Strange how many memories the human mind can store! If you really concentrate on a walk you've done lots of times, it's amazing how much detail can be recalled, even down to the location of individual rocks and plants.

And not just what could be seen, but heard and smelled, as well: the sylvan call of that ring ouzel on Napes Needle; the cak-cak-cak of the stonechat below Mellbreak; the sound of widgeon swirling down to the surface of Loweswater and, one of the most evocative of all, the honking of geese as they fly south for the winter. The smell of autumn leaves, the scent of heather in full bloom—

Memories? Oh, yes, a trunk-full from, I suppose, some thousands of miles walked in and around the fells over the last 40 years; a veritable feast in this glorious corner of England.

Oh, yes! Happy days, indeed!

Those Were The Days!

Oh! To be high in the fells again
'Neath a glorious blue summer sky,
Where the wilderness brings
A thousand things
To delight the walker's eye.

Oh! For the rattle of scree 'neath the boot
And those handholds on good solid rocks,
For the crunch of the snow
As the icy winds blow
And the comfort of extra thick socks!

Oh! For the sound of the raven above
And the musical beat of its wings,
For the peregrine's call
And, the sweetest of all,
When the white-collared ring ouzel sings.

Oh! For the days upon Grasmoor's steep sides
And the scramble to reach Pillar's top,
For old Scafell's fine heights,
The wildlife in our sights
Which has thrilled us, and never stops.

And here's to the health of those great guys and gals
Who we've tramped with for hundreds of miles,
For those pals good and true,
Right good souls, through and through,
With their broad happy fellwalker's smiles!

AJG

137. Mountain Rescue

'Go canny on the hill'

How difficult it can be to tread the narrow path between being sensibly safety conscious and totally over-protective. We all know of the 'nanny-state' syndrome, and how ridiculous rules and regulations can creep into our lives – like goggles for playing conkers! However, safety *is* an important factor out on the fells, at least calling for proper boots, map, compass and so on and, in my opinion, a stick or pole. I say that because on one memorable occasion we slipped simultaneously on a steep, wet grassy slope, and found ourselves careering down towards a cliff edge, beyond which was a drop of over 50 metres. A stick or pole, properly applied, is the only effective brake in these circumstances – and by the way, *do* use the wrist strap. Nothing worse than seeing a stick flying away from your grasp just when you need it most!

With the best will in the world, and even among the most experienced and well equipped walkers, accidents do happen, and much more frequently than many folk realise. One has only to look at the annual reports of the mountain rescue teams (MRTs) to see this. If ever there were to be a 'Walking Test', along the lines of a 'Driving Test', such reports should be required reading.

In 2009, for example, MRTs were called out to 649 incidents. Perhaps of even greater concern is the fact that the number of callouts is increasing year on year. While in 2003 the MRTs dealt with 348 incidents between them, in 2009 that figure was raised to 649. Of these, 115 involved minor injuries, but 183 involved serious injuries, i.e. needing hospitalisation for over 24 hours. This amounted to a total commitment of 27,000 man hours.

Needless to say, the MRTs keep detailed records of the incidents they attend, including location, ages of those involved, injuries and so on, and some of the details are enlightening. Of the 649 incidents in 2009, 156 were due to slips, 135 to falls and 118 to people being lost. One cannot but wonder how many slips could have been avoided by the use of a stick, and how many people who were lost could have avoided their plight by the use of map and compass. The chance of a mishap can at least be reduced with a little care. As for the injuries sustained in 2009, 114 were fractures, the ankle being the most common site, followed by lower leg, knee and head respectively. The combined statistics of the number of callouts and the number and type of the majority of injuries serve to emphasize the need for good boots, a stick or pole and general care and preparation. If that sounds 'nanny-like' it's perhaps worth remembering that not one of those injured last year expected to be!

All that apart, one cannot but admire the hard work and dedication of the MRTs which, although clearly a vital emergency service throughout the district, are manned entirely by volunteers and, amazingly, are charities which receive no government funding whatsoever. In addition to the many hours spent on callouts, a great deal of time is obviously spent on the maintenance of vehicles and the extensive range of equipment required for this work, and on the essential fundraising. Again, it must not be forgotten that, like a number of similar voluntary emergency services, the personnel have to be prepared for the disruption of turning out at any time of day or night, often in atrocious conditions, risking life and limb for the benefit of others.

Every fell walker owes them a debt of gratitude and should support their outstanding contribution to safety on the hill.

FINIS

Epilogue

Days spent fell-walking and scrambling in Lakeland have undoubtedly been among the happiest of my life. Although, strictly speaking, the fell country is not 'wild', in that much of it has been modified by the attentions of Man over the millennia, it is as wild as anywhere in England and much, much wilder than most of it. It encompasses extensive remote areas in which one may walk for many a mile without seeing another living soul. It is beautiful, fascinating and contains a wealth of wildlife to engage any country-lover or naturalist.

The benefits of fell-walking are many. They include the physical exercise, the blissful lack of man-made noise, the silence and the solitude which so replenish the mind, the wild flowers and the birds and, of course, the grandeur of the mountains in ever-changing light.

I sincerely hope that these jottings will bring back happy memories to many readers and that they may inspire others, as yet unfamiliar with this glorious corner of England, to explore and adventure here, and to savour its countless delights.

Walk on – through this, a magic place
Of Peace and Solitude and Space,
To body, mind and soul renew
And find God's presence here with you.

AJG

FINIS

Bibliography

Brown, Robert 1773-1858. Various treatises for the Linnean Society, of which he was Librarian, as also he was to Sir Joseph Banks and Keeper at the British Museum.

Culpepper, Nicholas. The English Physician Enlarged (Culpepper's Herbal) 1653.

Darwin, Charles. On the Origin of Species by Natural Selection. 1859.

Furneaux, W.S. Life in Ponds and Streams. 1935.

Halliday, Dr. Geoffrey. A Flora of Cumbria. 1997.

Holden, Elizabeth. Recommended English Names for Fungi in the U.K. 2003.

Tomkies, Mike. Golden Eagle Years. 1982.

Wainright, A.W. Guides to the Lakeland Fells. 1982

Walpole, Hugh. Herries Chronicles. 1982.

Williams, Michael. Deforesting the Earth; From Prehistory to Global Crisis. 2003.

The Friends of the Lake District. Flora of the Fells. 2003.